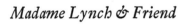

Madame Lynch & Friend

Books by Alyn Brodsky

Madame Lynch
& Friend

THE TRUE ACCOUNT OF AN IRISH ADVENTURESS
AND THE DICTATOR OF PARAGUAY WHO DESTROYED
THAT AMERICAN NATION

Alyn Brodsky

HARPER & ROW, PUBLISHERS
NEW YORK, EVANSTON, SAN FRANCISCO
LONDON

FIRST EDITION

Designed by Sidney Feinberg

Library of Congress Cataloging in Publication Data

Brodsky, Alyn.
Madame Lynch & friend.
Bibliography: p.
Includes index.
1. Lynch, Eliza Alicia, 1835?–1886. 2. López, Francisco Solano, Pres. Paraguay, 1827–1870.
3. Paraguayan War, 1865–1870. I. Title.
F2686.L9826   989.2'05'0924   [B]   74-15813
ISBN 0-06-010487-2

75 76 77 78 79 10 9 8 7 6 5 4 3 2 1

This one is for my nephews: Dennis, Donald,
Andrew, and Michael Burton

Contents

Acknowledgments

Where pertinent within the text, I have indicated—I hope with amplitude—my appreciation to those who showered me with assistance and, more, kindnesses during the course of my research for this book.

Unfortunately, as will become apparent to the reader, I am unable to cite here those of my friends among the Paraguayans who aided me in tracking down the truth concerning Madame Lynch and her Friend; those who, were their names to be recorded here, would suffer embarrassment in the eyes of, and possible retaliation at the hands of, their government, given the political climate which obtains in Paraguay today.

I wish also at this time to acknowledge publicly my debt of gratitude to Marie Rodell, my literary agent; Ruth Pollack, my editor at Harper & Row; and to a valued friend and sympathetic sounding board for writers, the late May Freedman—dear Manya.

Madame Lynch gradually and insidiously imbued López with the idea that he was the greatest soldier of the age, and flattered the vain, credulous and greedy savage into the belief that he was destined to raise Paraguay from obscurity, and make it the dominant power of South America. . . . The influence she exercised over a man so imperious, yet so weak, so vain, and sensual as López, was immense. With admirable tact, she treated him apparently with the utmost deference and respect, whilst she could really do with him as she pleased, and virtually was the ruler of Paraguay. . . . That lady occupied a very prominent place eventually in Paraguayan affairs, and, I believe, by her evil counsels and boundless ambitions was the remote cause of the terrible war which . . . utterly depopulated the country.

    —DR. GEORGE FREDERICK MASTERMAN,
       Apothecary General to the Paraguayan Army
       during the reign of Francisco López;
       My Seven Eventful Years in Paraguay [1869]

Heroes are created by popular demand, sometimes out of the scantiest materials. . . .

    —GERALD WHITE JOHNSON,
       American Heroes and Hero-Worship

Introduction

Between the years 1864 and 1870, the small landlocked nation of Paraguay fought against the combined forces of Brazil, Argentina, and Uruguay in the War of the Triple Alliance.

Also known as the Paraguayan War, it was the bloodiest ever waged in all of Latin America; indeed, with the exception of our own Civil War, the bloodiest ever waged in the Western Hemisphere.

And the most unnecessary.

And the most stupid.

But this book is not about that war.

Rather, it is about the two people who precipitated it: two people who shared a dream that became a nightmare for all concerned.

The dream they shared—a not entirely unrealistic one, given the circumstances of the time—was to convert Paraguay into the capital of an empire that would embrace the entire Río de la Plata region: Paraguay itself, the Argentine Confederation, Uruguay, and Brazil, the latter a Portuguese nation immensely larger than its mother country, which the dreamers hoped to hispanicize.

Both Uruguay and the Argentine Confederation, having shaken off the yoke of Spanish imperialism, were consumed by devastating civil wars. In striving to achieve birth as independent nations, they showed every promise of winding up as geopolitical abortions. Both feared Brazil, a cumbersome giant whose interior, vital to the development of the country, could easily be cut off by the rivers which Paraguay could have blockaded, and whose diplomats, without peer on the continent, felt that the nation's only hope for survival lay in preventing the entire region from achieving unification. Paraguay itself, though the least populated and most vulnerable geographically and economically, boasted the best-armed, best-trained, and best-motivated army not only among the combatants but in all of Latin America—indeed, in all of the Western Hemisphere, being superior even to the Union Army at the outbreak of the American Civil War.

It was a dream Napoleon Bonaparte and his Josephine might well have realized. But Francisco Solano López and Eliza Alicia Lynch were no Napoleon and Josephine, their illusions notwithstanding.

Madame Lynch was a physically appealing young Irish adventuress in search of wealth and glory. Her Friend was a physically appalling young Paraguayan megalomaniac in search of someone to feed his egregious ego.

Francisco Solano López, eldest son of the Dictator-President of Paraguay, envisioned himself as the emperor of the New World. That vision was nurtured—and shared—by Eliza Lynch, a young divorcee who envisioned herself as his empress. For the girl from County Cork, such an elevated station seemed infinitely more rewarding—and decidedly more respectable—than remaining, as she had been, just another successful courtesan plying her trade in Second Empire Paris.

At dream's end, Argentina, Brazil, and Uruguay emerged as unified nations; Paraguay's cities were in ruins, its economy utterly destroyed, its male population reduced by upwards of 90 percent. What began as a scheme to make Paraguay the most sophisticated and important power on the South American continent ended as a disaster which saw that unfortunate nation sink into a bog of insignificance and backwardness from which it has yet to emerge.

López had vowed that the war into which he rushed, through embarrassingly inept diplomacy and unfounded confidence in his talents as a military leader—encouraged along every step of the way by Madame Lynch—would not end until he was killed on the battlefield. He kept that vow.

His mistress had vowed to take vengeance on the aristocrats of Paraguay who had humiliatingly rejected her—another vow that was fulfilled.

López's last, defiant gesture was to declaim, "Yo muero con mi patria" ("I die with my country"—though a more appropriate declamation would have been "My country dies with me").

His mistress's last, defiant gesture was to flee back to Europe with the wealth of those who had scorned her—the wealth she and her Friend had expropriated shrewdly and shamelessly, ostensibly to help them construct their impossible dream.

Today, both are revered as Paraguay's greatest Hero and Heroine.

A Personal Note

I first became acquainted with the Lynch-López legend when I served with the United States Embassy at Asunción in 1955. Prior to moving into the house which had been put at my disposal, I lived for a few weeks at El Gran Hotel del Paraguay —at the time, the only habitable hotel in all of Paraguay. According to local tradition fiercely held to this day, the hotel's nucleus was the town house given Madame Lynch by her Paraguayan lover. According to fact, this "tradition" was begun by the hotel's builder, an enterprising Swiss-German, in hopes of attracting a clientele to what may well be the most execrable architectural monstrosity in all of Paraguay with the singular exception of the new U.S. Embassy (the address of which, it might be amusing to note, is 1776 Avenida Mariscal Francisco Solano López).

What first drew me to the legend—and I use the term advisedly—was the realization that two people who were so unmitigated a blight on Paraguayan history wound up being regarded, by the descendants of those whose deaths they had caused, with a reverence that is usually reserved for saints.

Having since then read every available book dealing with Eliza Lynch and Francisco López, many of which have never been translated into the English language and most of which are by now out of print, I found that comprehending the "real" López posed no problem. Only a few historians have attempted to portray him as other than the tyrant that more responsible scholarship has established him to have been; and these are taken seriously only by the present-day Stroessner dictatorship in Paraguay, whose purpose in glorifying both López *and* Lynch will be dealt with in its proper place.

But Madame Lynch was, to resort to contemporary argot, something else again.

There was no middle ground insofar as treatment of her career went: she was either absolutely loathed or absolutely adored by her biographers. None of them apparently saw fit to research her story with any degree of fidelity, preferring, instead, to let his or her imagination run wild in order to support a particular point of view.

One of her detractors, for example, determined to prove that she was no more than a common scheming whore, has Madame Lynch leading the Parisian doxies at the world premiere of Offenbach's *La Belle Hélène*—an action that borders on the transcendental, considering that this particular piece of musical fluff was not written until more than a decade after she had decamped Paris with her Paraguayan paramour.

Another—this time a defender—has Madame Lynch's father dying the glorious death of a naval officer off the coast of China in 1840, though records show that he was very much alive, and in mufti, when his daughter married a Frenchman, Xavier Quatrefages, ten years later.

Still another biographer—actually, this one could not quite decide whether she unabashedly admired or utterly abominated her subject—claims that Madame Lynch was a nymphomaniacal slut of superior intellect who had matriculated at Dublin's Trinity College at an age when even the brightest child, sexual proclivities notwithstanding, is matriculating in grammar school.

And so it goes.

About the only point on which all of her biographers agree,

detractors and defenders alike, is that Madame Lynch was buried in Paris's Père Lachaise Cemetery as a ward of the municipality—this despite the demonstrable facts that 1) by the time of her death in 1886, an eleven-year-old law strictly prohibited the inhumation of paupers in that august burial ground, and 2) her inhumation was in fact paid for by one of her three surviving sons by López (a son, it might be noted, whose existence has been completely overlooked by the majority of the Lynch-López chroniclers).

Those who wrote about her, and there have been many, were not alone when it came to bending (and in many cases warping) the truth. Madame Lynch, herself, in her only known autobiographical endeavor, *Exposición y Protesta* (*Statement and Protest,* published in Buenos Aires in 1875), laid down a few claims which can safely be consigned to the realm of self-serving fantasy. Many of these claims, plus many more that even Madame Lynch could never have dreamed up in her wildest flights of fancy, are accepted as gospel by her present-day descendants in the third and fourth generations.

After six months of extensive research in Washington, D.C., Dublin, Paris, London, Edinburgh, and Asunción, I have come to the following considered conclusion: While their accounts were undoubtedly colored by their own prejudices, those chroniclers who actually *knew* Madame Lynch were indubitably closer to the mark when it came to defining her personality and life style than could possibly have been her latter-day chroniclers, whose purposes smack suspiciously of having been less to serve history than to, in some cases, spin a lively *fábula* or, in other cases, to grind a particular axe.

Madame Lynch's detractors would have us believe she was the reincarnation of Messalina. Her defenders, including those present-day descendants, would have us believe she was all but a lineal descendant of the Son of Man.

Does the truth fall somewhere in between these two unsupportable extremes?

Hardly.

Messalina was, on balance, a truly demented human being, a charge which cannot be leveled against Madame Lynch; and it is by now historically valid to assume that the Son of Man left no known issue.

In many respects, Madame Lynch differed little from countless other adventuresses who have vamped their way across the stage of history from time to time, bent on avenging either ignominious origins or inflicted wrongs.

What, then, sets her apart from Agrippina, Du Barry, or even her contemporary the pompous Empress Eugénie, amongst others?

That, the reader must decide.

A Note on Nomenclature

There is no definitive rendering of our heroine's name.
The superscription of her *Exposición y Protesta* is signed "Elisa A. Lynch," while the postscription reads "Eliza Alicia Lynch." Her marriage certificate reads "Elizabeth Alecia [*sic*] Lynch"—which may have been the correct form. To one and all, she was known, at her insistence, as "Madame Lynch." To the aristocratic women of Paraguay, for whom she was anathema, she was referred to sneeringly as "Madama Lavincha." In her postwar claims against the Paraguayan Provisional Government and Dr. William Stewart, both of which were heard in the Scottish courts, she chose to be called "Mrs. Eliza Alicia Lynch." To her close intimates, she is believed to have been known as "Ella."

Since it is fairly safe to assume, on the basis of her marriage certificate, that her given name was Elizabeth, and since Eliza, for which she seems to have shown a preference, is a logical diminutive of Elizabeth, "Eliza" it shall be in this narrative. It might be interesting to note that her descendants in Paraguay, who venerate her, when referring to her do not say "my grandmother" or "my great-grandmother" but simply, and reverentially, "Madame Lynch."

PART ONE

THE ENCOUNTER

From *Exposición y Protesta:*

> I was born in Ireland in the year 1835, of honorable and wealthy parents belonging to an Irish family that counted on father's side two bishops and more than seventy [*sic*] magistrates, and on mother's side a Vice-Admiral of the British Navy who had the honor to fight with four of his brothers under the command of Nelson at the battles of the Nile and Trafalgar. All my uncles were officers in the British Navy or Army. My cousins are [likewise] today, and a number of my relatives occupy high positions in Ireland. On the third of June, 1850, I was married in England at the age of fifteen to Mr. Quatrefages, a person now occupying a high position in France. [It would seem that Madame Lynch fancied herself enjoying some spectacular affinity, whether through genealogy or matrimony, with individuals who managed to "occupy high positions."] I lived at his side three years, residing in France and Algeria, without leaving issue. Separated from him because of my poor health, I was reunited with my mother and sister in England, living for a time with them. I then lived with my uncle, Commodore William Boyle Crooke of the British Royal Navy, and his wife, who was my mother's sister. I [then] resided in Paris a short while, living with my mother and the Stafford family [which was] comprised of the mother and three daughters, whose father was at the time a magistrate in Dublin. [This would bring to more than seventy-one the number of magistrates who somehow allegedly figured in Madame Lynch's life.] A short time [*sic*] after being separated from my husband I met Marshal López, and immediately thereafter found myself in Buenos Aires in 1854, enroute to Asunción, which I did not leave until 1870, when I fell prisoner [to the Brazilian army].*

---

* Translated by A.B. from a copy of the first edition, now in the British Museum.

The Girl from County Cork

Though ample documentation abounds to prove that Eliza Lynch lived and died, we lack any evidentiary proof that she was actually born.

A careful check of birth and baptismal records at the Genealogical Office at Dublin Castle, the repository for all such records covering all the counties of Ireland and dating back more than three centuries, has proved fruitless; likewise the Dublin Public Records Office in the Four Courts, a treasure trove of marriage and death certificates, deeds, land applotment and taxation records, and the like.

Assuredly, records have a way of getting unintentionally lost; conversely, they have a way of getting intentionally destroyed. But there is a limit to how much one can destroy regarding one's ancestry—especially if that ancestry is an Irish one. The Japanese and Chinese merely worship their ancestors; the Irish *prove* theirs.

There is no evidence to indicate that Madame Lynch willfully set out to destroy all genealogical references to herself, in itself a formidable if not impossible task. She never returned to Ireland after leaving it as a young girl, though she had every opportunity to do so, especially in the postwar years.

No records exist to substantiate her more exalted ancestral

claims. A careful check of British Navy and Army records in London's Public Records Office has established that, while many an officer enjoyed the honor of fighting under Nelson at the battles of the Nile and Trafalgar, no quintet of siblings was entered in the lists. Nor, for that matter, do the records support Eliza's familial relationship with *any* British officers of flag or field rank, with the exception of William Boyle Crooke. And accepting this particular relationship is not so much a documentable fact as an act of faith. (I personally have accepted it, on the basis of claims made by many, including the descendants, that Eliza's mother was in fact Adelaide Schnock, sister of Mrs. Crooke. However, it should be noted that according to British naval records "Commodore" Crooke never rose above the rank of lieutenant.)

Logic would dictate that *some* shred of evidence surrounding Madame Lynch's ancestry would have somehow survived.

But after two visits to Dublin, poring over all available records under the skillful and highly appreciated guidance of Mr. Donal F. Begley, Director of the Genealogical Office, and the thoroughly delightful Ms. Margaret Byrne, Directress of the Public Records Office in the Four Courts, I am almost tempted to concur with Mr. Begley's thesis (as has Ms. Byrne) that "Either your Madame Lynch was a bloody liar or a bloody lunatic. Her claims are bloody rubbish."

It is a temptation I have managed to forswear.

Madame Lynch was not a lunatic, though some of her actions, especially toward the end of her life, may have bordered on lunacy in the clinical sense of the word. She was a liar, but not a complete liar. And only some of her claims could be categorized as rubbish, e.g., the claim that she returned to England following her separation from Quatrefages and lived, first with her mother and sister, and then with her uncle the spurious "Commodore," before moving on to Paris, where she met López. She did not in fact return to England until her expulsion

from Paraguay at war's end in 1870—twenty years after she had
left England as a bride. (And it might be of interest to note,
in all probability she lived in England at the time under an alias.)

More so than Madame Lynch, it was her most obdurate defenders and more antagonistic detractors who were the bloody
liars, the bloody lunatics, their claims bloody rubbish.

When writing the life of a historical personage, be he or she
of high or low estate, sinner or saint, it is the biographer's obligation to embark upon the undertaking with a fixed point of
view and then go on to support that point of view. But it is an
obligation that cannot and must not be adopted until all available
evidence has been exhaustively examined. If the writer does not
examine all evidence, and limits his research to reading only what
others with the same preconception have written on the subject,
then he is not supporting a viable point of view but merely rehearsing that of others.

After a careful study of the few authentic documents now
available in various records offices and libraries on three con-
tinents, and an equally careful sifting of all the material written
about her, including newspaper accounts, much of it while she
was still alive, I have arrived at the following point of view
about Madame Lynch:

She was reprehensible.

Yet, there was something tragic about her. One suspects that
if she had involved herself with someone less morally cretinous
than López—preferably a powerful leader from within her own
European culture—and had been accepted by her adopted people on *her* terms—which were not all that unreasonable—instead
of being treated as a pariah, Eliza Lynch might have gone down
in history as another Empress Theodosia. But the gods had decreed
otherwise. She did not set out to become a horror. But in choosing López, and Paraguay, she allowed herself, albeit unwittingly,
to be transmogrified into one.

Eliza Lynch was one of those whom Jim O'Malley, one of present-day Ireland's leading intellectuals, describes as "Those women of County Cork, all of whom were (and many of whom still are) eccentric—too much imagination and too many brains —and over-sexed. What can you do with such a combination— and believe me, they have little outlet for any of those qualities."

Eliza Lynch was certainly possessed of imagination: the manner in which she got her hands on all that Paraguayan jewelry and real estate is every bit as imaginative as Hannibal's celebrated transalpine excursion. And while she probably was not over-sexed, simple logic would dictate that any woman who could marry at fifteen, divorce at seventeen, take a string of lovers at eighteen, and bear her paramour seven children by the age of thirty-two could hardly be said to have recoiled from sexual encounters. As for the "brains" aspect, Eliza was demonstrably several cuts above the prototypal girl from County Cork: it is known that, among other accomplishments, she mastered French and Spanish and was highly fluent in the palate-twisting Paraguayan language of Guaraní, no mean feat.

If the O'Malley thesis holds true, then it was only when it came to having "little outlet for those qualities" that Eliza Lynch parted company with her sisters of the county, past, present, and probably future.

The question now obtrudes: How exactly did she find those outlets?

All evidence regarding Eliza Lynch's life prior to her arrival in Paraguay is, with the exception of her marriage certificate (now available at London's General Registry Office), admittedly circumstantial. All evidence regarding her postwar years is, with the exception of the records of her various lawsuits (now available at Edinburgh's West Register House) and her death and inhumation certificates (now available at the Mairie of Paris's Seventeenth Arrondissement), admittedly circumstantial.

But as Thoreau has pointed out, "Some circumstantial evidence is very strong, as when you find a trout in the milk."

She was born sometime during the first half of 1835 in County Cork (the actual city or village cannot be determined, nor can the exact date) to John and Adelaide Schnock Lynch. John is listed on Eliza's marriage certificate as a "Medical Doctor." It is fairly safe to suspect that the bride listed him so in order to imbue her father with some professional status; perhaps to outdo her French father-in-law, whose profession is given as "Merchant."

It is known that an older sister, Corinne, was at the time living in Paris with her husband, who may or may not have been a musician; and, though Eliza herself never mentioned them, two older brothers are believed to have been serving with the British Navy.

Therefore, although she was the youngest of two children, and quite possibly of four, Eliza was in effect raised as an only child.

The Lynch-López descendants persist in claiming that Adelaide Schnock counted on her family tree a variegated collection of twigs that included the Personal Confessor to Queen Victoria, three members of Parliament during the reign of Queen Anne, the Royal Executioner who beheaded Charles I, the rightful heir to the Duchy of Warwick, one of the leaders of the opposition to Cromwell's Roundheads, the favorite catamite of Richard the Lion-Hearted, the first white man to land in Ireland, and the man "who actually ghost-wrote" William the Conqueror's *Doomsday Book*.

All that can be deduced, on the basis of records and elementary logic, is that Adelaide Schnock was simply Adelaide Schnock. The name Schnock is not an Irish one; nor for that matter is the name Adelaide. It is fairly safe to conclude that Adelaide was an Englishwoman of Germanic descent. The questions of

when and under what circumstance she met and married John
Lynch are totally unanswerable, and need not detain us further.
The surname Lynch is the seventeenth most common in all of
Ireland. In County Cork alone, records show no less than nineteen John Lynches who flourished during the period under discussion, any one of whom might have been Eliza's father but
none of whom was either a medical doctor or was married to an
Adelaide Schnock (or any other Schnock). Also, none of the
John Lynches, nor any of the other eleven Lynches for that mat-
ter, can be shown to have enjoyed kinship, however remote,
with "two bishops and more than seventy magistrates." (Mr.
Begley of the Genealogical Office advises that there has never
been a man in all of Ireland, the surname notwithstanding, to
whom such kinships can be ascribed.) However, the various
Lynch clans, which were most predominant in County Cork
(Ireland's largest) at the beginning of the nineteenth century,
could well have boasted "relations who occupy high positions."
There have always been a covey of Lynches occupying such
positions at any given time in Ireland's troubled history; there
probably always will be.

The family were communicants of the Anglican Church. Many
of the Lynch clans were Anglican; Adelaide was certainly Anglican, and Eliza was married in the Anglican faith. Too, the
present-day descendants concede this, though they themselves
are practicing Catholics. (This is probably less out of deference
to López than to the fact that Catholicism is the state religion
of Paraguay, and all the Lópezes are, in one way or another,
closely tied in with the Stroessner Government.)

Little is known about Eliza's childhood, although one rather
curious set of circumstances, popular with her descendants,
merits examination. It is that father John died about 1840, at
which time Adelaide remarried, to a man named Kinkley,
whereupon Eliza was sent to Dublin to be raised by her maternal
uncle, the Archbishop of that city, with whose blessings Eliza
matriculated at Trinity College at the age of *nine*. We know that

John was alive when Eliza married in 1850; marriage and ec-clesiastical records fail to support any remarriage on Adelaide's part or any relationship to the Archbishop of Dublin; and there is the testimony of the Registrar at Trinity College that "We have had students matriculate here at an early age, but certainly *not* at *that* early an age!"

It is palpably more logical, and believed by the more respon-sible Lynch-López chroniclers, that Eliza did not leave Cork until her tenth year—when the family was forced to flee in the wake of the Great Famine.

If, as Eliza claims, her parents were wealthy, then the theory that she was sent to France for her primary schooling, a theory advanced by some of her biographers, is supportable. Eliza was an extremely bright, well-read, cultivated young lady whose formal education stopped at the age of fifteen; in short, hers was an education more readily obtained at a French school than at the hands of a local schoolmaster in the County Cork of the first half of the nineteenth century. However, it should be noted that in all contemporary newspaper accounts dealing with Madame Lynch, including interviews with the Argentinian journalist and social commentator Héctor Varela, who was often her guest in Asunción, no allusion has been made to a French education. Logic might dictate that, had she gone to school in France, Eliza would have boasted of it; she was a complete Francophile. (Indeed, one of the many stunts which brought her to grief in her adopted land of Paraguay was Eliza's attempt to impose French customs on a Guaraní culture.) Then again, there is always the possibility that Eliza was privately tutored at home. If so, the tutor must have been a fairly remarkable pedagogue.

Eliza was totally uncommunicative when it came to discuss-ing her childhood. One almost suspects that she hoped to con-vey the impression that she had simply joined the human race as a fifteen-year-old, much in the manner that Pallas Athena sprang from the cranium of Zeus fully clad and ready for battle.

The conclusion to be drawn, then, is that either her childhood was an unhappy one, or that she suffered some childhood trauma. Eliza's refusal to discuss her life up to the point where she married Quatrefages can quite conceivably be attributed to some form of convenient amnesia.

I am inclined to dismiss the idea that her entire childhood was an ongoing trauma; had that been the case, I suspect she would have denied her Irish heritage. It would have been easy for Eliza to claim she was born in England; too, it would have been just as easy for her to deny her name and claim French birth. It is my belief that either John Lynch was a wealthy man who did not know how to hold on to his money, or that the family was comfortable by the standards of the day, though by no means "rich." Supporting the latter thesis is our knowledge that the truly wealthy landowners of Ireland not only remained behind during the Famine, but managed to double, if not treble, their holdings; as was the case during the stock market crash of 1929, the Great Famine saw a handful profit from the misery of the masses. Supporting the theory that John Lynch was far from a clever businessman is our evidence (again, admittedly circumstantial) that he proved to be a failure in Paris.

That Eliza omits mention of her father in her immediate post-marriage arrangements ("I was reunited with my mother and sister in England"), taken in tandem with our knowledge that she did not in fact return to England at that time, does not so much resolve the question of John's ultimate fate as raise a few unanswerable questions. A careful check of the London Public Records Office, a veritable warehouse of minutiae on matters funerary, has failed to unearth any John Lynch being buried anywhere in the British Isles during the period of Eliza's marriage (1850–1853). Did he die in France? Did he *not* die but, instead, simply abandon his family (or perhaps have been abandoned by them)? Or was he perhaps killed off symbolically by Eliza, who might have resented his having been a failure and

having thus caused her to undertake a marriage that had proved
to be a disaster?

Henry Lyon Young, in his *Eliza Lynch, Regent of Paraguay*, has advanced a rather convincing conjecture which is
deserving of consideration:

> Looking back across the years Eliza could never forget the
> famine of '45. It had left its mark. It was as if she had been
> branded for the rest of her life. Ten years old at the time, she
> had witnessed scenes that had remained indelibly printed in her
> mind. Her chief recollection was one of hunger, a gnawing,
> lighthearted nausea that ate into her very vitals and made her
> vomit with emptiness. . . . Even if they had the means it would
> have been impossible to buy food. The shops were empty. Relief
> committees had been set up in Cork but they were forced to
> close after a few days as supplies ran out . . . How well she
> remembered her mother trying to make a stew with a handful of
> roots dug out of the garden. . . . The servants had long since
> disappeared to scavenge for themselves in the county districts.
> Then there was the night when Eliza, crying with distress, had
> been dressed hurriedly. With true Irish providence her parents
> had just abandoned the house. Corinne . . . had written from
> Paris suggesting that they come and stay with her during the
> present crisis, and pool their resources. The idea had taken root
> and John Lynch had decided that rather than face starvation in
> Cork he would collect every penny he could lay his hands on and
> take his wife and youngest child to France where he hoped to
> retrieve his vanished fortune.

Granted, the idea that Eliza was forced to flee with her
parents during the Famine does not in and of itself suggest that
she was the heiress of an aristocrat who had fallen on hard times,
whether as a result of his own ineptitude or otherwise. But
the fact that she was obviously a girl of breeding and sophistication, highly versed in the social and intellectual amenities, and
this without a formal secondary school education, strongly
implies that Eliza was hardly a product of the peasant class. (The

pathetic peasant class of early nineteenth-century Ireland could well have produced a genius, though any such accomplishment has thus far gone unrecorded, but not a woman whose fiercest detractors conceded that her sophistication and intellect were far from a veneer and seemingly congenital.) This implication is reinforceable by the inference to be drawn from Eliza's unwillingness to mention the ultimate fate of her father.

One need not be a Freudian to attribute Eliza's proven thirst for the finer things in life to some childhood trauma. I submit that Eliza's trauma derived from the conviction that her father had "failed her" by causing her, however unintentionally, to be deracinated from a life of luxury and forcibly implanted into the scabrous soil of poverty. Of one thing we can be sure: Eliza Lynch was determined that she would never again know the want of luxury, a determination that she fulfilled—at the expense of an entire Latin American nation.

The Paris of 1845 was the Paris of the so-called July Monarchy.

Fifteen years previously, the deposing of Charles X and the accession of Louis Philippe, the Citizen King, had finalized the victory of the bourgeoisie over the aristocracy. After striving for social ascendancy since 1789, and having seen their country suffer the justified French Revolution, the imperial dictatorship of Napoleon Bonaparte, and the restoration of the very monarchy whose overthrow had been the prime motivation for the Revolution, the upper and middle classes of France had at last secured that ascendancy. Within three years of Eliza's arrival, the great tide of revolution that swept across Europe would sweep the ineffectual Louis Philippe from his throne, and sweep into power the conniving Louis Napoleon, the Prince-President who presided over the transition of France from the Second Republic to the Second Empire.

The Paris of 1845 was assuredly the place where vanished

fortunes were to be retrieved, new fortunes to be made.
But John Lynch's was not one of those fortunes. His talent
for investing his carefully hoarded cash in the wrong stocks on
the Paris Bourse would appear to have bordered on the spec-
tacular. In short, the Lynch family was not much better off in
France than they would have been had they remained in Ireland. Compounding the family's fiscal plight, Corinne seems
not to have been as affluent as she may have led them to believe
she was.

(The "official" version of Madame Lynch's life, as perpetuated by the Stroessner Government in Paraguay, has it that
Corinne's husband, one Tamburini, was a major star in the
Parisian cultural pantheon of the mid-nineteenth century, that
he was an arbiter of matters musical on a par with Rossini and
Meyerbeer. Tamburini has yet to surface in any of the seemingly
countless histories and biographies that recorded this period. And
here we might note that this version of Eliza's life would have
us believe that Tamburini's "good friend" Victor Hugo considered her to be one of the most superior minds ever to appear
on his horizon, and that her "great friend" Franz Liszt all but
fairly collapsed in a lachrymose swoon because Eliza refused to
pursue a career as a concert pianist. It is known that Eliza enjoyed classical music, that she was able to execute the less complicated popular tunes of the day on the piano that traveled
with her wherever she went; the piano even went with her when
Eliza was forced to flee Asunción for the hinterlands ahead of
the invading Brazilian Army in 1868. But that Liszt ever encouraged her to follow in the steps of the legendary Teresa Ca-
rreño is as unsupportable as is the idea that Eliza ever considered
the suggestion, or was even capable of doing so—though from
the Paraguayan point of view, one is tempted to wish wistfully
that he had and she had. For the record, the only possible tie that
can be established between Eliza Lynch and Franz Liszt is that
they died within five days of each other: Eliza from stomach

cancer compounded by malnutrition, Franz from the infirmities of age compounded by attending a Wagner matinee.)

Father John was now faced with the problem of supporting, in addition to a wife and two daughters (and quite possibly his stockbroker, in a manner of speaking), a broken-down son-in-law whose identity and profession it is impossible to ascertain and who may quite possibly have never existed.

Being an aggressive, self-assured girl, Eliza had no delusions about herself. She was mature for her years, and she was exceptionally beautiful; what is more, she *knew* it. It should not be difficult to appreciate how a young girl well endowed both physically and intellectually, having been transported brutally from affluence to poverty in her most formative years, might seek out some means of achieving upward mobility. For a girl of Eliza's temperament and determination, upward mobility could be achieved only by following one of two routes: marriage or prostitution.

Prostitution was out of the question; it would have been a violation of her moral code. And here it must be emphasized that Eliza Lynch *never* became a prostitute. She sold herself, true. But she was a *courtesan*, never a prostitute; and there is more than a semantic difference between the two. We shall be having more to say shortly regarding Eliza's presumed attitudes toward sex, but first let us get her married off.

His name was Xavier Quatrefages, he was a career officer in the French Army, the scion of a respectable middle-class family; and, for those who would seek Freudian implications, he was almost old enough to be Eliza's father.

Many theories have been advanced as to how the two met; these range from the implausible (that they met and married in Cork) to the ludicrous. In this latter category belongs the version supported by the present-day Paraguayan Government. It is a version that merits our attention, less because of its inherent inanities than because it demonstrates how, in their attempt to glorify Madame Lynch, Government historians have chosen to dispense with considerations of logic and geography. According to this theory, then, Quatrefages, an old college mate of Eliza's eldest brother, came to Dublin on a secret mission for French Military Intelligence and wooed Eliza assiduously along the banks of the river Shannon; after a whirlwind courtship they were married by that putative ecclesiastical uncle the Dublin Archbishop.

It is highly improbable that a French Army officer and a British Naval officer would have attended university together. Xavier was not in French Military Intelligence, he was a veterinary surgeon with the French Army. Eliza and Xavier were married in Folkestone Parish, County Kent, England, "in the Rites and Ceremonies of the Established [Anglican] Church," Minister Thomas Pearce—no relative—officiating. And the river Shannon does not flow anywhere *near* Dublin.

The more acceptable theory, adhering to the general consensus, is that the two met in Paris. Where or how is not important. What *is* important is that, despite the disparity in their ages and the fact that Xavier was a Roman Catholic, father John would have been frantic that the marriage take place. Xavier was a career officer, which made him downright respectable; and he did not demand a dowry, which made him downright desirable.

That Xavier fell instantly in love with Eliza is understandable: the one surviving picture from this period reveals her to have been an extraordinary beauty. That he was eager to make her his bride is more than implied by the fact that in agreeing to marry Eliza in contravention of the French Code, he willingly put his military career in jeopardy.

Whether Eliza was madly in love with Xavier, as is claimed by some, or whether, as seems more logical, she saw in marriage an escape from the rim of poverty on which the Lynch family tottered is speculative. Be that as it may, all parties directly concerned were in favor of the marriage.

But as much could not be said for the French authorities.

Even were Eliza to convert to the Roman faith, the law decreed that no girl could marry until she had celebrated her sixteenth birthday; and we have no way of knowing whether Eliza had yet celebrated her *fifteenth* birthday. The French authorities did not prohibit the marriage; they simply ordered that it be delayed until Eliza reached sixteen. Eliza—showing that streak of determination which was to carry her to unknown heights (and her adopted country of Paraguay to unknown depths)—simply dragged Xavier off to England, where, as has been established, she became Madame Quatrefages.

The manner and haste in which they were married more than suggest that Eliza and Xavier simply could not "wait." This is not to imply that Eliza was pregnant; she was not. Rather, the implication here is that Eliza was desperate to escape from her poverty-stricken family through the legal route, while Xavier, anxious to "have" Eliza, was, in jeopardizing his career, willing to put passion before pragmatism.

Both got what they wanted out of the marriage; and after they had achieved their respective wants, they seem to have allowed the marriage to die. Of the various reasons which have been advanced regarding the dissolution of the marriage within three years, two deserve repetition. Both contain more than a nugget of plausibility.

According to the first, Eliza, while stationed with Xavier in Algeria, was seduced by his commanding officer, a lecherous old colonel, and was aggrieved beyond measure when Xavier, fearing to stand up to the colonel, if only to protect his wife's honor, suddenly and conveniently discovered that Eliza was not in fact his wife according to the French Code. Eliza's "grief," the story goes, was mitigated when, while out horseback riding one day—she is known to have been an accomplished equestrienne —Eliza chanced upon a dashing young Russian Cavalry officer of the patent nobility named Michael, who just happened to be cantering across Algeria in search of adventure. When Michael learned that Xavier was not going to defend the honor of the beautiful young matron with whom he seems to have fallen in love at first sight, he killed the colonel and took Eliza off to Paris, where he established her in a town house in the fashionable Boulevard Saint Germain. The two nuggets of plausibility here: seeing his advancement blocked, it was indeed convenient for Xavier to "discover" that he was not legally married, even though it took him more than two years to make that "discovery"; and it is believed by the more responsible chroniclers that before her third wedding anniversary Eliza was "established" in Paris by a Russian Cavalry officer.

The second theory, as she claimed in her *Exposición y Protesta,* is that Eliza was indeed suffering "poor health"—but that the "poor health" (the nugget of plausibility here) was emotional as opposed to organic in nature. Logic would dictate that the provincial life of Algerian garrison towns, with restricted duties imposed upon the free-willed child bride of a minor officer charged with overseeing the health and welfare of a cavalry regiment's horses, held few attractions for an ambitious girl; more so in the case of Eliza, who had tasted both the horrors of the Irish Famine and the glitter of Paris, and who might well have galloped into the arms of a dashing Russian and/or decided she could no longer suffer the taunts of the other garrison wives, in whose eyes she was not legally married.

While visiting Scotland to research Madame Lynch's postwar claims against Dr. William Stewart and the Provisional Paraguayan Government, the present writer stumbled across an extraordinary document in Edinburgh's West Register House which has gone unnoticed by every biographer of Eliza Lynch, and which has led me to arrive at still a third theory regarding the breakup of the marriage.

On October 19, 1854, Quatrefages, who had by then been promoted to "senior inspector at the Military Hospitals in Algiers," while on a leave of absence in Paris signed a notarized statement giving "all necessary powers and authorities to Madame Elisa Alice Lynch, his wife, *residing with him* [italics added]: In order that she may manage and administer, actively and passively, all properties and matters whatsoever, real and personal, present or future, of the said Madame Quatrefages in England . . ."

This power of attorney was affirmed by the British Consul in Paris *more than a year after* Eliza had left Quatrefages in Algeria, and barely *three weeks before* she left Paris for Paraguay. It tactfully implies that Eliza was "Madame Lynch" in France, "Madame Quatrefages" in England; and it gave her power of attorney only in England, where Eliza had no property or claims to any. Why, then, this extraordinary document? Surely Eliza was not "residing with him" at the time.

It is my belief that the breakup of the quasi marriage was a mutually agreed upon maneuver. Perhaps Eliza had in fact taken another lover; certainly she did not enjoy living in some Algerian outpost, especially at this point in her life. After four years of pretense at presiding over a republic, Louis Napoleon had seized the government and restored the monarchy; Paris was by now the place for aggressive young matrons concerned less with respectability than upward mobility. Too, Xavier had probably by now had it brought home to him that if he hoped to advance in his career, he had better do something about his "marriage." It was perfectly proper, in the French scheme of things, for an officer to live openly with a mistress, even if that mistress were married to one of his fellow officers, but it was *malséant* to pass off a mistress as a wife.

But why, the reader would be justified in asking, why would Xavier swear before a notary that he was still living with Eliza, when he must have known—as just about everyone else in Paris knew—that she was by now the acknowledged mistress of the Paraguayan Ambassador, Francisco Solano López? It is my belief that Xaxier had already met the woman he was to marry and wanted a legal termination of his relationship with Eliza, and that Eliza, who considered her marriage a valid one, French Code to the contrary, coerced him into signing a document that would give her the respectability of a married woman. Or—and this is admittedly a bit farfetched—that the document was a forgery undertaken at Eliza's behest seventeen years after the fact. When Madame Lynch sued in the Scottish courts, the defendants claimed immunity from prosecution on the grounds that a married woman could not sue without the cooperation of her husband—at which point Eliza's solicitors produced "proof" that Eliza's husband had in fact removed himself legally from any involvement in the litigation.

While visiting Asunción to research this book, I showed a reproduction of that power of attorney to the Lynch-López descendants and members of the Stroessner Government, none of whom had known of its existence. It was immediately seized upon as "proof that Madame Lynch was a respectable married lady until she met López." When I pointed out that a scant three weeks separated the execution of the document and Eliza's departure for Paraguay, and that even Eliza admits that she did not meet López until a while *after* her separation from Quatrefages, I was told, "Well, maybe the date on the document was forged by the Scottish authorities. Who knows? It is a great mystery."

Thanks to the capable assistance of Ms. Lesley Horn at Edinburgh's West Register House, I have been able to ascertain that if the power of attorney, originally executed in French, was a forgery, the crime cannot be ascribed to Scottish authorities.

Having raised the question of the power of attorney, perhaps it is as well that we dismiss it, as do even Madame Lynch's staunchest partisans, with a simple Who knows?—It is indeed a great mystery—and pick up where we left off with Eliza: in Paris.

By whatever route she or the fates chose to transport her there, Eliza Lynch celebrated her eighteenth birthday in the city which the Goncourt brothers were to disparage as "the brothel of Europe."

Within a year, she was to meet her destiny in that brothel.

2

All evidence seems to indicate that during Eliza's absence in Algeria, her father had either died or abandoned the family (or both), and her mother had returned to Ireland (or perhaps England); sister Corinne may have left Paris, either with or without her presumed husband; and Eliza's brothers were pursuing their naval careers. And if that Russian cavalry officer Michael had in fact set her up in a mansion in the Boulevard Saint Germain, he seems to have abandoned her precipitously (perhaps to gallop off to help his country lose the Crimean War, which was just about getting under way).

Eliza was now faced with two alternatives: returning to Ireland (or even England) and living in genteel poverty; or staying on to partake of all that the Second Empire, still in its first year, had to offer.

Her marriage to Quatrefages had been a means toward an end: escape from poverty. And now she was right back where she had started. Is it possible that, being the strong-willed woman she was, Eliza realized that she could never make any one man happy, or find one man who could make *her* happy? Perhaps. But highly doubtful. For Eliza was probably incapable of loving any man. Her protests notwithstanding, she never loved López. He, like everyone else and everything else in Eliza's life, represented, as had Quatrefages, a means toward an end.

Wealth, power, independence. These were Eliza's goals—goals she would exploit every means to achieve.

And high on her list of "means" was self-exploitation.

The only surviving picture of Eliza dating from this period reveals a stunning young girl with a provocative smile who seems to be saying unabashedly and unashamedly, I'll get what I want, and my way. In the one surviving picture of Eliza dating from her days as empress-consort over Paraguay in all but name, we see in her Gioconda-like smile and those penetrating eyes—eyes that do not so much stare at the camera as through the photographer—a woman who seems to be saying unabashedly and unashamedly, I got what I wanted, and my way. From both pictures, and from what we know of her career, it is safe to suspect that Eliza Lynch, not unlike so many demimondaines down through the ages, was, in all probability, asexual: a woman who would sell her body—but with discrimination, and only so long as it took her to get what such self-exploitation could bring her.

Héctor Varela, who knew her well and who had no reason to give her more than her due, describes Eliza as having been

> tall and of a flexible and delicate figure with beautiful and seductive curves. Her skin was alabaster. Her eyes were of a blue that seems borrowed from the very hues of heaven and had an expression of ineffable sweetness in whose depths the light of Cupid was enthroned. Her beautiful lips were indescribably expressive of the voluptuous, moistened by an ethereal dew that God must have provided to lull the fires within her, a mouth that was like a cup of delight at the banquet table of ardent passion. Her hands were small with long fingers, the nails perfectly formed and delicately polished. She was, evidently, one of those women who make the care of their appearance a religion.

(Varela has omitted to mention that she was also Junoesque in stature.)

One almost suspects that, had Varela addressed his appraisal to Eliza instead of to his reader audience, she would have smiled languidly and murmured, Thank you, but I already know that.

Eliza knew a few other things. Quite a few. She knew that she could never be just another beautiful cocotte, drifting from customer to customer until premature aging had dethroned Cupid from the depths of that ineffable sweetness; rather, she would—she *must*—metamorphose that God-given dew into more tangible liquid assets. She knew that, while it was no problem to find men eager to swamp her with francs in return for favors, it was nevertheless logical to assume that the high-priced demoiselle of today is invariably the bargain-basement hag of tomorrow.

She knew that she was, in the idiom of the theater, which was one of her great cultural passions, a quick study. How to dress, how to charm, how to fend off undesirable suitors (and equally undesirable creditors)—these she knew. A flair for languages, a talent for finding in the most boring of gentleman callers brilliant bon mots where less discerning ladies found only feeble pseudo witticisms, a nodding acquaintance with the classics, a gift for conversation and flattery, a knowledge of the proper foods, the correct wines, the right furnishings and appointments—these were talents which, if not by now atavistic attributes, were certainly rapidly acquirable. Above all, she knew that she would avoid at all costs the fate that befell, to cite but one classic example, her contemporary in commerce, the ill-fated and tragic Marie Duplessis, the model for Dumas's *La Dame aux Camélias*. Eliza Lynch had *no* intention whatsoever of coughing *her*self to death at the age of twenty-one.

She went to bed with many men; she accepted money. But Eliza Lynch was not a prostitute. She was a courtesan. Prostitutes sell themselves to any man willing and able to meet their price. Courtesans sell themselves only to men who can advance them socially as well as materially. Prostitutes seek out customers, while courtesans seek out protectors. But as there are societal gradations in the world of the prostitute, so are there to be found societal gradations in the world of the courtesan: those who seek out *temporary* protectors, at the one end of the scale, those who seek out *permanent* protectors at the other end. In the first category of courtesan were such contemporaries of Eliza as, in addition to the above-mentioned Lady of the Camelias, the notorious Cora Pearl and the legendary La Belle Otero (who specialized in temporary but fruitful alliances with many of the crowned heads of Europe).

But it was another contemporary whom Eliza chose to emulate: the Empress Eugénie.

The careers of these two women—the most successful adventuresses of the nineteenth century—are as remarkable in their similarities as in their dissimilarities.

Similarly, both used sex solely as a means of advancing themselves to the stratospheric heights of the milieus in which they flourished. Both, though not French-born, were thoroughly French-orientated. Both were accomplished equestriennes. Both had Gaelic blood coursing through their veins. Both suffered the tragedy of seeing their offspring die. Both exercised tremendous influence over the men who had raised them to high estate. Both bound themselves to physically unappetizing and morally reprehensible men who were *soi-disant* emperors to the purple born. Both encouraged their men to embark on disastrous wars that caused their downfall as well as that of their nations. Both achieved the pinnacle of success at the age of twenty-seven. And both died in lands other than their own.

Dissimilarly, Eugénie was pompous to one and all, whereas Eliza practiced egalitarianism—to those willing to accept her. Eugénie married her man (wags claimed, with some merit, that Eugénie had "held out," that Louis Napoleon married her only to bed her down),* whereas Eliza did not marry hers. Eugénie lived to be ninety-four, whereas Eliza died at the age of fifty. Eugénie's place in history has long since been fixed; yet Eliza, decidedly the more "interesting" of the two, has, with the exception of a handful of historians, been ignored.

In the same year that Eugénie married her Permanent Protector (quite possibly the same month), Eliza Lynch, aged eighteen, embarked upon the quest for *her* Permanent Protector. It was a quest undertaken with the inherent conviction that she would succeed. She did not know who he would be, *what* he would

---

*When the love-struck Napoleon asked her to "tell me the way to your heart," Eugénie is said to have replied coyly, "Through the chapel, sir."

be, whence he would come, or whither he would take her. Nor did she know how long she must wait until he hove into her line of vision.

But she knew she would find him.

And she knew she could not have found a more fertile ambience in which to seek him out.

The Second Empire had been officially proclaimed on December 2, 1852—one year to the day after his coup d'état of the republic over which he had presided for three years as President —by Napoleon Bonaparte's nephew (and step-grandson), Louis, who adopted the regnal cognomen Emperor Louis Napoleon III. (The by now dead Duke of Reichstadt and erstwhile King of Rome, Bonaparte's only legitimate son—by the Austrian princess Maria Luisa—was held to have been "Napoleon II," though he never reigned.) The new Emperor was a lascivious, untidy little man whom Théophile Gautier aptly described as looking like "a ring-master who has been sacked for getting drunk." Sharing his imperial prerogatives and pretensions (but rarely his bed) over what Karl Marx dismissed as "a ferocious farce" was Louis Napoleon's shrewish, clothes-conscious, and hypocritically prudish consort the half-Spanish, half-American adventuress, who absolutely reveled in being the Empress Eugénie (and who was properly characterized by Nestor Roqueplan as "the best kept kept-woman in all of France").

Paris was by now a city where the average workingman commanded a mere three to four francs for a twelve-hour day— while the Countess of Castiglione commanded one million francs for a night with an English visiting fireman; a city where, in the words of Pierre Larousse, "Cocottes were women kept by rich idiots bent on destroying themselves."

(One such idiot chose to destroy himself in the living room of Cora Pearl—née Emma Crouch, an English cockney who spoke execrable French, was possessed of a magnificent figure and a miserable face, danced in the nude on a carpet of orchids and bathed in champagne in the buff before her guests, and gulled between five thousand and ten thousand francs per session from men who vied for the pleasure of enjoying her body and, an added dividend, being reviled in Cora's well-heralded billingsgate. When the rich idiot in question shot himself before Cora and a handful of friends because he had been told that he should not consider himself her *only* lover, the best that Cora could come up with in the way of an epitaph was "The fucking pig has ruined my beautiful carpet!")

It was a city—nay, an empire—where one million francs were spent on the birth of the Prince Imperial, while a thirteen-year-old serving girl earning four francs a month was sentenced to a four-year term in the house of correction for having stolen a bit of jam and syrup from her mistress (the presiding judge's rationale: "to imbue her with a moral sense").

It was a city where, so Mark Twain observed, assassins were hired for seven francs, while fashionable women changed costumes seven times a day; where young officers in the Garde Impérial were passed around as male prostitutes, and popular actresses and society women dabbled in lesbianism. One of the emperor's courtiers was arrested by the police at a *bal masqué* where half the Guardsmen present were decked out as nuns; one stage-struck noblewoman divided her time between rehearsing for court pageants and passing along her gonorrhea only to her closest female friends.

In short, Paris was the hub of a universe of which Émile Félix Fleury was to remark in nostalgic retrospect, "It was not exactly a proper empire, but we did have a damn good time."

Eliza Lynch was not above having a damn good time. But so far as she was concerned, there was no law, juridical, moral, or otherwise, which precluded the pursuit of her ultimate objective while thus comporting herself.

First came the question of the proper circle in which to travel. And here she was faced with a brace of alternatives. Was it to be the circle whose ringmistress was the notorious Cora Pearl? Hardly. Cora and her crowd confined their extra-boudoir activities to the bohemian haunts of the demimonde. Here wealthy scions out on a fling and daredevil husbands straying temporarily from the hearth frequented raffish dance halls in the company of gay Guards officers, homosexual actresses *manquées*, hunchbacks, dwarfs, and variegated grotesques. All tumbled their way riotously through the unsubtle vulgarities of the can-can while screaming the popular ditty of the day, which summed up both their philosophy toward life and their justification for polluting the environment: "Sans la toilette et le plaisir, faut en convenir, la vie est bête" ("Without finery and pleasure, we must agree, life is just a stupidity").

Eliza Lynch had nothing personal against grotesques and hedonists. She could kick up her heels with the best of them, and her prejudices—nay, her hatreds—were reserved only for those who would not accept her on her terms. But besotted scions and daredevil husbands did not Permanent Protectors make.

These were to be more frequently encountered, Eliza quickly observed, among the old and new nobility. Let Cora Pearl and her motley crew while away their off-duty hours at the Bal Mabille; Eliza would patronize the more elevated Variétés and the Comédie Française, to name but two of the "in" spots on the circuit presided over by the Emperor's cousin and erstwhile hostess, the redoubtable Princess Mathilde.

Ere long, Eliza had maneuvered herself into the charmed circle presided over by this egalitarian and fun-loving princess to whom prospective and quite eligible protectors were drawn as lemmings to the sea, and for whom one of life's supreme pleasures, other than getting in her knocks at cousin Louis's wife, was to introduce her young lady friends to those lemmings. Thus as Cora Pearl and the other less pragmatic girls raised hell in some *boîte-bas*, Mathilde's new-found Irish friend made the rounds of the theaters and *maisons* whose clientele was restricted to what might be described as the Empire's "beautiful people."

Soon there was no event of import going on in Paris—be it a soiree at dear Mathilde's palace, the opening night of a raunchy revue at the Variétés, or the revival of some turgid Racine tragedy at the Comédie Française—that was not attended by Eliza, superbly bedecked, and more often than not in the company of some eager aspirant to the delicious favors which she was prepared to bestow for a proper fee. Being, as has been indicated, a quick learner, Eliza soon mastered the rather subtle art of flattering her escort of the moment while dividing her vision between what Mathilde was saying (or the onstage soprano or tragedienne was singing or declaiming) and the well-turned-out *homme éligible* seated across the parlor (or in the neighboring box).

As the money began to pour in (and pour out: to the local dressmaker, the respectable landlord, the major-domo who supervised her household, the caterers who appeared regularly with the best in viands), Eliza came to another realization: No one ever caught a fish simply by walking along the water's edge and hoping for the best. Or as the Spanish say, "Quien busca halla—He who seeks finds."

Eliza launched a campaign. It was a campaign worthy of an aggressive salesman who achieves the acme of success in his chosen field merely by flooding the mails periodically with impeccable résumés to the right corporate executives. Having evaluated the ambience, Eliza seems to have concluded that the Permanent Protector for whom she was convinced that the gods had intended her must be a foreigner. Eliza was flexible; she could live anywhere—so long as she was living with a Permanent Protector. Her contacts had been, for the most part, with Frenchmen of affluence; but these were either married men or men who did not think in terms of long liaisons. Paris was in a sense the metaphorical Rome to which all roads led. Down that metaphorical road trooped princes, potentates, patricians. Surely, thought Eliza, possible Permanent Protectors also trod that road. Had she had any idea which direction he was coming from, Eliza would probably have gone to meet him halfway. But possible Permanent Protectors came from all points of the compass. And although Eliza was capable of contravening laws when the occasion demanded, she was incapable of contravening the law which dictates that a person can be in only one place at one time. Thus her decision to make sure that those roads which led to Paris led ultimately to Chez Lynch; thus her campaign.

Eliza's servants were instructed to fan out through the city's more fashionable arrondissements and leave her cards at the more respectable hotels and foreign embassies. Obviously the cards could not read simply "Madame Lynch" and give her address; there was no telling *what* might turn up at her door. Nor could they read "Madame Lynch, Solicitor of a Permanent Protector."

With a stroke of imagination, she had the cards inscribed: "Madame Lynch, Instructress in Languages."

Soon Lynch Chez Elle was counted among the most popular and glittering of all Parisian watering holes. There was witty conversation (more often than not at the emperor's expense, e.g., "The only thing he's inherited from his Uncle Bonaparte is his insatiable sexual appetite"). There was food and wine galore.

And there was Madame Lynch, hoping that out of all this might come some semblance of permanence.

No visitor of substance dared leave Paris without having paid his respects to the young Irish charmer who, preferring to pretend that M. Quatrefages had never crossed her path, adopted the sobriquet by which she wished to be known to all but her most intimate of friends: Madame Lynch.

To be sure, many of her male visitors, rather amused by those devilishly wicked calling cards, played the game and sought Madame's assistance in conjugating a noun or two. But their hostess was not a dedicated pedagogue. As soon as she realized that the evening's catch had not turned up any possibilities, she would quickly and tactfully suggest that should any of her pupils wish, while currying the favor of their preceptress, to indulge in a round or two of harmless gambling, they could repair to the magnificent baize table over which she would graciously preside (and over which she would tenaciously hold the bank).

But time was flying by. Eliza was getting impatient. She was almost nineteen.

And though she had met—and dangled a few participles with—numerous men of wealth and position (and had managed to stash away a not inconsiderable sum at that baize table), she had yet to snare her pigeon.

Fortunately for Eliza, though not for the Paraguayans, time and the gods were on her side.

3

It was a classic encounter of Beauty and the Beast.

From Charles Ames Washburn, United States Minister to Paraguay during most of López's reign, and whose two-volume *History of Paraguay, with Notes of Personal Observations, and Reminiscences of Diplomacy Under Difficulties* is one of the primary sources for this book, we learn that Francisco Solano López

was short and stout, always inclining to corpulence. He dressed grotesquely, but his costumes were always expensive and elaborately finished. His eyes, when he was pleased, had a mild expression; but when he was enraged the pupil seemed to dilate till it did not appear to be that of a human being, but rather a wild beast goaded to madness. He had, however, a gross animal look that was repulsive when his face was in repose. His forehead was narrow and his head small, with the rear organs largely developed. His teeth were very much decayed, and so many of the front ones were gone as to render his articulation somewhat difficult and indistinct. He apparently took no pains to keep them clean, and those which remained were unwholesome in appearance, and nearly as dark as the cigar that he had almost constantly between them. His face was rather flat, and his nose and hair indicated more of the negro than the Indian. His cheeks had a fulness that extended to the jowl, giving him a sort of bulldog expression.

On balance, hardly the sort of specimen that might ordinarily appeal to Eliza Lynch.

But more than offsetting López's multitude of deficiencies were three considerations not to be dismissed lightly: he was immensely rich, he was malleable in the hands of a strong woman (history has demonstrated that most megalomaniacs usually are), and, an added fillip, he had fallen instantly and madly in love with her.

As if to show just how imaginative those girls from County Cork can be when it serves their purpose, where others saw only decayed teeth Eliza Lynch managed to see jewels.

Sources are unagreed on just how the meeting came about. (Eliza's version: "a short time after being separated from my husband I met Marshal López.")

Some claim that it was a chance encounter on the platform of La Gare St. Lazare; others, that the two literally bumped into each other while stumbling through a quadrille at an Imperial Ball in the Tuileries.

Washburn, on the other hand, drawing on contemporary and presumably more authoritative accounts, maintains that "this woman of abandoned character [who] was at the time a member of that class of public women so numerous in Paris, always on the watch for strangers with long purses and vicious habits," had "made the acquaintance" (in a whorehouse) of one Brizuela, a member of López's suite, "and learning from him of the circumstance under which he had come to France, and the magnificence and princely munificence of his chief, contrived to make his acquaintance. Brizuela boasting to his patron of the conquest he had achieved, López was anxious to meet the lady whose charms were so vaunted by his subordinate."

(Washburn's account would have to be taken rather judiciously. He was often eager to see both Madame Lynch and her Friend in the worst possible light. And given López's character, if Brizuela had enjoyed Madame Lynch's favors, which is highly doubtful, he would undoubtedly have been eliminated by López when she became his mistress.)

More likely than not, the fateful meeting took place Chez Lynch, whither López had been taken by his courtiers. Perhaps each had indeed, as many responsible writers have claimed, observed the other at the railway station, and López's being brought to her salon was Eliza's determined follow-up to that chance encounter.

It is most probable, however, that the introduction was arranged by the two parties acting independently of each other. Eliza had heard—as had just about everyone else in Paris with the possible exception of that pathetic thirteen-year-old who was still in the house of correction being "imbued with a moral sense"—that the newly arrived *sauvage* was scattering money about as if it were buckshot. López had heard (possibly from Brizuela) that La Lynch was one of those attractions for the well-heeled *visiteur* that was simply not to be missed.

Militating in favor of this calamitous meeting was the fact that López's command of the English language was as deficient as his command of the toothbrush, and La Lynch was touted up and down the more fashionable arrondissements of Paris as the best "instructress in languages" to be found.

It is logical to assume that, had López been told that Eliza Lynch was just another beautiful whore, he would have stayed away. López never frequented brothels; he considered such activity beneath his dignity. Some chroniclers claim that he agreed to go meet Eliza simply because she was heralded as a beautiful woman of breeding and sophistication, and López considered it only right that he favor her with an hour of his precious time. It is a claim to which the present writer subscribes. Baldly stated, López set out to bed down this beauty, and wound up being seduced by her; what began as a diversion to last a few hours evolved into a relationship that lasted for the rest of Lopez's life.

Within hours of entering Madame Lynch's salon López entered Madame Lynch's boudoir.

By the following morning, they were lovers in the biblical sense.

By the following afternoon López had declaimed on the glories of the Paradise beyond the Seas whence he had come and whither he wished to transport her.

By the following evening Eliza Lynch had given notice to her landlord.

Any revulsion Eliza might have felt (*must* have felt) at the very sight of this physical atrocity was more than mitigated by the reputation of his affluence that had preceded him to her bed, and by the torrent of promises (and gilded half-truths) that issued forth from his obviously unattractive mouth. Too, it did not take her long to size López up for what he was: a fabulously wealthy, vain, and megalomaniacal little man of twenty-seven desperately in need of a cultivated beauty to encourage him in his dreams of glory and to give those dreams a whopping dollop of culture and class.

In essence, he was, in Eliza's scheme of things, the perfect Permanent Protector.

Francisco Solano López had encountered many beautiful women before, even many with class. But he had never encountered one willing to go to bed with him without putting up a fierce struggle. Initially, the idea that this Irish beauty might become his mistress, much less his consort, was probably the last thing that entered López's mind. But it was probably the first thing that entered Eliza's.

Like so many victims of the so-called Napoleonic complex, López was not aware that he projected to the astute observer what he could not or would not admit to himself: that he was suffering a congenital and colossal inferiority complex, a complex rooted in his physical imperfections. However, it is an established fact that many of these victims overcompensate for their inadequacies by masquerading behind an outrageous and obnoxious egomania. López carried off the masquerade to perfection. Also carried off to perfection was the manner in which Eliza shrewdly manipulated him without his being aware that he was in many respects a marionette in her hands.

She told him—and convinced him she really meant it—that he was, in her considered opinion, the very apotheosis of masculine appeal. The idea that a truly beautiful woman such as she, so obviously possessed of intelligence and élan, could have miraculously drifted into his life was probably more than López, in the darkest recesses of his twisted ego, had ever dared hope for.

To be sure, López was the first person to allow as how he was the paradigm of sophistication and breeding, the perfect mate for Eliza.

To be sure, Eliza was the last person to deny his convictions.

He told her he was determined to be the emperor of South America.

She saw no earthly reason why he should not or could not.

Would Madame consent to being his empress?

She would.

Eliza had never heard of Paraguay (neither had most other Europeans). But from the size of López's suite, the manner in which he was spending money, the opulent (and laughably garish) uniforms he wore (modeled, with grotesque Lópezian touches, on those of his Corsican idol), and the middling-to-tall tales he told of the paradisiacal nation to whose leadership he was heir apparent, it all sounded to Eliza like a dream that even the most ambitious adventuress should not in all common decency dare to dream.

She had sought one man—a Permanent Protector—who would give her opulent security. She had found one man who would make her an empress. Eliza Lynch had never thought in imperial terms; adventuresses rarely do. But once the seed had been planted in her mind, it bloomed like an aspidistra run amok. As Francisco talked, Eliza listened; and as she listened, her thoughts became a maelstrom.

It did not take long for her rationale to move from the incredulous "Is it possible that *I* could be an *empress?*" to the affirmative "But of course; *I* was *meant* to be an empress!"

Eliza realized she had her work cut out for her. She must give López the encouragement he needed in his mad ambitions. And she must reassure him that he was the renaissance man he unabashedly considered himself to be. At the same time, she must attempt, with utmost tact and subtlety, to smooth out at least some of those rough edges.

That she managed to live with his gaucheries is testimony to Eliza's fortitude. That she managed to smooth out a few of the rough edges is testimony to her talent. That she succeeded with López where any other woman might well have failed is testimony to her genius.

As one historian well versed in nineteenth-century France remarked to the present author when he was in Paris researching this book, "If your Madame Lynch had married Louis Napoleon, the course of French history would have taken a different turn. Why, the monarchy could possibly have survived!"

Admittedly, the historian is a neoroyalist who still defers to the Count of Paris, the incumbent Pretender. But the idea of Eliza Lynch having been Louis Napoleon's wife instead of the Empress Eugénie is a most intriguing one. The Second Empire would undoubtedly have fallen eventually; thanks to Bismarck, that was historically inevitable. But with Eliza Lynch sharing the helm, it might well have not collapsed with such a thud. Eliza was in many respects a born empress, though the idea never entered her mind until she met López. The fact that she failed to become a bona-fide one was certainly not for her want of trying.

She just had the misfortune to snare the wrong "emperor."

To state that each was loyal to the other to the very end is to state the obvious. Even when, not long after her arrival in Paraguay, Francisco started dropping at Eliza's doorstep his various bastards by sundry concubines, Eliza remained loyal. And even though López had other mistresses, Eliza was still the Favorite; his loyalty to her never wavered. Among the many afflictions López was cursed with, one of the more pronounced was an incipient case of satyriasis. So far as Eliza was concerned, if he needed other women, all well and good; far from tolerating his peccadilloes, she would go one step further and, like Pompadour with her Louis XV, she would *encourage* those peccadilloes.

Some sources claim that Eliza did so as a means of, bluntly stated, keeping López from her bed. Others claim that she had no choice but to accept his philandering if she hoped to maintain her status. Both theories are extremely improbable.

Why, then, did Eliza not only accept López's philandering but go so far as to procure for him? And why did López seek out other women when Eliza was unequivocally the most beautiful woman in the realm? The answer to the first question should by now be obvious: Eliza had found a substitute for sex: wealth and power. As for the second question: López soon came to look upon Eliza as a coequal—his only coequal in all the world; in his psychologically twisted mind, to look upon Eliza as merely a sex object could well have been tantamount to entertaining some form of incestuous feeling toward her.

And to claim, as do so many of their biographers, that Eliza had to accept López on his terms as a means of self-preservation is unsupportable. To maintain her position in Paraguay, yes; but she could have left Paraguay as a wealthy woman any time she wished to. But she never wished to.

Far from adopting the attitude "I've made my bed, now I must lie in it," Eliza's attitude seems to have been "I've discovered the lode, now I must mine it."

Thus, the myth perpetuated by their staunchest defenders that Eliza and Francisco belong in that pantheon of great lovers whose shining lights include the likes of Héloïse and Abelard is palpably ridiculous.

They admired each other and complemented each other, but they did not *love* each other.

They *needed* each other.

4

The two set off on a marriageless honeymoon in Europe, and as López plied her with diamonds and crinolines—and promises of wealth that was his and glory that would be theirs—this physically repulsive and distressingly uncouth creature became transformed into the prototype of masculine beauty through the compromising and imperial prism of Eliza's smiling Irish eyes.

The Grand Tour included, among other stops, an audience with the notoriously scandalous Queen Isabella II of Spain (who incurred López's wrath by tactlessly suggesting that Paraguay hold a plebiscite on the question of returning to the Spanish fold); a visit to Rome (where Madame Lynch bought her table service plus a few more trunkloads of gowns and assorted accessories, and where she probably did *not*, as some claim, toss "a wickedly obscene dinner party" for the incumbent Pope); and a tour of the Crimean battlefront.

Dropping in on the area was considered a "must" among the fashionable tourists of the time. The gentlemen and their ladies, lavishly turned out in the latest Parisian fashions, would camp for an hour or two under a hastily erected pavilion atop a safe promontory overlooking the arena, and while sipping champagne and nibbling on a cold bird or a dish of caviar (smuggled through the Allied lines), would look down with a connoisseur's eye as the combatants below engaged in wholesale slaughter—usually between the hours of sunup and sundown, weather permitting. Eliza considered their time would be better spent in the less sanguinolent pursuit of shopping, but López was anxious to observe the action (and probably to root for the Russians; he had been snubbed by Queen Victoria, and he was never one to forget a snub). He was commander-in-chief of his nation's armed forces; had been, in fact, since the age of eighteen, though he was as ignorant of the science of war as Madame Lynch was of Paraguay. Nevertheless he had long since made up his mind that Paraguay was going to be involved in a war with at least one of her neighbors, just as soon as his less bellicose, more rational father accommodated him by passing on, and he wanted to be sure not to miss any new innovations, either in tactics or weaponry, which might by chance have escaped his attention.

Francisco's curiosity (and Eliza's thirst for bargains) now fairly satisfied, the two returned to Paris. There, hand in hand, they paid their respects to the memory of López's Corsican hero, gazing down in wonder—and perhaps a touch of envy—on the sarcophagus in the Invalides that contains what are now only alleged to be Bonaparte's remains. Francisco decided on the spot that an exact replica of the Invalides was to be constructed in Asunción, as a repository for his own remains. It was.

It was time for López to return to Paraguay.

Urgent messages had been coming in a steady stream from his aging, sickly father wondering when his favorite son was coming home. Francisco had been putting his father off, claiming that he was busy "attending scientific lectures" when in fact he was being "lectured" by Eliza on myriad variations devolving upon one theme: You *can* be greater than Bonaparte!

But the old Dictator-President was not to be put off any longer. And militating in favor of an early departure, Madame Lynch was consumed with a desire to see the promised paradise over which she was to reign as empress-consort.

At ten-thirty in the morning of November 11, 1854—practically ten years to the day before the beginning of the war that was to destroy that empire before it was properly launched—Madame Lynch & Friend sailed for Paraguay aboard the *Tacuarí*. The ship, a newly constructed five-hundred-tonner, fairly groaned under its cargo of countless gowns and miles of lingerie and house linens for Eliza (not to mention that elaborate table service plus a veritable warehouse of the finest in Limoges and Sèvres china), an outrageous number of meretricious uniforms for Francisco (including seventy pairs of hand-crafted leather boots trimmed with silver and mounted on elevated heels), tons of opulent furniture and carriages, a Pleyel piano—and a pregnant Eliza.

As the *Tacuarí* pulled out of the harbor of Bordeaux for its six-week run from the Old World to the New, Eliza had ample time to contemplate, not her past but her future. A year before, she had been the quasi wife of an insignificant French Army officer. Now she was the mistress of a savage who would make her an empress. This savage, who hovered over her, boasting through all his waking hours of the glories of the paradise to which he was transporting her, was fairly insatiable (which would explain why Eliza did much of her contemplation in a recumbent position). While she managed to convince López that he was another Napoleon, Eliza managed to hide from him the fact that the passion she feigned was far from felt.

Eliza had learned that Paraguay's natural resources—most notably wood, animal hides, tobacco, and that indigenous tea of sorts called *yerba maté**—made it one of the wealthiest nations on the South American Continent. Her Friend was heir apparent to the presidency of Paraguay. And in the scheme of things which obtained at the time—and which, to a degree, obtains to this day—whichever man *governed* Paraguay *owned* Paraguay.

Francisco was convinced that when his father, the old President-

---

* A mildly narcotic, positively bilious concoction that, as the present author can testify from experience, works wonders with the digestive tract—once one manages to get, and keep, it down.

Dictator, was dead he would succeed, through an alchemy compounded in equal doses of political acumen and military genius, in converting the dress of quasi republicanism into the gold of imperialism. Eliza concurred wholeheartedly. She also had a few ideas along monarchical lines.

To imply, as have so many of her detractors both in and out of print, that Madame Lynch set out for Paraguay with the express intent to destroy the country is ridiculous. She wanted to reign as consort over a mighty nation, not over a Hispanic slum. Far from wanting to tear down Paraguay, she wanted to build it up. Thanks to her lover's position and his seemingly limitless funds, she had the wherewithal; thanks to her own innate talents, she had the imagination. Before the *Tacuari* was midway across the Atlantic, Eliza had it all worked out in her mind.

She would bring European culture, in all its more respectable manifestations, to the Paraguayans. She would make herself popular with her and her lover's subjects—even more popular than were Napoleon III and Empress Eugénie with theirs. López had promised that his people would love her. Eliza had accepted this promise, probably less because he had made it than because she just *knew* they could not help *but* love her. She had style, she had class, she had refinement, she had taste; too, she assumed that she was superior to any Paraguayan in the areas of art and literature.

And above all, she had an overriding eagerness to dole out to her adopted people more than a mere soupçon of all that she had to offer them. Eugénie offered her subjects advice only on how many crinolines it was proper to wear when receiving a foreign envoy, or the proper etiquette for conducting a levee. Eliza would offer *her* subjects more elevated advice: how to appreciate the finer things in life, as exemplified in the Second Empire, which she had abandoned in favor of this remote, backward land.

Tragically, as events were to prove, Madame Lynch's great error was in overestimating the Paraguayans.

Their great error was in underestimating Madame Lynch.

The Man from Asunción

To paraphrase Carlyle's thesis that "the history of the world is but the biography of great men," the history of Paraguay is but the biography of dreadful dictators. Demonstrably, the most dreadful was Madame Lynch's Friend. There is something indefinable in the nature of the Paraguayan people, most notably among the indigenous Guaraní stock, that sets them apart as the gentlest and kindest in all of Latin America—and, when it comes to the leaders they have tolerated and continue to tolerate, the most masochistic. Francisco Solano López was confident that he could pursue his insane concept of leadership with impunity. A superficial examination of what was, until his advent, Paraguay's brief history, would demonstrate that López's confidence was well placed.

When the various South American states declared their independence from Spain at the beginning of the nineteenth century, Paraguay came under the hegemony of the Province of Buenos Aires. In 1813, Paraguay declared its independence from Buenos Aires and constituted itself as a republic along the ancient Roman lines, with leadership vested in two consuls.

Within a year there was only one consul: José Gaspar Rodríguez Francia—the first in a line, which extends down to the present day, of self-serving despots under whose guidance, and at whose indulgence, the average Paraguayan would pursue the often painful task of merely getting through this life without incident. Francia was named by the people Dictator when he seized the Government; two years later he was named Perpetual Dictator for Life.

Known to one and all (at his insistence) as El Supremo, he was a solitary, austere, misanthropic, misogynistic, absolutist, extremely well educated and decidedly charismatic loner. (Portraits of the excessively lean, beak-nosed Francia in his habitual garb—a black swallowtail coat and modified tricorne hat—readily summon to mind every American schoolboy's notion of Ichabod Crane.) His twenty-eight-year grip on the nation is generally referred to as "Francia's reign of terror," although Carlyle's remark that it was more properly "a reign of rigour" is more supportable. Unlike his immediate successors, Francia never condemned people to death out of sheer arbitrariness or because of imagined "conspiracies." He was many things, but he was neither a paranoid nor a psychotic. He always managed to find viable, though not necessarily moral or legal, grounds for dispatching his enemies.

El Supremo expropriated all Church property and turned a deaf ear to papal protests ("If the Holy Father should come to Paraguay, I would do him no other honor than to make him my personal chaplain"), thereby retaining so much of the wealth that had been finding its way to Rome ever since the Jesuits established their short-lived hold on the country in the early eighteenth century. (Unlike Henry VIII of England, Francia did not break from the Church and declare himself Defender of the Faith. Though an anti-clericist, he permitted—perhaps tolerated is more appropriate —the practice of Catholicism in the realm, so long as it was not practiced in his presence. And to Francia's credit, the tithe money that had formerly gone to Rome went into the state treasury instead of into his pockets.)

He turned the nation into a veritable hermit kingdom—thereby steering Paraguay clear of the turbulence going on in all the neighboring lands, most notably among the feuding Argentinians. (What we now define as Argentina was a collection of mutually antagonistic provinces vying for leadership of the overall Argentine Confederation.)

He broke the power not only of the Church but of the Spanish and mestizo upper classes—though he himself was probably of the patrician class—thereby winning over the fealty of the long-oppressed Guaranís who constituted the vast bulk of the population. (With the exception of Negroes, no person could marry anyone possessed of even a hint of Spanish blood.)

He developed a small yet powerful army, no more than four thousand in number and strictly for purposes of keeping out all foreigners—thereby imparting a strong sense of nationalism.

He encouraged agriculture—thereby making his nation self-sufficient.

And he was *feared*. (When Francia died in 1840 at the age of seventy-nine, the populace at first refused to accept the news, panicking in the suspicion that the announcement was merely one of The Supreme One's ruses to test their fealty and obedience; surely, they reasoned, no mortal so omnipotent, so absolute could actually *die!*) All citizens were compelled to hide behind closed shutters when he rode through the streets. All adults were compelled to wear hats, to doff when encountering a militiaman or government functionary; those too poor to afford even a hat had to wear a brim. (In addition to the hats, or brims, many of the men—even those who could not ride a horse much less own one—followed the rather intriguing custom of wearing silver spurs on their ankles. The custom continued during the reigns of the Lópezes; in the capital city of Asunción, as well as in the other major cities of Concepción, Encarnación, and Villarrica, it was not an uncommon sight to behold a Guaraní walking the streets dressed only in hatbrim and ankle spurs.)

Francia's favorite reading were the works of Voltaire and Rousseau (especially *Social Contract*), and he professed abject admiration for Benjamin Franklin: "That man is the first democrat of the world . . . the model whom we must imitate," he told the

Argentinian statesman Manuel Belgrano shortly after his assumption of power. When reminded tactfully that the philosophy espoused by Franklin, not to mention those French rationalists, was rather alien to his concept of government, the Perpetual Dictator replied, rather paternalistically and perhaps a bit hypocritically, "Within forty years, it may be that these [Latin American] countries will have one like Franklin, and only then shall we enjoy the liberty for which we are not prepared today."

El Supremo refused to entertain the idea of grooming a successor—a common shortcoming among dictators past, present, and probably future. But ironically, when he died following an apopleptic seizure—a death that was surely hastened along by his refusal to allow any human being, physicians included, ever to touch him—the people remained docile. Such was the almost mesmerizing hold he maintained over the nation.

Immediately following Francia's death his secretary, Polycarpo Patiño, called together a junta to govern the constitutionless country—a junta whose first act was to throw Patiño into prison (where he proceeded to hang himself). Six months later, by which time the nation at large was finally convinced that El Supremo was indeed dead and buried, a national congress was called. Following the precedent set in 1813, it established another consulate, composed of a nonentity named Mariano Roque Alonso and Carlos Antonio López. Three years later, with the tacit acquiescence of Alonso, a new congress established a presidential system for Paraguay according to the constitution López had drafted, and López was elected to fill the office for a ten-year term. He was reelected, constitutionally, at ten-year intervals for the remainder of his life.

It was quite a constitution. The executive and judiciary branches were embodied in the authority of the President; the third branch, the legislative, was not so much dependent on the President as totally subservient to him. Congress had the power to make and interpret laws, the execution of which was vested in the President.

However, the Congress, composed of a representative from each of the ninety-two *partidos*,* could not discharge its constitutional powers unless it had been called into session. And it could only be called into session by the President. With one or two exceptions, and then only to serve less as an organic body than as a rubber stamp, under the Lópezes the Congress was called into session only to "elect" a new chief magistrate.

The military was at the absolute disposal of the President, who was further empowered to conduct all foreign relations. Also, he was empowered to appoint and remove all civil, military, and political employees, nominate business agents and diplomatic envoys, decide on all salaries, and act as final arbiter in all cases of a juridical nature. In sum, he could run the country as a personal fiefdom, but under the guise of constitutional republicanism. And he did just that.

Being less the philosophical rationalist than his predecessor, Carlos Antonio López decided upon as his first order of business a renewal of ties with the Holy See, which had been suspended during Francia's reign. (Washburn: "López, more wise than Francia, and yet as eager for absolute power, instead of arraying whatever was left of a religious element in the country against him by persecution of the priests, sought to make the church a support to himself.") Determined to be the head of the Church within his own dominions, and on his own terms, the President requested the Pope, Gregory XVI, to name his brother Basilio López as Bishop of Asunción. It was a choice that was rooted less in nepotism than pragmatism on Carlos Antonio's part. As described by Washburn, Basilio "was an eccentric, good-natured priest, without ambition and without avarice, the two qualities that were the guiding principles of Carlos Antonio. He lived in extreme poverty, and gave away nearly all his income to charity [and] ridiculed the pretension of his brother to royal honors and dignities. As bishop

---

* The word translates as "party," in the sense of political party, but in Paraguayan terminology it designated a geographical district.

he had no authority or power beyond what was conceded by the President, with whose arbitrary rule he never pretended to interfere."

(When brother Basilio died in 1859, Carlos Antonio requested that Gregory's successor, Pius IX, name to the vacant office the aged, infirm, and totally subservient Juan Gregorio Urbieta. Pius, in a blistering letter, reminded López that when Gregory had agreed to a resumption of ties with Paraguay, he had stipulated that the payment of tithes was to be resumed and the confiscated Church treasures and property were to be accounted for. After allowing that he would not name a successor to Basilio unless López promised to account for the tithes—which had not been paid for fifty years—as well as the treasures, Pius further stipulated that the new Bishop would not be a Paraguayan but a man of his choice who would be responsible directly to him. And to emphasize his position, Pius informed López that unless these terms were met, the entire Paraguayan nation would be subject to excommunication. López replied with a letter expressing his confidence that, should the Holy Father close forever the Gates of Heaven against himself and his people, he was most confident that God Almighty would manage to find *some* means by which the excommunicants, loving and dutiful children all, would find ingress to His Kingdom. Involved up to his miter in the Risorgimento movement that was to see the papacy stripped of the outrageous and near absolute temporal authority it enjoyed over much of the Italian peninsula, Pius gave in and issued the bull authorizing Urbieta's appointment.)

Sir Richard Burton, that ubiquitous nineteenth-century English adventurer and chronicler of little-known places and peoples, describes Carlos Antonio as "hideous, burly, and thick-set. . . . With chops flying over his cravat, his face wears, like the late George IV, a porcine appearance. . . . He generally received visitors sitting in an armchair, probably to conceal the fact that one leg was shorter than the other."

Unlike his predecessor, Carlos Antonio permitted his minions to view him whenever he made the rounds of his capital. Washburn advises that on these occasions, which were often, he

> was always attended by a numerous guard, all well-mounted and generally composed of large, fine-looking men, so that his squat, uncourtly figure appeared more ridiculous from the contrast. . . . Though he had no military rank or title and regarded himself in no respect as a military man [he preferred the cognomen "Citizen López"], when he went out in his carriage (as for a long time before his death, owing to an immense obesity, he never went on horseback) he was dressed in a uniform [that was] fantastic. . . . The appearance of the old man as he rode through the streets in his low carriage, with his cocked hat and blue coat with enormous epaulets, holding his sword by the hilt, would have led one to suppose that some harmless, demented buffoon was playing king for the diversion of the rabble.

But clownish as he must have appeared, Carlos Antonio López can be said to have been the Organizer of independent Paraguay, just as Francia was the Founder (and Francisco Solano was the Destroyer).

Born November 4, 1790, to a Creole father and a mother who was part Indian and part Negro slave,* Carlos was educated, despite his humble background, at the *Colegio* in Asunción. Here he subsequently taught philosophy and theology and then went on to the practice of law—at which point he ran afoul of Francia. El Supremo refused to tolerate any educated person other than himself within the borders of his hermit kingdom. Withdrawing discreetly to the estancia that came to him in the dowry of his wife, the equally obese Doña Juana Pablo Carillo, Carlos Antonio read, engaged in agricultural pursuits, sired a brood of nasty children, wrote that constitution—and otherwise bided his time. With the death of Francia, his time had come.

---

* It was probably his heritage more than any sense of egalitarianism that led Carlos Antonio to be the first Western Hemisphere chief of state to grant manumission; however, it should be noted that the slaves were not to be freed until they reached adulthood.

Rejecting the closed-door policy of his predecessor, Carlos Antonio López opened the country to trade and established diplomatic relations with, among others, the United States as well as the major European powers of England, France, and Sardinia. Also, he imported foreign technicians to build up the country (one such project: the first railroad on the South American continent). More often than not—until he was old enough to know better, by which time it was too late to avoid the disaster which overtook Paraguay under the aegis of his son and successor— Carlos Antonio's handling of foreign relations skirted on the edge of near disaster. Among other accomplishments, he became caught up in imbroglios with the United States and Great Britain. Worse, he made that one cardinal error that Francia had so scrupulously avoided: he injected himself into the Argentinian civil war and antagonized his other powerful contiguous neighbor, Brazil.

But his greatest failure—and the aspect of this corpulent autocrat which most concerns us—was in his relations with his own children. He literally spoiled them rotten, at the expense of the nation at large. The profits from Paraguay's lucrative export trade were scooped up into his pudgy hands and doled out generously to his five spawn, especially the three boys.

Of the three, the most rotten by far was the eldest, Francisco Solano.

And it is questionable whether Francisco was actually his son.

As Washburn has recorded the tale for posterity, with just the proper touch of delicacy:

There was living at this time [1826] in one of the districts to the northeast of Asunción, a rich estanciero by the name of Lázaro Rojas. . . . A part of [his estates] he had received with his wife, who at the time of his marriage was a widow by the name of Carillo. At the time of this marriage the widow had but one child, a daughter named Juana. It appears that Don Lázaro had an eye for the person of the daughter as well as for the estate of the mother. The result was that he found, after a time, that it would be convenient to have the young woman married off;

and casting about for a suitable match for his step-daughter, he selected Carlos Antonio López as the most eligible person, inasmuch as he was a man of intelligence above the average, and, having some negro blood to boast of, the union would not be a violation of the law which Francia had promulgated. . . . The marriage was therefore permitted, and the first fruit, not of, but after, the union, was Francisco Solano López. The putative father always recognized the child as his own, and it was only known to a few Paraguayans that he was not so.

That Francisco became the old President's trusted and closest adviser could, without violating the theory that they were not truly father and son, be explained away on the grounds that 1) Francisco assiduously promoted himself into the old man's confidence, 2) he was the only one of the three sons capable of leadership, and/or 3) Carlos Antonio honored the debt he owed both Don Lázaro and Doña Juana, whose fortunes provided the springboard for his bounce to leadership (and ownership) of the country. It should be noted, however, that many historians, including López's severest critics, tend to dismiss the tale, though militating in its favor are these considerations: Francisco Solano bore no physical resemblance to his siblings; and the siblings were among the first to fall victim to his paranoia. Francisco Solano took immense pride in being free of any strain of Spanish blood —a fact (or at least it was to him a fact) that he exploited in order to curry the favor of the Guaraní masses, whose hatred for the Spanish was monumental though repressed. There is, of course, the possibility that Don Lázaro, a man of Spanish descent, was in truth Francisco's natural father, that Francisco was aware of it, and that his boasts to the Guaranís that he was "one of their own" was either a calculated ploy or a case of the gentleman protesting a bit too much, if not a combination of the two factors. However, I am inclined to go along with the more responsible historians who prefer to await more conclusive evidence as to Francisco's true paternity. Though circumstantial evidence, and rather convincing evidence at that, tends to support the tale of Carlos Antonio's cuckoldry, there is as much, and as convincing, circumstantial evidence to dispute it.

The other children were, in order of birth, Inocencia, Venancio, Rafaela, and Benigno. Since all were destined (perhaps doomed would be more appropriate) to play major supporting, and for them disastrous, roles in the Lynch-López drama, a few words about these dreadful siblings would not be out of order at this point in our narrative.

The two girls were thoroughly repulsive nonentities who made a great display of enjoying what they considered to be the royal prerogatives of having been born to Citizen López. (They also made a great profit in cashing in used banknotes at above par value, a perquisite granted to them by the Citizen.) Though both married men who rose to prominence in Francisco Solano's government, their first loyalty seems to have been to their mother, a drab, semi-illiterate, uncompromising, and hideously obese peasant in the most pejorative sense of the word.

The López boys have been variously described as "coarse and sensual," "mean and vindictive," "avaricious and grasping," and "heinous and thoroughly despicable"—to cite but a few of the blander adjectival groupings. And all were the richest men in Paraguay, thanks to Carlos Antonio, who granted them what amounted to monopolies on the nation's export trade, and made sure that many of the largest and finest estancias in the country fell into their hands through outrageous expropriation.

Venancio, the middle son, appears to have been the least wretched, if only because, as Washburn reports, he "did not aspire to the honor or dangers of the government. He would have preferred a life of ease and license on one of the estancias obtained for him by his father at the expense of others. His father, however, forced him into the military service, and compelled him to reside in the capital." Though gross and massive, Venancio went beardless and spoke in a high falsetto voice; he is believed to have been sexually underdeveloped and may well have been impotent, although this did not inhibit him from raping (or attempting to rape) any maiden who caught his fancy.

Benigno, on the other hand, was, in Washburn's words, "universally detested." In addition to being gross in mien, he was elephantine and syphilitic. He was also Doña Juana's favorite child. One of Benigno's favorite pastimes, as well as that of most Paraguayan men of affluence, was playing cards. To the merchants who indulged in this sport, "the appearance of Benigno was always unwelcome. They did not dare to refuse to play with him or to win his money. In either case they would incur his ill-will [and] injure their business, either by prejudicing his father . . . against them, or by [his] intimidating subordinate government officials, and inducing them to embarrass their mercantile operations." Probably because he was his mother's pet—God knows he lacked the mind of even a merchant—Benigno was allowed by Carlos Antonio extraordinary privileges in the collecting and exporting of products without having to pay the duties to which others were subjected.

2

Francisco Solano López was born on or around July 24, 1826, at the family estancia near Trinidad in the outskirts of Asunción, where he spent his early years. He was probably named for Francisco Solano, a Franciscan priest who flourished toward the end of the sixteenth century, and who became the first canonized saint in the Americas.

When, following the death of El Supremo, the schools were reopened, Francisco Solano was sent to an academy run by one Juan Pedro Escalada in Asunción. Here he "studied arithmetic, grammar, and a little Latin," in addition to learning Spanish. (When Washburn questioned Escalada "as to the aptitude and abilities of this pupil, Escalada declined to speak except in terms that left it to be inferred that, if he was not a dunce, he was not a desirable pupil to have in his school. The teacher evidently took no credit to himself for having aided in developing a character like that of López.")

A year after enrolling in the Escuela Escalada, Francisco Solano ended his formal education. He was fifteen years old. His personality and character had by then been formed. He was coarse, vulgar, megalomaniacal, solipsistic, and, toward the end of his life, certifiably mad. And if he was not, as Escalada claims, a "desirable pupil," he was certainly not "a dunce."

Like Eliza Lynch, whose formal education also ended at the age of fifteen, Francisco Solano was far from the illiterate fool many historians would have him be. More than ample proof exists that he enjoyed a flair for articulation, both oral and written, that one cannot associate with an illiterate. Also like Eliza, he seems to have had a flair for languages. In addition to being totally fluent in Guaraní and Spanish (and here it should be noted that Paraguay was at the time, and remains to this day, the only bilingual nation in the Western Hemisphere), thanks to Eliza he learned to handle himself creditably in French and English.

The fact that he had no knowledge of the classics—literature, music, art—can be attributed to the fact that these did not interest him. Francisco pursued only those areas of knowledge which most commanded his curiosity; of these, the area in which he concentrated, practically to the exclusion of all others, was history. In addition to being well versed on the career of his all-time hero Bonaparte, Francisco was extremely articulate when it came to discoursing on the tangled historical threads that bound together, at the same time separating, his country's neighbors. It is logical to assume that he gained much of his education from poring through his father's private library, which was the largest one in Paraguay and probably the only one worthy of the term.

On leaving the Escalada school, Francisco entered the Army. Within less than three years he attained the rank of brigadier general, the highest grade in the Paraguayan military service. Shortly after becoming a brigadier general, Francisco became a national hero. The validity of his heroism is as open to question as was the validity of the elder López's logic in choosing to involve the nation in the turbulent affairs of the civil war–ridden Argentine Confederation.

The Confederation was divided between the provinces of Misiones, Entre Ríos, and Corrientes (Paraguay's contiguous neighbor) on the one hand, and the coastal province of Buenos Aires on the other. Juan Manuel de Rosas, dictator of Buenos Aires, had refused to recognize the independence of Paraguay, which had been reaffirmed by Carlos Antonio López upon entering office. Nevertheless, in his determination to keep López out of Argentinian affairs, Rosas had assured his "friendly disposition," agreeing to the principle of free navigation for Paraguayan shipping. Though Paraguay enjoyed free access to the Paraguay and Paraná rivers, her shipping was at the mercy of Buenos Aires. The two rivers empty into the Río de la Plata, which in turn gives on to the Atlantic Ocean. Thus, by closing the port of Buenos Aires to Paraguayan vessels, Rosas could strangle Paraguay economically.* But Rosas was anxious to secure Paraguayan neutrality in the civil war which saw Buenos Aires pitted against the other provinces for leadership of the Argentine Confederation. He had even gone so far as to agree to sell López a thousand each of carbines, pistols, and sabers—with the understanding that López was *not* to involve himself in the Argentinian conflict.

Unfortunately, Carlos Antonio had not yet learned the characteristic caution that was to come only with old age, especially as regarded his Argentinian neighbors. When López unwisely recognized Corrientes as a geopolitical entity independent of Buenos Aires, Rosas became enraged and closed his port city to Paraguayan shipping. Also, he made formal protest to Brazil over that empire's recognition of Paraguayan independence; and he prevailed upon Manuel Oribe, his confederate who was leader of the

---

* Paraguay was cut off from the Pacific by land-locked Bolivia and the Andes Mountains.

anti-Brazil (hence pro-Argentine) faction in Uruguay's civil war, to prohibit Paraguayan commerce by way of the Uruguay river. As a result of Rosas's Bonaparte-like "continental system," Paraguay was now effectively blockaded, its commerce cut to the merest trickle.

Meanwhile, Brazil negotiated a treaty with López whereby the Paraná and Paraguay rivers—vital to Brazilian economic development of its vast interior—were opened to Brazilian shipping. In return, Paraguay was to stand firm in its support of Corrientes, thereby putting her on the side of Brazil, which was anti-Rosas. As an added inducement, Brazil promised to negotiate with Paraguay a definitive settlement of their long-disputed common boundaries, and to secure a general recognition by the European powers, as well as the other Latin American states, of Paraguay's status as an independent nation.

What it all added up to was that Paraguay now became the cat's-paw of the brilliant Brazilian diplomacy.

Francia would have handled the entire situation (provided he would have allowed the situation to deteriorate that far, which is doubtful in the extreme) by simply pulling in his horns and reasserting total Paraguayan noninvolvement in the affairs of *any* of her neighbors. But the clever Brazilians were quick to see that López was less penetrating than Francia.

On November 11, 1845, encouraged by Brazil, Carlos Antonio López, without even realizing what a mess he had gotten himself into, concluded an offensive and defensive alliance with Corrientes. In return for the surrender to Paraguay of some utterly worthless territory, López obliged himself to aid Corrientes and her allies in their fight against Rosas with a force of 10,000 men. Overall direction of the campaign was to be in the hands of José Elitazia-Paz, Rosas's major antagonist from the province of Entre Ríos, and at the time universally acknowledged as the foremost military tactician in all of Latin America.

On December 4, 1845, proving what a Brazilian cat's-paw he could really be when the occasion demanded, Carlos Antonio

declared war on Rosas; shortly thereafter a Paraguayan force of
5,000 men (half the number promised) under the command of the
nineteen-year-old Brigadier General Francisco Solano López, invaded Corrientes to meet the Rosas army that had come up from
Buenos Aires. (Carlos Antonio took pains to point out that the
war was a personal one against the tyrant Rosas and not against
the Argentinian people. The compliment was returned twenty
years later when Argentina declared that it was not making war
on the Paraguayan people but only on the tyrant Francisco Solano
López.)

Like the proverbial Duke of York, who marched his troops up
the hill and then back down again, Francisco Solano, after a brief
period of "cooperation" with his allies, returned with his army to
Paraguay—without having fired a shot. In an interview with the
Chilean writer Federico de la Barra, he allowed that "The military
art has no secrets for me. General Paz cannot teach me nor have
I anything to learn of his science."

Indeed, Francisco had much to learn, but little reason to so exert
himself. *Semanario,* the only newspaper in all of Paraguay, which
was controlled (and written) by the López family, extolled "the
young hero of the Corrientes war" as the greatest warrior of
modern times. Unblushingly, he was compared favorably with
Alexander the Great. The newly acclaimed Hero of the Corrientes believed what he read (and probably wrote) in *Semanario.*

Unfortunately, so did the Paraguayan people.

But fortunately for the Hero, he did not have to prove that the
military art "had no secrets" for him. Because of international
complications with France and England, Rosas chose not to follow up his victory at Corrientes with a punitive expedition against
Paraguay. (Even had he been in a position to, it is doubtful Rosas
would have invaded Paraguay. Like Lloyd George, Rosas was one
of those leaders who believed in solving one crisis by precipitating
another; thus he was content with making Carlos Antonio López's
flesh creep from time to time until the old dictator got the message and kept clear of the Argentinian chaos.)

On his triumphant return to Asunción, Francisco Solano was named by his father to be Minister of War. Lest the other sons feel left out of things, Benigno was named Commander in Chief of the garrison at Asunción, and Venancio was promoted to the rank of major in the Army. When Venancio made known to his father that the Army held no fatal attraction for him, the old man named him Grand Admiral of the Fleet. The fact that the Grand Admiral had never been on a ship and, furthermore, was in no way interested in pursuing a naval career was of no consequence: Paraguay did not have a fleet.

In addition to being a self-proclaimed military genius, the Hero of Corrientes was an outrageous profligate. Along with the syphilitic Benigno and the sexually underdeveloped Venancio, Francisco was the terror of those First Families of Asunción who boasted of beautiful daughters. If the advances of the young Lópezes were resisted and the victims were daughters of men who lacked any influence with the President, their fathers were jailed and the boys' coffers were enriched through confiscation of property. Carlos Antonio's sons were in effect licensed ravishers.

Francisco Solano's particular predilection seems to have been for aristocratic virgins (as opposed to Venancio and Benigno, who took what they could get). Whenever the intended victim declined his overtures (which was often), the future dictator found ways to assuage his pique (which was as easily aroused as was his libido).

There was, for instance, Pancha Garmendia, "the pride and jewel of Asunción." Suitors abounded—but all were frightened away by young López. On being rejected by Pancha, who is said to have threatened suicide if he came any closer, Francisco decided, rather perversely, that his revenge must be an extended one. It was.

After ordering the execution of her brothers on trumped-up charges of being enemies of the state (her father had already met a like fate under El Supremo) and, with the permission of Carlos

Antonio, confiscating their properties, Francisco had the poor girl put out of circulation—and into chains. Twenty years later, when López was forced to evacuate Asunción in the wake of the Allies, whom he led on a not-so-merry two-year chase through the jungle interior, poor Pancha was dragged along in his tatterdemalian train at the express command of her quondam suitor—who further ordered that she was, in the words of Washburn, "to be kept alive apparently with no other motive than that she might bear the floggings that were almost daily visited on her once fair round, but now emaciated and shrunken shoulders" before she was mercifully lanced to death in the closing days of the war.

And there was Carmencita Cordal, with whom Francisco fell passionately in love shortly after returning from his celebrated "victory" at Corrientes. Carmencita was about to be married to her cousin Carlos Decoud, scion of one of Paraguay's leading families. Francisco's determination to make Carmencita his concubine was exceeded only by her determination to avoid such a fate. The tragedy was compounded when young Decoud had the temerity to engage his adversary in physical combat—and thoroughly humiliate him publicly. Francisco persuaded Carlos Antonio to imprison Decoud on trumped-up charges of plotting a coup d'état. (Perhaps "asked" is closer to the mark than "persuaded," for Carlos Antonio had had his eyes on the Decoud properties for quite a while.)

On the night before the wedding, young Decoud was executed and his bloodstained corpse flung into the street before Carmencita's house (some sources claim it was flung into the poor girl's living room). Carmencita spent the remainder of her life shrouded in black, gathering flowers in the moonlight and praying nightly at deserted shrines, not unlike some pathetically demented Hispanic Ophelia.

Things were coming to such a pass, many of the well-established Asunción families possessed of beautiful daughters began to ask for their passports. Carlos Antonio made no objection to their going into voluntary exile—so long as they left their assets behind. Faced with this Hobson's choice, many opted for exile.

With the complaints now coming in daily, if not hourly, over the behavior of his sons, most notably that of the young general, Carlos Antonio deemed it wise that Francisco Solano absent himself from the country for a while, until tempers had cooled among the aristocrats.

It was decided that the Hero of Corrientes should undertake a diplomatic mission.

3

Having by now successfully negotiated commercial and diplomatic treaties with France and England, Carlos Antonio decided the time had come to send an ambassador to represent him at these courts—and to purchase weapons, ships, and munitions for the defense of his country. Accordingly, as Washburn informs us,

> the young diplomatist was . . . dispatched on his mission with an outfit and an escort such as in modern times has seldom, if ever, accompanied a single ambassador to any court. His suite consisted of some forty persons. His secretary was Juan Andres Gelly, who . . . had been abroad on different occasions as a sort of special agent of the government, and in this way had had considerable experience in diplomatic affairs, and was, in fact, the minister, as young López, though nominally head of the embassy, had yet to learn everything that regarded diplomatic usages and duties. The other members of the escort consisted of military men and naval officers of different grades, his brother Benigno, and a large following of servants. [By now Carlos Antonio had decided that his riparian nation needed a navy; one of Francisco's purchases was to be some ships.] [In addition to] the large retinue which the young minister took with him to give importance to his mission, he had ample means provided to support the style and equipage becoming a general, ambassador, and prince of the blood. The old man put to his

credit in England and France a sum of money sufficient to maintain him and his suite in a style such as no other ambassador at Paris or London could pretend to rival.

On arriving at Paris, young López left the details of all business to his secretary, and gave loose rein to his naturally licentious propensities, and plunged into the vices of that gay capital. With an unlimited bank account and . . . making such a display of wealth, it was not difficult to create the impression that he must represent a country of immense resources; and, as little was known of Paraguay, it was thought, by some persons of influence and official position, that immense commercial advantages were to result from the cultivation of intimate relations with the newly opened country.

Included in those numbers who so thought were many merchants eager to sell López the materiel he sought and many brokers anxious to gain a monopoly on imports from Paraguay, especially the woods and animal hides in which the country abounded.

López had long since been more than kindly disposed toward France. Had it not, after all, given the world his all-time hero, Napoleon I? (Technically, it had not; to Corsica goes that singular honor.) As a worshiper of Napoleon I, López was eager to meet his lineal and political descendant; as Ambassador of Paraguay and son of the President, he deemed it only befitting that Napoleon III grant him an audience.

Many of her partisan biographers claim that it was Madame Lynch who arranged with "her good friend the Emperor" to receive her new Friend. In fact, López met the Emperor before he met the Madame. The brokers and merchants had suggested that Louis Napoleon make the proper fuss over the young visitor. It was good for business. And the Emperor was not about to ignore the advice of those who had helped raise him to, and were helping to keep him in, power.

López habitually wore his uniforms a size smaller than sartorial decency demanded, in the mistaken assumption that he might thus disguise his awkwardly formed physique. Stuffed into his most meretricious number, a gold- and silver-trimmed variation on one of Bonaparte's more outlandish costumes, the young Ambassador fairly glowed with self-importance as, in the words of Henry Lyon Young, "he was conducted down a long series of connecting drawing rooms, the doors of which were flung open by liveried servants. The Emperor stood behind an ormolu desk to receive him and he was not alone. He was accompanied by the Empress, who made herself charming and spoke to him in her native Spanish."*

After an exchange of pleasantries, López presented Louis with a hundred boxes of the best Paraguayan cigars and a sample of tobacco which the Emperor promised to exhibit at the following year's Paris Exhibition. (Louis kept his promise; the tobacco took first prize in its category. As for those cigars, one fairly reliable source claims that they were immediately disposed of on the orders of Eugénie, who found them "vile, disgusting—and an *extraordinary* gift for the Emperor of the French!") The audience concluded,

> General López then kissed the Empress's hand and the Emperor personally conducted him to the door of his study and dismissed him with the words "j'espère que vous vous amusez à Paris, Monsieur," and entrusted an equerry with the task of seeing that the young General's stay in the French capital should be made agreeable. As he took his leave the Emperor kissed him on both cheeks and presented him with the Legion of Honour. Francisco's bosom swelled with pride and he was filled [again] with the ambition of becoming the Napoleon of the New World.

With that ambition now firmly fixed in his twisted mind's eye, López saw to the purchase of spanking new uniforms both for

---

* One Lópezian scholar has written that when, on being ushered into the Imperial Presence, López leaned over to kiss the Empress's hand, she promptly turned away and "vomited all over the ormolu desk." It all sounds more inspired than factual. The author of this report goes on to claim that "Eugénie excused herself on the grounds that she was suffering morning-sickness, being *enceinte* at the time with the future Prince Imperial." In fact, the Prince Imperial was born more than two years after López's audience, and while Eugénie set many a record, long-distance pregnancies was not one of them.

himself and for the Paraguayan Army, and then crossed the Channel to present himself as his country's first Ambassador to the Court of St. James's and to see what the English had to sell. Here, though he spent his money as profusely as he had in Paris, Francisco was not as successful in impressing upon Her Majesty's Government the importance of himself and of his mission.

It seems that as a result of some minor bollix in the arrangement of her Prime Minister's appointment book, Queen Victoria became "quite too busy" to grant "the little savage" an audience. This may well have been an intended snub on the British Government's part, as it was still irritated with López's father over the so-called Canstatt Affair. (Canstatt, a British businessman born in Montevideo, had been condemned to death by Carlos Antonio for taking part in an imagined anti-Lópezian conspiracy. Committing an act of piracy on the high seas, a squadron of the Royal Navy's South Atlantic Fleet subsequently intercepted the ship carrying Francisco Solano home from his Buenos Aires triumph—of which we shall be hearing more shortly—and held him as hostage against Canstatt's release. Carlos Antonio gave in and decided that Canstatt was probably innocent after all.)

Her Government may have been unimpressed with López, but Victoria's businessmen were highly impressed, most notably the Blyth Brothers, London's leading arms merchants. After courting the visiting potentate assiduously, they wound up with a handsome long-term contract that included, among other items, construction of an arsenal in Asunción and two steamers "of a superior quality," one of which was sent out to Paraguay under the command of an English captain, the other of which "was to be ready to cross the Atlantic whenever [López] should himself wish to return home." This latter ship was, of course, the *Tacuarí*, which carried López and Madame Lynch to Paraguay. (The Blyth Brothers also wound up with a sheaf of unpaid bills for all the arms and munitions they subsequently shipped out to Paraguay prior to and during the War of the Triple Alliance. More often than not, López responded to their repeated demands for payment with worthless specie and equally unredeemable IOU's bearing his signature.)

The slight of not being received by Queen Victoria left a lifelong antipathy in López toward the British. However, he was able to compromise antipathy with practicality when the occasion demanded. The French could make the slickest uniforms, but when it came to armaments and munitions, the English suffered no peers. Too, while the French were good at advising on the proper wine or practicing the arcane art of keeping a soufflé from collapsing of its own weight, it was the English who provided the best talent in those areas which were López's immediate concern: in addition to stockpiling war materiel, the constructing of shipyards, arsenals, fortresses, and lines of communication. (To Francisco Solano goes the credit of building the first telegraph system on the South American continent.)

After attending to his various purchases and engaging the services of a number of British specialists in various fields, most of whom were to regret they ever left home, López returned to Paris to pick up the uniforms he had ordered and, as has been duly recorded, to make his most consequential—and expensive—of purchases: the girl from County Cork.

"That Irish Concubine"

While Francisco Solano knew that he enjoyed the widest latitude when it came to counseling his father on (and in many respects supervising) the affairs of state, he knew there was one kind of affair on which the old man frowned: that of any of his sons with a foreign woman. Domestic mistresses were quite acceptable. Francisco, not to mention Venancio and Benigno, had already built up quite a stable prior to his European sojourn, and though Carlos Antonio had not welcomed to his pendulous bosom his various little *nietos bastardos* scattered in and around Asunción, neither had he proscribed them. The old dictator was not a xenophobe. Unlike his predecessor El Supremo, he welcomed the introduction of foreign technicians into Paraguay. But he did not welcome foreign concubines into the family.

Too, Francisco must have suspected that his sisters, who considered themselves the Royal Princesses, and their equally drab and pretentious mother—all of whose lack of refinement was the butt of the more daring wits in the foreign colony—would resent the intrusion into their midst of a cultivated, sophisticated, and extraordinarily beautiful young European who could not but make them appear even more bucolic than they already were in the eyes of Asunción Society. And the old dictator was easily swayed by the López Ladies, especially when their attitudes conformed with his own. Even brother Benigno, while in Paris with Francisco, had tried to talk him out of taking his "plaything" home. In fact, it was brother Benigno who had sent along word to the old dictator that his favorite son was not "attending very important scientific lectures" but was attending to the wants of *una ramera irlandesa*, and, what was worse, had determined to bring the Irish strumpet to Paraguay as his Favorite.

Most sources claim that Francisco left Eliza behind in Buenos Aires to have her baby, while he went on to Asunción to pave the way for her coming. But records show that the child was born in Asunción. This would support the theory that Francisco remained in Buenos Aires, Carlos Antonio remained in Asunción—and the rest of the family remained on tenterhooks, wondering which of the two strong-willed men was going to give in first.

The López Ladies worked assiduously on the old dictator to prohibit Eliza's entry. Surrounded by her daughters, La Presidenta (as Doña Juana demanded that she be addressed) fondled her rosary and wailed determinedly that she would "never accept La Irlandesa." But weighed against Carlos Antonio's loyalty to the women of his family, and to his own convictions, was the realization that he was getting older (and fatter) and was not in the best of health. He not only *wanted* Francisco back home, he *needed* him back home.

Thus, he sent word that he would not make too much of a fuss over his favorite son's acquisition. Francisco assured the by now somewhat apprehensive Eliza that his entire family would take her to their collective bosom once they had actually met and gotten to know her. The two reboarded the *Tacuarí* early in January 1855 and began the slow thousand-mile voyage upriver to Asunción. Francisco was in his thirtieth year, Eliza was on the verge of entering her twenty-first year, and their first-born son, to be named Juan Francisco, was on the verge of entering the world.

Eliza's physical discomfort must have been unbearable. Coming from France, where the climate is rather temperate, she was now entering a land that lay in a low latitude, with nearly half its territory within the tropical zone, the temperatures of which were extreme. It was now the height of the summer, when the temperature ranged between ninety-two and a hundred and two and the humidity ranged between the impossible and the incredible; too, the nights were almost as hot as the days. Reclining beneath an awning on the deck of the *Tacuarí*, Eliza sought to refresh herself with cool liquids as she got her first glimpses of the paradise her lover had promised her.

It was in fact Eden-like in many respects. Floating islets of water lilies, the *nenúfares*, competed for space on the narrow, winding river with the sand banks on which the *cocodrilos* lay log-like as do all crocodiles, while overhead toucans and herons flew at low level, ready to pounce on the flying fish executing their balletic movements alongside the boat. Along the banks grew a veritable profusion of wild fruits and vegetables, most notably the oranges that provided the natives with their basic and favorite *dulce*. Off in the distance could be seen the uncharted wasteland that was the Gran Chaco. At this time of the year it was a rain forest whose foliage hid the lagoons that crisscrossed the area haphazardly like the veins of a patriarch's wrist. Among these lagoons roamed semi-barbaric Indians on horseback who stood naked before the world save for the long spears they carried and the tufts of ostrich feathers that seemed to sprout from their heads.

Of the half-million inhabitants of this primitive nation that was more than half the size of Eliza's beloved France, the overwhelming majority of them were either pure Guaraní or of Guaraní stock. The Guaranís were mild, tractable, gentle in manner, hospitable in character, docile and peaceable yet somber, sad, and subdued; they were a race of aborigines who spoke little, cried or complained rarely, and did not know the trait of jealousy. They spoke in a nasal grunt, which must have sat uneasily on the ears of one such as Eliza, who was accustomed to the mellifluousness of spoken French. And they bathed religiously once a day, which must have seemed rather extraordinary to a young woman coming from a land whose inhabitants bathed religiously once a month. They had made some feeble attempts to throw off Spanish domination in the sixteenth century, but had given it up as a bad go, and, accepting the Spaniards as the dominant race, had in many cases intermarried with them to produce the Paraguayan.

The Paraguayans were a simple people, and their tastes were simple. The women had a great love of jewelry, but this was less a pretension than a way of life. Even the poorest among them managed to acquire quantities of beads, earrings, and finger rings, and none would dare appear in public unless she was wearing everything she owned. For those who could afford them, there were combs, either tortoise shell or gold-mounted, which they wore along with roses or plumes of leaves in their jet-black hair that was usually dressed in two dangling plaits. The Paraguayans were superb goldsmiths as well as embroiderers. The gold was not an indigenous metal; it came into the country as payment for the *yerba maté*, woods, hides, and tobacco that were now filtering onto the world markets. The Government carefully watched the goldsmiths and prevented them, under pain of heavy penalty, from manufacturing their wares in any way inferior to the average ounce in circulation. The amount of gold in Paraguay prior to the war for a population of such general poverty was enormous.

Those who could afford to wore European dress, and only in the capital city of Asunción; in the other cities—Concepción, Encarnación, Villarrica—as well as in the suburban settlements (and here it should be noted that the population as a whole was a rural as opposed to an urban one), the Paraguayans by and large preferred their own less complicated and actually more attractive native dress. For the men, in addition to the omnipresent silver ankle spurs and straw hats that harkened back to the days of Francia, there was a kilt of white cotton, a double apron of dressed leather, a white shirt handsomely embroidered, and, during the cold season, a simple woolen poncho of about two square yards with a hole cut through the center. The women wore a long cotton chemise, called the *tupoi*, cut very low in the neck with a deep border of embroidery in black or scarlet wool to its upper edge, and loose lace sleeves; the skirt was a simple affair of muslin or silk, puffed out by stiffly starched petticoats and fastened around the waist by a broad embroidered sash. Except in the capital, and then only among the aristocracy, very few Paraguayans wore shoes; and even the aristocrats loved to kick off their shoes while dancing. With the coming of foreigners after the death of Francia, many of the merchants and government functionaries took to wearing patent-leather boots, thus leading to the term *gente calzada* ("people with footwear"), by which they were differentiated from the masses.

The cuisine of the average Paraguayan was quite simple. The poorest among them subsisted on oranges, an occasional *asado* (the native barbecue), and a boiled manioc root. (This is a tuber similar to the sweet potato, but more nutritious, and was the principal starch of the Paraguayan diet, potatoes having not yet been introduced into the country. It was eaten either boiled or roasted, and was rather tasteless; then, as today, it was also used to starch petticoats.)

Those who could afford to do so did not eat much better. A typical meal served even to the Lópezes would begin with a *puchero*, a stew of beef or chicken with rice; then would come the *sopa paraguaya* ("Paraguayan soup"), a tasteless solidified concoction based on the manioc root that cannot quite make up its mind whether it is a pudding or a brick. The meal would end with the *dulce*, usually guavas or pomegranates drowned in syrup, after which a gourd of water was passed around to each person. Tea or coffee was scarcely known to the Paraguayans, and wine was taken only at public festivals, never in the home.

A favorite of all Paraguayans, their station in life notwithstanding, was, as remains to this day, the flourlike pancake, the *chipá*, which, along with the *yerba maté*, was then, as today, constantly being ingested even on the streets. And common as the sight of someone sipping *yerba* and chewing on a *chipá* was the sight of men and women smoking the long reedlike native cigar. Children of both sexes learned to smoke as soon as they could walk. Except among the aristocrats, all girls were taught to carry water jugs on their heads as soon as they could walk steadily, so that when grown they carried enormous burdens with effortless grace. And even among the aristocrats, all boys were initiated into the mysteries of gambling, perhaps the paramount Paraguayan vice, if vice it be. The children, who were allowed to go naked in all but the coldest weather until the age of nine or ten years, had no toys. George Masterman records how, while out walking in the suburbs of Asunción one day, he "found a group of children engaged in burying a live baby; they had scooped a hole in the middle of the road, and had covered the little creature as far as its neck. It looked somewhat scared, as might have been expected, but lay quietly enough in the warm sand. Two or three of their companions, about five years old—too old, I suppose, to take part in such childish amusements—were sitting on the edge of the path, smoking their cigars and watching the proceedings with utmost gravity."*

For a people who prided themselves on their cleanliness, the Paraguayans lived in dwellings that were more often than not appalling, depending on one's station in life. The poorest, of course, lived in hastily erected (and just as hastily demolished) lean-tos. Except for the most aristocratic, such as the Lópezes themselves, the average Paraguayan home was a simple one-story adobe house with tiled roof, sparsely furnished and rarely cleaned. The homes of the López family were also one-story dwellings, but differed only in that they might contain more rooms and have less of a Spartan look about them; in the event, they were also rarely cleaned.

All Paraguayans loved to dance; in the cities it was the greatest pleasure they knew. Masterman speculates that "one reason why the señoritas like it so much is, perhaps, that it is the only oppor-

---

* Masterman notes that, although the smoking habit was universal—"men, women, and children of both sexes and all classes indulge in it"—the women of the higher class, perhaps as a result of the infusion of foreigners due to Carlos Antonio's open-door policy, "were getting ashamed of it, and only smoked in secret."

tunity they have of listening freely to their admirers; for at all other times they are subjected to the strictest surveillance by their mothers—I am sorry to add, not without good reason; so much so, that before marriage one can scarcely speak to them for a minute alone, and they never walk in the streets with their male friends, not even with their brothers."

Paraguay was, on balance, a nation of contented people whose wants were few, whose basic needs were satisfied even among the most lowly. It was a nation where little was learned in the schools Carlos Antonio López had reopened; but the people assumed that what little they were taught was all that they were supposed to learn. It was a nation whose inhabitants may have been a bit lax in their morality—especially out in the hinterlands, or in the cities when the duenna's back was turned—but the only illnesses known to those inhabitants prior to the war were, on rare occasion, fever and ague.* It was a nation where the greatest pleasures were to be found in dancing or in strumming the guitars and the indigenous haunting *arpas;* but such pleasures in no way involved the baser human instincts such as avariciousness and aggressiveness. It was a nation where the overwhelming majority assumed that no peoples existed beyond their own borders; but this was out of ignorance, not conceit. It was a nation that accepted the despotism of its government, as personified in Carlos Antonio López; but his was a benevolent despotism. It was a nation where more than 99 percent of the people had no earthly ambitions beyond the hope that they would not starve.

It was a nation that is hardly the material of which empires are made.

The *Tacuarí*, bearing Eliza and Francisco, docked at Asunción on January 21, 1855. A public fiesta had been declared, and most

---

* Syphilis and gonorrhea, today Paraguay's most prevalent diseases, swept the country in epidemic proportions after the war broke out, as did measles, cholera, and smallpox, all of which were brought in by the invading Allied armies.

of the city's population of twenty thousand crowded the water-front at the foot of the Plaza de Palma to welcome home the Hero of the Corrientes. As Francisco appeared at the top of the gang-plank, the crowds cheered: "Taita Guazú. Caria Guazú" ("Great Lord. Big Lord"). López usually was seen around Asunción in military uniform, but for this special occasion he had stuffed himself into one of his more colorful "civilian" ensembles: tight-fitting trousers of a pastel shade strapped over one of those seventy pairs of handcrafted elevated boots, a blue frock coat, and a stovepipe hat of monumental proportions.

As Francisco acknowledged the cheers of the normally staid and taciturn populace, he glanced off to the side of the quay where three carriages were parked surrounded by a colorfully clad escort, each carriage seeming to sag almost to the ground under the weight it had to bear. In the lead carriage, his sword across his lap, his omnipresent hat on his head, sat Carlos Antonio López. Directly behind was the carriage bearing Doña Juana and her daughters Inocencia and Rafaela; the three were dressed, as was their wont, in black shroudlike gowns that, in the words of one observer, "were stained with sweat under the armpits." Bringing up the rear was the third carriage "with its springs sagging under the weight of Benigno and Venancio, who bulged out of their tropical suits as they lolled back on the padded seats."

Only the First Family knew that Francisco was not traveling alone. Therefore when Madame Lynch appeared at the top of the gangplank, clad in a pale lilac gown with matching bonnet and a stole of lace which hid well the figure swollen with pregnancy, the natives stared in astonishment. With the exception of the very few who had come into contact with the wives of the European envoys, the people of Asunción had never seen a woman with blue eyes and golden hair; and even those who had seen European women had never seen one so commandingly exquisite.

As Francisco took her arm and led her down the gangplank and over toward where his family stared down from their respective carriages, Eliza beamed beatifically upon her new subjects, who, in the words of Masterman, "thought her charms were of more than earthly brilliance, and her dress so sumptuous that they had not words to express the admiration they both excited."

Francisco presented Eliza to his father. Eliza, a radiant smile on her face, held out a gloved hand—whereupon the old dictator grunted a few unintelligible words and ordered his coachman to get moving. It was the last "conversation" Carlos Antonio and Eliza ever held. As the presidential escort, crack cavalrymen all, raised clouds of dust that quickly transformed his beloved's lilac gown to soot gray, Francisco, choking down his humiliation and fury, next introduced Eliza to his mother and sisters. Before he could even complete the introductions, Doña Juana screamed at her driver to move on. The carriage shot away with such a lurch that Eliza's dress (and Francisco's boots) were splattered with excrement. Benigno, a smirk of satisfaction on his face, ordered his and Venancio's carriage to move off without even acknowledging their brother's return.

So much for Madame Lynch's acceptance by the First Family.

If Eliza was disappointed by the reception given her by her putative in-laws, she must have been downright appalled by the sight of their realm. Asunción, by then more than three hundred years old, was a community which even by the standards of the day looked less like a nation's capital than a classic argument for urban renewal. From Masterman's perceptive word portrait of the city, we are justified in assuming that surely Eliza, coming from the architectural miracle into which Georges Eugène Haussmann had begun to transform Paris, must have wondered why at least *some* of the wealth Francisco boasted of had not gone into *some* form of civic improvement:

> From the river Asunción makes a poor appearance, owing to the absence of lofty buildings, and as the houses are one story— a ground-floor—in height, there is little to be seen from a distance but red-tiled roofs. The quay, the first point seen by a

traveler, shows but little appearance of business, and except for a few lounging soldiers or smoking market women, was often nearly deserted, and the ships seemed to be rotting at their moorings, rather than taking on or discharging cargo. The wharves, built on the outside of a bend which the river makes there, are being gradually abandoned by its waters, the opposite bank is compensatingly eaten away by the current, and the channel will soon be far from the city. A hundred years ago the landing-place was more than a mile above its present site. Now it is far from the business part of the town (for the merchants have not retreated with the river), with a sandy waste, a shallow muddy brook, and a dilapidated bridge intervening.

Close by is the Aduana or Custom-house, which, like all else in the country is unfinished, and is, moreover, so hideous, that one can only regret that it was ever commenced. The ground on which the entire market and business areas is built slopes at an angle of about ten degrees, and, as a Paraguayan sees no beauty in, nor necessity for, level lines, the whole front of the long building follows the slope of the ground! To make matters worse, there is not a single break or projection to hide the defect, and the entire piazza looks as if it were sliding into the river!

It was obvious to Eliza that before she and Francisco could make Paraguay the capital of an empire, that capital's capital city would first have to be made habitable. Keyed up by what he had seen being accomplished in Paris under the direction of Haussmann, Francisco had already determined, even without having it suggested to him by his mistress, to undertake a model-cities program.

Fortunately, Carlos Antonio was amenable to the idea of building a new city, and gave his son the go-ahead (and the wherewithal) to start construction.

Unfortunately, Francisco Solano was addicted to embarking on a new scheme with enthusiasm, tiring of it, and moving on to something else. A new palace, a new cathedral, a railway station, a new arsenal, a new custom house, a post office, a national library, a block of government offices in an esplanade—all were started, none was completed.

The hastily constructed railway station started crumbling to pieces even while it was under construction; the façade of the custom house was half demolished when a heavy hailstorm roared through Asunción one night. Buildings were started, and the laborers were summarily dragged off to start yet another building. It was not so much insanity on López's part as sheer impatience. Frantic to get everything done at once, he splattered his minions and his monies in all directions, so that nothing was finished.

All the labor on the various building projects was carried out by slaves, most of whom were boys between the ages of six and ten. Washburn has left us assurances that it was "a sad sight to see the little fellows made prematurely old by the labour to which they were condemned. They were constantly watched and in passing through the ground where they wrought, they appeared like worn-out gnomes in whom all hope was so utterly extinguished that they never looked up or ceased for a moment in their labours. They were scantily fed. The poor little wretches were only allowed [the equivalent of] six or eight cents a day to buy their food." To the gnomes, it was a matter of supreme indifference on what particular structure they might be asked to work on any given day. If commanded to stop laying stones for the custom house and rush off to dig ground for the new Palacio, off they rushed to dig.

Within weeks of Francisco's return from Europe, Asunción was as busy as an ant colony under construction—a colony in which all the ants have taken leave of their senses. Francisco was all over the city, ordering this to be done, that to be done. As a consequence, nothing much got done. The foreign colony stood by appalled, wondering if any building would ever be completed. The buildings were all completed—but long after her Friend had died and Madame Lynch had fled the country.

(Most of these buildings are still in use today, notably the Palacio, which was intended as the imperial seat of the Empire of the Río de la Plata and which today houses the offices of the incumbent dictator, Alfredo Stroessner.)

Symptomatic of the manner in which Francisco's building mania manifested itself was the opera house Eliza wanted built; to her the idea of an imperial capital without an opera house was unsupportable. When Francisco mentioned to his father that he would build the greatest opera house on the continent, he met with stiff resistance. Who needed an opera house? But as it happened, the López Ladies also felt that Asunción should have an opera house, and made this known to Carlos Antonio. Carlos Antonio gave in. His family wanted an opera house, they would have an opera house.

Construction was begun on the opera house, which was to be a miniature replica of La Scala in Milan. Drawings were imported from Italy, and López's imported Italian architect (the same designer of the crumbling railway station and the hail-prone Aduana) copied the celebrated La Scala down to every last detail. But there was one problem: The architect did not know how to construct the roof! Close to a decade later, one observer was to describe the opera house as "a mere wilderness of lofty walls and arches."

(The building was finally roofed years later and now stands, somewhat precariously, as El Teatro Nacional; almost a century passed before it was the setting for its first opera. The present author had the distinction of being in the audience on that historic occasion in 1955. For the record, the opera was Puccini's *Suor Angelica*, a bit of treacle which deals with a society girl who abandons her bastard child and enters a convent in expiation. The work was performed, with much enthusiasm if little else, by a local girls' parochial school. When asked why this particular work was chosen as the bill of fare, the school's director replied, "Pardon me, Señor Brodsky, but is it not obvious? The opera is very short, it is easy to sing, it has theo-

logical connotations, and it calls for no male roles." It was
not "obvious" at the time, but it should have been.)

Also started (but never completed) at the suggestion of
Madame Lynch, who liked to read and who believed that her
future subjects should be exposed to the habit, was a public library, although here Uncle Basilio, the Bishop of Asunción, appears to have injected himself, for "the books were nearly all
theological, and I [Masterman] never heard of anyone reading
there. López found, however, a most uncharacteristic use for
them: he had the ponderous tomes cut up for rocket and squib
cases! I saw them one day serving thus a folio Hebrew Bible, with
an interleaved Latin translation—a most South American mode of
diffusing useful knowledge!"

When it came to shipyards, arsenals, and fortifications, however, López had better luck—probably because he entrusted the
responsibility of their construction to the English artisans and
technicians he had imported. (Carlos Antonio assumed that the
fortresses—especially the magnificent complexes at Cerro Corá
and Humaitá—were intended solely for the defense of the
country. Francisco did not bother to disabuse the old man of
this assumption.) And, probably due in large measure to Eliza
taking a more direct interest, the various mansions he built in
and around Asunción for himself and his Favorite managed to
get up—and stay up.

Francisco had ordered constructed, and in record time, a *casa*
for Eliza in the heart of Asunción (it now houses the Colegio
Carlos Antonio López), in addition to the one he built for himself. For appearances' sake, the two had decided to maintain
separate residences. Also, Eliza had decided to maintain a low
profile. It was hoped that eventually the López family would
accept her, so long as she did not flaunt herself and managed
to convince them that she had come to Paraguay to help the
nation, and not, as they had decided was her real purpose, to
"bleed the nation dry," to "turn Francisco against his family."

Shortly after giving birth to their first son, Eliza decided that she must have a country home as well. What Eliza wanted, Eliza got. Work on all public projects was halted temporarily, and the pathetic gnomes, working round the clock, constructed in record time "Patiño," a country quinta a few miles from downtown Asunción, in the suburban community of La Recoleta. Here lived the upper-class merchants and foreigners; also the López family, scattered about in the various quintas they had extracted from their original owners through means less fair than foul.

Eliza had not yet given up on winning at least some measure of acceptance from the First Family, though she had given up on Francisco's assurances that eventually they would love her. In fact, the knowledge that Francisco doted on the son Eliza had given him only made the Lópezes hate Eliza all the more. To his credit, Francisco had tried his damnedest to get them to be at least *civil* to Eliza; but on this one point they remained obdurate. Doña Juana, it was said around Asunción, spent the better part of every day fingering her rosary and screeching a capella with her daughters Inocencia and Rafaela, "I will *never* accept that woman! I will *never* accept that woman!"

Being a courtesan of the world, Eliza could accept that she must remain discreetly in the background. She had abandoned the prospect of being embraced by the López Ladies, whom she considered to be, with justification, beneath the dignity of scrubbing her floors. She had in fact turned their hatred of her to her own advantage. As she was seen around Asunción, in the latest Parisian fashions, making it a point to show her magnificent figure to every advantage, she relished the knowledge that even those among the aristocrats who disliked her simply because they envied her had to admit that the López Ladies more than paled by comparison.

Eliza realized that Francisco was in a difficult position. Once his father was dead and he had acceded to the presidency, his mothers and sisters could be shunted aside and Eliza allowed to take her rightful place in society. But with Carlos Antonio still alive, Francisco had to swallow his bile and keep Eliza in the background. Eliza realized that this savage to whom she had bound herself had enough sensitivity to feel awkward for her. Thus it was less for her sake than for Francisco's that Eliza requested that he build her quinta at La Recoleta, in the hopes that proximity would break down the barrier his family had erected against her.

It didn't. The Lópezes simply abandoned their quintas there and relocated a few miles down the road at Trinidad.

The quinta, a pink and white marble palace built to Eliza's own design, was the first habitation in Paraguay to have two stories. For some unknown reason, it is about the only major building dating from this period of which no traces remain. With its exotic air, its imported Empire furniture, and, according to Héctor Varela, "French tapestries and Oriental rugs distributed with excellent taste and in a manner to delight the eye," the total ambience led more than one observer to suspect that Madame Lynch had hoped to transplant to Paraguay, if not the Tuileries then certainly the Petit Trianon. (According to one fairly reliable source, included on the estate was a corral "where cows were kept and Eliza could play at being Marie Antoinette.") The quinta was connected with the capital by a specially constructed straight road, also a "first" for Paraguay, "built in record time to enable Francisco to mount his horse at the Cabildo [Government House] and be with his mistress within half an hour." (The road is today Avenida Mariscal Francisco Solano López, Asunción's "Embassy Row.")

Shortly after settling into the quinta, in the summer of 1856, Eliza gave birth to her second child, a girl whom she named Corina Adelaida (the Spanish forms of her sister's and mother's given names). According to creditable sources, Eliza, not particularly oriented to motherhood and inordinately vain about her figure, rode her horse around the countryside constantly and in a demonic fury in hopes of precipitating an abortion.

If this is true, the birth of a daughter would seem to have aroused some dormant maternal feelings, for when Corina Adelaida died six months later (February 13, 1857), Eliza was prostrate with grief. After ordering the infant dressed in a white frock on which had been sewn a pair of gauze wings, she had the body interred under an ornate tombstone which stands to this day just to the right of the main entrance to the cemetery at La Recoleta on the airport road out of Asunción. Some degree of Eliza's grief may be discerned from the sentiments she had inscribed on the stone:

> Ere sin could blight or sorrow fade
> Death came with friendly care
> The lovely bird to Heaven conveyed
> And made it beossom [*sic*] there.

(Many of her biographers identify Eliza herself as the author of these sentiments, although the "true author" is identified on the stone as "B.M." When the present writer asked one of Eliza's descendants the identity of "B.M.," he was told, "It's the poet John Milton, but the engraver made a mistake." [The descendant also conceded that the engraver had made a mistake in spelling the word "blossom."] Advised by the present writer that the poem is by Samuel Taylor Coleridge, and that, furthermore, "lovely bird" should read "opening bud" and "made it beossom" should read "bade it blossom," the descendant replied most graciously, "Forgive me, Señor Brodsky, but you are totally in error." Señor Brodsky murmured politely that perhaps he was.)*

Two months after her second child was buried, Eliza's first child was baptized. He was now in his second year. Had Eliza's insistence on little Juan Francisco's rather belated reception into the Church derived from a reawakened religiosity precipitated by the death of little Corina Adelaida? Or did it derive from a determination on Eliza's part to assure Francisco Solano's recog-

---

* See Coleridge's *Epitaph on an Infant.*

nition of the little boy as his only "legitimate" heir? Perhaps it was a combination of the two factors. At any rate, her insistence precipitated the first no-holds-barred showdown between Madame Lynch & Friend.

It was also the last such showdown.

While enroute home from his celebrated "victory" at Corrientes, Francisco had fallen in love with—and taken as his concubine—one Juana Pesoa, who had borne him two children prior to his departure for Europe. It was hardly a secret that he had established La Pesoa and her bastards, Emiliano Victor and Adelina Constanta, in an Asunción town house. Francisco had probably told Eliza about his other family even before her arrival in Paraguay.

Eliza had accepted the situation, knowing, as everyone in Asunción was shortly to know, that she was "the Favorite." Juana Pesoa posed no threat; she accepted the new Favorite's ascendancy and kept to the background. (Considering Juana's ultimate fate, she would have been better off fleeing the country. Washburn claims that she fell afoul of Francisco in the last years of the war and, like so many of his enemies both real and imagined, was dragged along in his train during López's flight from Asunción into the Paraguayan wilderness, where "she was exposed to the most terrible hardships, and, it is supposed, perished of want and exposure.")

More than merely accepting Francisco's relationship with Juana Pesoa, Eliza encouraged it; she even took Emiliano under her protection when Juana fell from favor. (Emiliano was the only surviving child of this particular union; the little girl died, as did another son, José Félix, who was born in September of 1860.) Thus to claim, as do so many of Eliza's detractors, that Juana Pesoa fell from favor at her insistence when Eliza became First Lady of Paraguay, and that her quasi-adoption of Emiliano was an act of expiation, is unfounded. Eliza Lynch reserved her fierce hatreds for, and took vengeance on, only those who wronged her. And far from "wronging" her, Juana Pesoa was, in a sense, an ally: she did not submit to the pressure of the López Ladies that she somehow coerce Francisco into marrying her.

As for marrying Francisco, Eliza suspected that any woman who became his wife would lose all power over him. Conversely, she did not want anyone *else* to marry him. As William Barrett has noted with great perception in his *Woman on Horseback:*

> He had a peculiar mental slant that would make his wife a woman forever obligated to him. A mistress was different. He had to give and to continue to give to a mistress in order to hold her esteem if he wished that esteem; it was a rule that he understood and obeyed. Constancy and responsibility, the twin rules of marriage, were beyond his comprehension entirely. Ella Lynch had understood all of that long ago. López might marry some day—and she would fight that eventuality with every resource that she possessed—but she would not be the unlucky woman.

Eliza succeeded. López never married.

Eliza was, in the broadest connotation of the term, Francisco's procuress. However, it should not be inferred that she strewed his path with whores every time the biological urge overtook him, which was often. Francisco was quite capable of finding his own whores. And, in his own way, he seems to have respected Eliza too much to flaunt these transient peccadilloes openly. Rather, Eliza sought out respectable girls who were willing to enter into concubinage with Francisco without demanding the prerogative of trying to exert an influence on him, and the respectability of marital ties. Just as Eliza had been able to perceive that there is more than a semantic difference between a cocotte and a courtesan, she was able to appreciate what separated a concubine from a mistress.

Since Francisco Solano seems to have enjoyed a penchant for concubines, Eliza determined that she would have a hand in their selection, and she determined that they would enter into concubinage with Francisco on *her* terms. In addition to her tacit fostering of Francisco's relationship with Juana Pesoa, Eliza fostered his relationships with all the others who joined the López stable. In some cases, she went so far as to arrange these relationships. A case in point would be that of La Burgos (her first name is lost to history), described by one contemporary as "a tall and rather fine-looking young woman."

Francisco had fallen in love with La Burgos, but she did not reciprocate in kind. He could not resort to his old ploy of threatening to confiscate her father's properties lest she submit. Her father was Pedro Burgos, a magistrate from the small provincial city of Luque, and a man held in high esteem by Carlos Antonio. From Eliza's part in the episode, it would appear that Francisco had by now arrived at the point where he openly discussed his amorous intentions with her (that is, intentions other than those involving a transient whore). Eliza sought out the Burgos girl and ascertained that she had no desire whatsoever to marry Francisco Solano. She then contacted Judge Burgos and promised that if he were to encourage his daughter to accept Francisco's nonmarital proposal, he would be amply rewarded when Francisco inherited the presidency.

If it is true, as evidence seems to indicate, that the magistrate did in fact coerce his daughter into prostituting herself for his own eventual advancement—it has been definitely established that La Burgos became one of López's concubines—then the fate that befell him was justified, if only from a moralistic point of view. He was one of the many put to death when, shortly after the war broke out, López began to see "conspirators" behind every bush. (As for the young girl's fate, Washburn speculates that she probably died "like a hundred thousand others in the wilderness, or may have been one of those unhappy wretches whose sufferance had been such that, on being rescued from the power of López [by the Brazilians after his death], the very instincts of modesty had been almost destroyed.")

So far as Eliza was concerned, Francisco could sire a battalion of sons (though he failed to sire a battalion, López's male issue by the various concubines added up to a rather respectable platoon), but she was determined that *her* son was going to be protected. She took no small comfort in the knowledge that Francisco considered little Juan Francisco his favorite child; nicknamed Pancho, the boy was transformed by his overindulgent father into a thoroughly spoiled and abjectly rotten youth (he did not survive to adulthood). But, López's mercurial temperament being what it was, Eliza realized that there was always the possibility that even young Pancho could one day fall from favor.

Thus it came about that shortly after Corina Adelaida's death, Eliza demanded of Francisco that their son be properly baptized. Francisco agreed. To announce, rather belatedly, the glorious event of Juan Francisco's birth, the proud father commanded the firing of a hundred-and-one-gun salute (during the course of which eleven buildings collapsed in downtown Asunción, including five under construction, and one of the imported English field artillery pieces which had not been properly cleaned backfired, putting half the battery into the hospital and the other half into the cemetery). He then proclaimed that the little boy would be christened, ostentatiously, in Asunción's Catedral de la Encarnación.

Carlos Antonio was furious, the López Ladies were apopleptic —and Francisco Solano was made to see that he could not have *everything* his way. For Uncle Basilio announced that the child could not be baptized in the Cathedral; furthermore, any priest who officiated at any rite resembling a baptism would be excommunicated. Francisco appealed to his father, who could have overriden Uncle Basilio's ban. Predictably, the old dictator sided with Uncle Basilio—less because he was all that religious than because he would not tolerate official recognition of any bastard by La Irlandesa.

Francisco then turned to Padre Fidel Maiz, described by

Washburn as "the only one of all the priests in Paraguay, so far as I had any knowledge of them, who was respected for his morality. He was about the same age as Francisco Solano, and was early distinguished for his application and scholarship . . . respected . . . for his talents, learning, and correct deportment, and . . . for his piety."

Though the two had been childhood friends, Francisco Solano must surely have realized that soliciting Padre Maiz's services was futile in the extreme. Padre Maiz was the only clergyman in all of Paraguay, Uncle Basilio included, whom Carlos Antonio respected; also, he was the personal confessor to the López Ladies. As was to be expected, Maiz declined to baptize the child, even in secrecy, despite Francisco's promises that 1) he would take the priest under his personal protection if word got out that Uncle Basilio's proscription had been contravened, and 2) the priest would live to regret denying his boyhood chum this one request.

Eliza was furious when informed that her son was to be denied baptism. Allowing that she was willing to compromise by not insisting that the child be baptized in her own Anglican faith, she threatened to return with the child to Europe unless he were baptized into *some* faith.

Eliza must have known that she was walking a precarious road. Francisco loved her, respected her judgment, convinced her that she was the only person with whom he could "talk," the only person in all of Paraguay who "understood" him. But even Eliza was not too sure how far he could be pushed before turning on her.

Some historians argue that Eliza's forcing of the issue was in reality a means by which she hoped to determine to find out just how far Francisco *could* be pushed; for to Francisco's way of thinking, whether or not his son was received into the Church was a matter of supreme indifference. It was still his favorite son; the sprinkling of holy water over the boy could not endear him any more to his father. In all probability, Francisco had agreed to all this baptism business only at Eliza's insistence; he personally could not care less about religious conventions one way or the other.

Nor, for that matter, could Eliza have cared less. Thus, the theory that her insistence on the baptism was in effect a calculated risk, aimed at determining once and for all the extent of her hold on Francisco, is a valid one.

When Francisco coolly informed her that he was not one to be handed an ultimatum by anybody, Eliza immediately went on the offensive, attacking him as a coward who would be Emperor of South America but would back down in the eyes of mere priests.

Francisco indignantly asseverated that the Church was the *last* thing he feared. Need he remind her that he was not above suborning—and in some cases threatening on pain of death—many of the priests to turn over to him secrets entrusted to them in the confessional booth? But Paraguay was still a Catholic country, and forms must be adhered to, if only in terms of public relations. Eliza countered that she did not mean to imply that he should ignore the Church; rather, that he should follow the pattern established by his father of having the nation render unto God what was God's, and unto López what was López's.

She then ordered Francisco from her house to ponder his dilemma. But so far as Francisco was concerned, there was no dilemma. The child would not be baptized. Ultimatums notwithstanding, Francisco doubted strenuously that Eliza would leave him.

Eliza decided to take matters into her own hands; she was not prepared to return to Europe save only as a last resort. Casting about for the stupidest, most malleable priest in all of Paraguay, Eliza was led by her faithful Indian servants to the mud hut of one Manuel Antonio Palacios—a man described by those who knew him as "very limited in education, very sinister and forbidding in appearance," a man who "was never accused of a good act."

Father Palacios had never been able to make a go of it in his chosen profession; when Eliza discovered him, he was reduced to preaching, halfheartedly, the gospel of Jesus to a small village of Guaranís in the outback who found in him a butt of constant derision.

When Palacios balked at defying the ban of Uncle Basilio, his ultimate superior in the hierarchy, and, into the bargain, incurring the enmity of the President, Eliza promised that if he baptized her son he would not only be protected against Uncle Basilio but would eventually wind up *succeeding* Uncle Basilio. Father Palacios agreed to baptize the *niño*—provided Francisco Solano took him under his personal protection. Eliza then gave him a fistful of coins, ordered him to take a bath and shave, change his motheaten and odoriferous habit, and told him to stand by.

Eliza called Francisco back to the quinta and told him that the problem was solved: their son would be baptized. But still Francisco balked. After all, his father was still alive, and Uncle Basilio . . .

But Eliza had had enough of this nonsense. She ordered her maids to start packing and turned on Francisco in a cold fury. She knew that he had set his spies on her from the moment she landed in Asunción. She had accepted this, knowing that she had no secrets to hide from him (and knowing, furthermore, that she had by now established the nucleus of her own little spy network). But being spied upon had rankled her. She now presented Francisco with a two-tined ultimatum: either allow Father Palacios to baptize their son, *and* call off the spies, or she was leaving for Europe immediately.

Eliza's fury was matched by Francisco's; he now literally screamed that, if he wished to, he could keep her from leaving Paraguay. To this Eliza calmly replied that if it became known that she wished to leave, Francisco's own father would not only see her safely out of the country but would probably give her a bounty into the bargain.

Without making any promises, Francisco said he would interview Father Palacios.

Carefully coached by Eliza, and now tidied up a bit, Father Palacios made the sign of the cross over Francisco Solano and proclaimed him not only the Hero of the Corrientes but the coming Savior of Paraguay. Francisco listened to the priest's litany of encomiums and decided that Father Palacios was his kind of Father.

After returning to the quinta at La Recoleta, Francisco informed Eliza that their son would be properly baptized, though for obvious reasons not in the Catedral de la Encarnación; furthermore, the spies would be called off. Eliza ordered her servants to halt packing and start stitching up a proper robe in which to carry the child to the baptismal font (though, in truth, the child was by now old enough to make the journey to the font under his own steam).

All of Asunción Society, including the Diplomatic Corps, was commanded to appear at the baptism, which was to be held at Madame Lynch's quinta. All of Asunción Society, including the Diplomatic Corps, was in a quandary. No one wanted to offend Francisco Solano by snubbing him on this joyous, albeit belated, occasion; yet no one wanted to antagonize the López family. Francisco was going to be President—but he was not President yet. The dilemma was resolved to a degree when Carlos Antonio let it be known that he would cast a jaundiced eye on anyone who attended the ceremony.

The proud Francisco seethed with rage for days on end (his rages were legendary, both in degree of ferocity and of duration). But there was little he could do save to see his favorite son baptized before a congregation that was limited to Eliza's household staff of Guaraní Indians. It was enough that Society, not to mention his own family, had refused to recognize his Favorite;

now they had gone to the ultimate in refusing to recognize his favorite son.

Madame Lynch had little difficulty convincing her aggrieved Friend that Society, the First Family, and now the Mother Church must all pay eventually for this outrageous disrespect.

Eliza was secure in her hold on Francisco, and she suffered not from the want of material comforts; she was even prepared to remain in the background, as it were, so long as Carlos Antonio López lived. Eliza did not need Francisco to remind her that when the old dictator died she would come into her own. And she was prepared to wait (though she must have wondered ruefully if Carlos Antonio ever would in fact die). But she was deeply wounded; and while Francisco could shower her with luxuries, he could not mitigate the wound.

The López Ladies had by now realized they could not force Francisco to send his Irish mistress back to Europe. Nor could they prevail upon Carlos Antonio to do so. So far as the old man was concerned, they should just ignore La Irlandesa, as he ignored her, and let Francisco Solano concentrate on more important matters, such as getting those arsenals and fortifications built. However, the López Ladies assumed they could force Eliza to leave Paraguay of her own volition once they had made it palpably obvious to her that she was not welcome. It was a false assumption: Eliza was determined not to give in to them, as she was determined that they would be at her feet when Francisco came into power in his own right.

No, it was not the attitude of the López Ladies that wounded Eliza; rather, the knowledge that so many of the foreign wives, especially the English and French, went out of their way to ignore her. Worse yet was the attitude of the old aristocratic families, who, despite none too subtle hints from Francisco, persisted in treating Eliza as if she were a common whore. They even went so far as to practice the ultimate in humiliating rejection: making the sign of the cross and quickly averting their eyes whenever she rode through the streets of Asunción in her imported coach-and-four.

On the other hand, the foreign diplomats and businessmen assiduously courted her. True, many did so only as a means of gaining favor with Francisco Solano, who was rapidly assuming direction of the nation's destiny, notwithstanding the fact that Carlos Antonio refused to die. But there were also those who, seeking no personal aggrandizement, found her home a veritable oasis of European élan (and superlative foods, beverages, and conversation) in the wasteland that was Asunción. For many of the foreigners, attending an *asunto* at the Cabildo was an obligation, whereas attending a soiree at Chez Lynch was a profound pleasure.

For Eliza, the pleasure was twofold. She enjoyed the company of people with whom she could converse, especially men who flattered her in an asexual way; and she enjoyed knowing that the wives of her courtiers were beside themselves, knowing that their men would have anything to do with her. So far as Eliza was concerned, let the López Ladies play at being royalty; in her own home, she was queen, and she relished the role.

And the servants absolutely adored her; Madame Lynch had few peers when it came to practicing the subtleties of noblesse oblige.

But those Ladies of Asunción—the Paraguayan aristocrats, the foreign wives, the whole pack—not one of whom was possessed of one tenth of her breeding and cultivation . . .

It was probably around the time of young Juan Francisco's controversial baptism that Eliza began her friendship with Colonel Enrique von Wisner de Morgenstern. They would have met as soon as Eliza came to Asunción: Von Wisner was almost an adjunct of the López family. But Von Wisner had held off from pursuing any relationship with Eliza beyond mere politeness; his loyalty was still to Carlos Antonio.

However, there came a time when Von Wisner realized that

he had better ingratiate himself with Madame Lynch. His patron, Carlos Antonio, was showing signs of physical deterioration. He would have to tread cautiously; he dared not antagonize the President and the López Ladies by openly consorting with Madame Lynch. Conversely, there was much to be gained by currying Madame Lynch's favor. First, the obvious: it would make Von Wisner's position with Francisco Solano all the more secure when he inherited the presidency. Second, to Von Wisner, Madame Lynch was the only person in Paraguay whom he considered his intellectual and cultural coequal.

Von Wisner was a sixty-five-year-old Hungarian who had fled the court at Vienna years before under a cloud of scandal. After drifting about the Western Hemisphere, he had wound up in Paraguay as military adviser to the López family. He was urbane, snobbishly cultivated, and, presumably, suffering the *Weltschmerz* and *Heimweh* of an outcast who would rather be part of the glitter and *Gemütlichkeit* of the court of the Emperor Franz Joseph than of the comparative primitiveness and privation of the court of Carlos Antonio López.

Far from resenting Von Wisner's friendship with Madame Lynch, her Friend encouraged it. The old baron was an astute engineer. He had much to offer Francisco when it came to constructing fortresses and emplacing guns. Also, Francisco realized Eliza's loneliness and was thankful that she had at least one person (other than himself, of course) who was her intellectual equal. And he entertained no fears that this rather suave European would ever make any gesture toward attempting to seduce the affections of his Eliza; it was common gossip that the Hungarian was interested only in young boys.

Once or twice a week Von Wisner would ride out to the quinta and take tea with Eliza. Their favorite pastime was to look down on the entire Paraguayan population, plus accredited envoys and visiting entrepreneurs, from their heights as, in their considered opinion, the only two truly civilized people in the entire country.

Washburn reports how "the old Baron played the courtier to Madame Lynch by agreeing with her in all her ambitious schemes, and seconding her efforts to influence the mind of López." Along with Eliza, Von Wisner agreed wholeheartedly with López in the latter's contention that it would be ludicrous in the extreme to declare Paraguay an empire before steps—drastic steps—had been taken to make the world know that such a country existed. Thus, the Hungarian began to argue, not only with López but with anyone who would give him an ear, that the landlocked country would never be respected abroad, would have no standing as a nation, until she had demonstrated her capacity "to defend her rights and chastise her enemies."

Francisco Solano was making admirable progress in building up his armed forces, perfecting his fortresses (most notably the strategic one at Humaitá that was to hold back for a long time an invading army that equaled in number the entire Paraguayan population), dabbling, through the stream of editorials he wrote for publication in *Semanario*, in the chaotic politics of the Río de la Plata region—and, to be sure, overseeing the construction of still more grandiose, and never to be completed, edifices.

Soon, encouraged by Eliza, Von Wisner, and even old Carlos Antonio himself, Francisco Solano became convinced beyond doubt that he was the God-proven arbiter *ne plus ultra* between the various factions operating in Paraguay's neighboring states. Incredible though it may seem, Francisco succeeded in halting the civil war that was consuming Argentina. Was it not obvious, Francisco Solano declaimed rhetorically, that his having pulled off such a miracle was proof that there was no stopping him now? Eliza and Von Wisner both agreed that it was obvious. *Anyone,* they argued, who could get the warring Argentinians to so much as break bread together, much less agree to a cease-fire, was *destined* to be Emperor of the Río de la Plata region. And once the Empire of the Río de la Plata was a political reality, could the rest of South America be far behind?

2

Students of history are familiar with the claim made, only half in jest, by Lord Palmerston regarding the incredibly complex Schleswig-Holstein Question that kept Europe's major powers on their toes (and at each other's throats) throughout much of the nineteenth century: "There are only three people who have ever understood this Question: the Prince Consort, and he is dead; a German professor, and he is insane; and myself—and I have forgotten all about it!"

The political origins of the War of the Triple Alliance can be analogized to the Schleswig-Holstein Question, both in complexity and incomprehensibility.*

As Professor Harris Gaylord Warren, the foremost contemporary authority on Paraguayan history, has pointed out,

> Paraguayans could have been happy had it not been for their political immaturity that gave rise to oppressive dictatorships, and the interplay of rivalry between Brazil and Argentina. The Brazilian historian, Antonio Baptista Pereira . . . cleverly states: "Francia was the major premise, Carlos Antonio López the minor, and [Francisco] Solano López the conclusion of the Paraguayan syllogism." This syllogism ended in the War of the Triple Alliance, a conflict caused by power politics in the Plata basin. What López might have done had there been no war is an interesting and, of course, entirely useless conjecture. One must not suppose that Francisco Solano López alone caused the war that all but destroyed his country. . . . That disaster . . . had its origin in Brazilian encroachments upon Paraguayan territory, in Brazilian and Argentine meddling in Uruguay, in Paraguay's desire to play a decisive role in the politics of the

---

* For a superb exegesis of this conflict, *The Origins of the Paraguayan War* by the late British historian Pelham Horton Box is still in print and highly recommended.

Río de la Plata. But López precipitated the war, and upon him must rest much of the blame for what happened to Paraguay.

Simply stated, the causes of the war were threefold: long-standing disputes between Argentina, Brazil, and Paraguay over boundaries and navigational rights on the major rivers which empty into the Río de la Plata; the meddling of her neighbors in the internal affairs of war-torn Uruguay; and Francisco Solano López's imperialistic ambitions.

Also, there were two ancillary factors: Carlos Antonio López's political naïveté in allowing his nation to become the cat's-paw of Brazil in the latter's attempt to put down the Argentinian dictator Rosas; and the political unreality manifested by both Lópezes, who thought they could negotiate their border disputes with Brazil through military instead of diplomatic activity.

On two occasions (1850, and again in 1855) the Lópezes had ejected Brazilian garrison forces from frontier territory claimed by Paraguay. As Warren points out, "These matters alone would have been enough to cause war. Add to them . . . the Uruguayan political vortex, and one wonders why war had not come sooner." La República Oriental del Uruguay, the Eastern Republic of Uruguay, was in effect the Balkans of the Río de la Plata region: the powder keg. For more than a generation, it had been going through "birth pains agonizing in the extreme." (Even so astute a historian as Professor Warren confesses, "There is no way to make this complicated account either simple or sensible.")

Uruguay, which separates Brazil and Argentina, had originally been part of Brazil, which was now attempting to reclaim it; this in turn forced Argentina to involve itself in Uruguay, less to conquer it than to secure it as a buffer state against Brazil. Argentina was, of course, waging a civil war of its own, in addition to trying to fend off the much larger and very much encroaching Brazil. And to compound matters, the Uruguayans were themselves divided into two warring factions: the conservative Blancos (Whites) and the liberal Colorados (Reds).

Brazil supported the Blancos, Argentina supported the Colorados. As we have already seen, by steering clear of any foreign entanglements, El Supremo had wisely avoided, among other complications, any involvement in Uruguay's political chaos. Carlos Antonio López had, by joining the league to overthrow Rosas, come dangerously close to getting caught up in "the Uruguayan political vortex." But he had wisely pulled back and, with great luck—the feuding powers were not interested in Paraguay—succeeded in maintaining a precarious neutrality. Unfortunately, Francisco Solano lacked both Francia's wisdom and his own father's good luck.

As we have also seen, Francisco, abetted by Eliza and Von Wisner, had decided that Paraguay simply *had to* make war on her neighbors in order to construct the empire that was the fixed, tropismatic, and ultimate goal in their collective mind's eye. Simple logic would dictate that a leader—especially of a small, landlocked, and thus vulnerable country—no matter how bellicose, no matter how confident, no matter how irrational, simply does not suddenly announce to one and all, "I now declare war on my three most powerful neighbors." Even Francisco Solano realized that one cannot expect orchids to grow in cement.

But he realized the garden was cultivable. His problem was twofold: how to move into the garden, and how to start digging. The first problem was resolved when Francisco Solano, far from moving in, was invited in.

In 1852, General Justo José de Urquiza, the governor of Entre Ríos who had helped Rosas send Francisco Solano scurrying home from Corrientes, overthrew Rosas and assumed the presidency of the Argentine Confederation, which was now supposed, by treaty, to include *all* the provinces. But Urquiza was faced with a rather profound embarrassment: Buenos Aires had refused to ratify the very treaty which made it the capital of the new nation. Thus for seven years the heart fought with the rest of the body for control of the Argentinian geopolitical corpus that threatened to become a geopolitical corpse. When, in 1859, the United States representative at Buenos Aires, after trying to work out a viable solution, withdrew in frustration and disgust, Francisco Solano—encouraged by his myopic father, his Irish mistress, and his Hungarian adviser—offered his services as mediator.

Mirabile dictu, his services were readily accepted.

Foreign observers, not excluding Argentinians representing all factions, were aware that Francisco had built up a powerful army—the best-trained, best-armed in the entire Río de la Plata region. But their mistake was in believing, as did old Carlos Antonio, that Francisco's arming of his nation was purely a defensive measure against Brazil. And since none of the Argentinian factions were interested in subduing Paraguay —which they could readily do, should Paraguay threaten to become rambunctious, simply by closing the Río de la Plata to Paraguayan shipping—they took Francisco Solano at his word: that his *only* aim in offering to mediate the Argentinian crisis was to bring stability to the entire region.

Accompanied by a colorful retinue that looked less like a traveling embassy than a touring gypsy carnival, López arrived at Paraná, the seat of the anti–Buenos Aires Confederate Government—only to learn that in the meantime Urquiza had routed the Federalist *porteños* (as the people of Buenos Aires were called) commanded by General Bartolomé Mitre (the Battle of Cepeda) and was now besieging Mitre's stronghold at Buenos Aires. Moving on to Buenos Aires, López managed somehow to get the combatants to call a truce and submit to arbitration, and through a combination of Lópezian rhetoric commingled with Argentinian exhaustion, both factions were persuaded to end the civil war. Buenos Aires was reincorporated into the Argentine Confederation, Urquiza agreed to retire as President and accept the governorship of Entre Ríos, and Mitre—who was eventually to become President of a unified Argentina, and López's most hated enemy—became Governor of Buenos Aires.

It was Francisco Solano's moment of genuine triumph. As he was paraded through the streets of Buenos Aires, which but for his mediation might well have been demolished by Urquiza's forces (who themselves would undoubtedly have been decimated in the attempt), confetti and flowers fell on his head, beautiful young *porteñas* fell at his feet, and a scroll was presented to him

Dedicated with due respect and in grateful thanks to his Most Excellent Señor Brigadier General don Francisco Solano López, Minister Plenipotentiary of the Republic of Paraguay and saviour of Argentine blood, through whose friendly intervention we owe the satisfactory conclusion of the peace negotiations, a peace so wholeheartedly desired by our entire family.

When Francisco returned home, the jubilation that ensued was as heartfelt—and as undeserved—as that accorded Neville Chamberlain when he returned from his meeting with Hitler to proclaim to the British that there would be "peace in our time." So deliriously proud were the Paraguayans—and especially Madame Lynch and the ever-present Von Wisner—that Francisco Solano had scored his first major diplomatic coup, they could not possibly have conceived that it would prove to be his last such accomplishment.

As the cobblestoned streets of Asunción all but gave way under the pounding from the dancing and marching and general hoopla that went on for days on end, Carlos Antonio López was convinced that Paraguay was now safely launched on the road to tranquility, and Madame Lynch & Friend were convinced that Paraguay was now safely launched on the road to empire.

Francisco Solano resumed building up his war machine (and sending out still more IOU's to the Blyth Brothers, who were shipping out munitions and arms in a never-ending flow); Argentina and Brazil continued to support the opposing factions in Uruguay, all the while rattling sabers at each other, metaphorically speaking; Brazil and Paraguay continued to haggle over their common borders; and Buenos Aires and the other Argentinian provinces continued to bicker, bloodlessly, over who was to lead a (hopefully) unified nation.

Madame Lynch was also busy. She was determined to acculturize Paraguay. Toward that end, two extraordinary projects had already been set in motion. The first of these involved the importation of three of Eliza's friends from her Paris days: Monsieur de Cluny and Mesdames Luisa Balet and Dorotea Dupart.

After succeeding Francia as dictator, Carlos Antonio López had ordered the opening of all schools and the building of even more. It is questionable why he even bothered. Though more than four hundred schools were now in operation, with a total enrollment of approximately twenty thousand children, very few bothered to attend on a regular basis, and even those who did were not learning very much. The curriculum was confined to the most basic elements of reading, writing, and arithmetic; worse, the basic text, so to speak, was the Catechism of St. Albert.

This was a shrewd move on Carlos Antonio's part (so shrewd, in fact, that Francisco Solano continued the policy when he became dictator). By organizing the educational system along the dogmatic lines laid down by St. Albert, the Lópezes—who managed to be religious when it suited their purpose—were able to perpetuate their tyranny on a moral basis by conditioning the people to the idea of accepting all order without protest. An article published in *Semanario*, titled "Paraguayan Lesson," preaching doctrines similar to those found in the Catechism of St. Albert, was intended to edify the schoolchildren and their parents, and is illustrative of the Lópezian approach to education: "without morals, without religion, the perfection of society cannot be achieved. . . . A good Christian does not attack his legitimate superior, because he obeys the voice of religion which tells him that all authority comes from God and that therefore he should obey and respect it; because he who resists his superior resists the order of God. . . . A good Christian respects the law and venerates the magistrates, because whoever does this loves his country, loves peace, loves his equals . . ." ad infinitum and ad nauseam.

Madame Lynch realized there was little to be done with the overwhelming majority of the "good Christians." But she assumed, as logic might dictate, that *somewhere* among those twenty thousand were to be found a handful who had possibilities. An empire needed men who could do more than fight battles, strum *arpas*, and while away their hours sipping *yerba maté* and eating *chipás*.

The elder López had, in fact, established a scholarship program of sorts: the more promising sons of the aristocrats were sent to Europe for study—but only in the areas of commerce and engineering. Where, Eliza wondered, were the *cultured* ones to come from: the artists, the musicians, those who would make an intellectual contribution to the realm? And what of those who were not from the aristocratic families? Why, she reasoned, there could well be another Gautier, another Liszt, another Delacroix among her future subjects who, but for her determination to *discover* him, to develop his innate talents, to give him the opportunity which he had been denied by birth and the lack of governmental concern for the aesthetic, would go totally unnoticed!

Monsieur de Cluny was commissioned to open an Academy of Music and French Language and Literature.

Eliza anticipated no problems. Both she and Francisco were held in high esteem by the indigenous Guaranís.

Francisco always went out of his way to endear himself to the masses by speaking and joking with them in their own language, and making known his contempt for the Spanish and the mestizo aristocracy. The realization that the Hero of the Corrientes was, in a manner of speaking, "one of their own," and would, furthermore, make them masters of the Río de la Plata, was to the Guaranís an ecstatic one; their ecstasy was compounded by Francisco's thinly veiled hint that eventually all traces of Spanish blood would be expunged from the nation.

Eliza had gone out of her way to endear herself to the masses by, in addition to practicing noblesse oblige, shrewdly exploiting the fact that she was by now the implacable enemy of the Guaranís' implacable enemies, the aristocrats. Militating in favor of her acceptance by the Guaranís was their knowledge that she was the Favorite of their beloved Francisco Solano. Also, and more encouraging, Eliza realized that while the Guaranís might *look* like savages and *behave* like savages, they were nevertheless open to improvement: they were kind, they were gentle, and they were willing (or so assumed Eliza) to be "improved." They had met her halfway by accepting her. She would go more than halfway to express her appreciation of that acceptance by exposing them to the finer aspects of civilization which geographical remoteness and lack of opportunity had denied them.

She erred in her reasoning.

Not only did the Guaranís prefer to pursue the less academic pleasures of smoking, sipping, and strumming, they were adamant on two points: they preferred their own truly lovely Indian melodies to the alien convolutions of a Bach fugue; and the Guaraní language was a source of particular pride to these fiercely proud people, who did not even want to learn *Spanish*, much less *French*. Monsieur de Cluny returned home, where his talents were undoubtedly more appreciated. Eliza, conceding that perhaps she had overestimated the natives, now turned to give Mesdames Dupart and Balet encouragement in *their* particular commission.

Luisa Balet and Dorotea Dupart were, as the reader would be justified in suspecting, a pair of rather threadbare *filles de joie* who were having a rough go of it among the Parisian salons. Their commission, from a sister under the skin who had struck it rich, was to start a finishing school for the daughters of Asunción's First Families. Perhaps, reasoned Eliza, were she to demonstrate the efficacy of having their daughters inculcated with the finer aspects of education and deportment, the First Families would realize that she truly wanted to be their friend.

So enthusiastic were Eliza and Francisco in their belief that she had finally hit upon a way to win over her antagonists, and at the same time lay the foundations for a viable court over which they would one day preside in imperial splendor, they overlooked one fact that doomed the project before it could get airborne: in addition to wanting absolutely nothing to do with Madame Lynch *or* any of her friends from across the sea, the Ladies of Asunción were *not* about to entrust the "finishing" of *their* daughters to a pair of antediluvian sluts. Mesdames Balet and Dupart fled back to Europe, where, though they were not encouraged to frequent the leading salons of Paris, neither were they discouraged from frequenting its leading saloons.

But still Eliza persevered in her attempt to bring culture to her adopted nation. It was during the course of the second—and perhaps only slightly less unrealistic—of her major projects that she began to cross swords openly with her archenemy, Madame Laurent-Cochelet, wife of the French Minister.

To the prim and provincial Madame Cochelet, the fact that Eliza Lynch was Parisian by training if not by birth was a source of embarrassment. In her position as doyenne of Asunción's Corps Diplomatique, La Cochelet had quickly assumed the role of torchbearer for the anti-Lynch segment of Society—a segment which was overwhelming in number, extraordinarily vocal in sentiment, and highly indignant that Madame Lynch had not yet been deported.

When Madame Lynch decided to found a national theater, Madame Cochelet—egged on by the López Ladies—decided to get into the act.

Eliza had prevailed upon Francisco (who had in turn prevailed upon Carlos Antonio) to invite Ildefonso Bermejo, a Spanish actor well known among a large circle of unknown people, to come out from Madrid to organize the national theater. So far as Carlos Antonio was concerned, it all sounded like utter nonsense. But his wife and daughters, having learned from their dear friend Madame Cochelet that a national theater was a sure sign that a country had "arrived," seconded Francisco's arguments that Paraguay *must* have a national theater; *every* country had a national theater. Carlos Antonio was not one to deny his family a request—especially a request in which the entire family displayed a rare moment of total unanimity.

Señor Bermejo was not long in Asunción before he realized that Madame Lynch's Friend, as well as his father, absolutely loathed Spaniards. But Bermejo was a persevering soul; ere long, he managed to ingratiate himself with both Lópezes, so much so that he was given, in addition to his duties with the theater, the added positions of Superintendent of Schools and (nominal) editorship of *Semanario*.

While Señor Bermejo was ingratiating himself with Francisco, his wife Doña Pura was following suit with Eliza. In fact Doña Pura was given the honor of being godmother to Eliza's and Francisco's third child and second son, Enrique Venancio, who was born October 2, 1858, and from whom all the Lynch-López heirs descend.

Shortly after Enrique's birth, his godmother had it brought home to her that she was jeopardizing her husband's position by her open friendship with Madame Lynch. Being rather flexible, Doña Pura now allowed herself to be drawn into the orbit of the López Ladies and Madame Laurent-Cochelet, who succeeded in poisoning her mind against "that Irish concubine." Worse, thanks to Doña Pura and her new-found friends, Eliza's patronage was not invited, nor was her advice sought, in the formation of the national theater she had single-handedly initiated.

Francisco sympathized with Eliza. But short of making known his displeasure to his family, there was little he could do save to advise her to forget the whole thing. *He* certainly had—consumed as he was with less cultural but decidedly more pressing projects: building up his fortifications, training his troops, and keeping an eye on the political turmoil in the neighboring states.

Seething with rage, Madame Lynch took her Friend's advice

and kept herself aloof from the entire enterprise. Von Wisner urged her to fight Madame Cochelet *and* the Bermejos *and* the López Ladies. (Both La Cochelet and Doña Juana publicly shared credit for having conceived the idea of a national theater; Doña Pura concurred wholeheartedly in the joint claim.) Eliza would have liked to follow Von Wisner's advice, but she realized this would only put Francisco in a difficult position with his father, who openly proclaimed that Doña Pura Bermejo was a revelation of sorts to him: the old dictator never realized that *any* Spaniard could be so intelligent, so worldly, so culture-oriented. (In truth, Doña Pura was none of these, but Carlos Antonio was hardly the best judge when it came to evaluating talent.) As the plans moved ahead rapidly for the formation of the theater, Eliza swallowed her anger . . .

. . . although she did manage to impose one condition, through Francisco: On pain of expulsion from the country, Bermejo was absolutely forbidden to import any actors.

Even Francisco was aware that no Paraguayan, other than the handful who had served abroad on diplomatic or commercial missions, had ever seen a play performed, much less trod any boards. But when Bermejo pleaded with him to intercede, López was swayed by Eliza's rather shrewd argument that if this were going to be a *national* theater, then the players must be Paraguayan *nationals*. Protests were then made to Carlos Antonio, who was encouraged by a delegation composed of Madame Cochelet, Doña Pura, and the López Ladies to import professional actors (and, again, to deport Madame Lynch).

But Francisco had gotten to his father first and had convinced him that if this were to be a *national* theater then the players must be Paraguayan *nationals*.

Score one for Madame Lynch.

(One wonders whether Eliza's insistence on this point was truly aimed at proving her pro-Paraguayan chauvinism and thus gaining some measure of acceptance by the Royal Family, which could only lead to her acceptance, albeit begrudgingly, by Asunción Society; or whether it was little more than a calculated attempt to abort the entire project. Eliza was still trying desperately to be accepted. Conversely, she was not one to trifle with when her hackles were up; and being excluded from the very project she had initiated must surely have raised Eliza's hackles to stratospheric altitudes.)

For months all of Asunción digressed on only one topic: the opening of the new Teatro Nacional. (A new auditorium was not projected; it was decided to use the roofless miniature of La Scala, and pray for clement weather.) Bermejo had written a play especially for the occasion: a monumental epic dealing with a pro-Paraguayan Spanish maiden who, during the time of the Conquest, was befriended by a lion cub.

It is a question who was busier: the Ladies of Asunción or Señor Bermejo. If the Ladies were indeed busier, driving their seamstresses in a frenetic fury to execute the gowns and wraps (based on the latest European fashions) that would be worn on opening night, it is nevertheless poor Señor Bermejo who must command our admiration for industriousness. Between putting the finishing touches on his stupendous composition and overseeing the construction of scenery and costumes and installation of stage equipment, the overworked Spaniard pursued with a demonic fury the herculean task of transforming Paraguayans into Thespians.

Whereas he and Doña Pura (who played the Spanish maiden to her husband's lion cub) had only detested Madame Lynch, now they loathed her beyond redemption. But Madame Lynch could not have cared less. She was too preoccupied with selecting from her vast treasure trove the costume and accessories *she* would wear on opening night.

Since protocol, and her anomalous position, decreed that she must sit alone, Eliza had insisted that her box be the focal point of the entire audience's attention. Francisco Solano had so ordered —over the strenuous objections of his mother and sisters, who felt *they* belonged in the center box. (As for Carlos Antonio, he probably could not have cared less where *he* sat. It is said on reliable authority that he did not even want to attend.)

The López Ladies would not give an inch on this point. They reminded Carlos Antonio that the center box was the Royal Box, and that protocol demanded that the First Family sit in the Royal Box. Carlos Antonio bowed to protocol (he probably bowed more to the whining of his wife and daughters) and informed Bermejo that the First Family would sit in the Royal Box.

Francisco Solano then informed Bermejo that if his parents and sisters wished to sit in the Royal Box, that was all right with him. But the Royal Box was to be *left* of center. He also informed the frantic Bermejo, who had just overseen the finishing touches of the roofless theater's interior, that whereas protocol might demand that the center box be the Royal Box, the demands of Francisco Solano superseded the demands of protocol.

As if he did not have enough problems, poor Bermejo had to redesign the interior of the theater. Fortunately, he was busy climbing into his lion's cub ensemble when the López Ladies arrived for the opening and discovered they had been upstaged, or rather upboxed, by their archnemesis.

Score one more for Madame Lynch.

We are indebted to Héctor Varela—who always seemed to be boating up from Buenos Aires whenever anything of interest was transpiring in the Paraguayan outback—for this eyewitness account of the opening night:

> The High Society of Asunción attended. In the box of honour, the broad faced and corpulent dictator sat with his equally corpulent wife and two obese daughters decked out like Bavarian Eggs. In the next box sat General Francisco López and Baron Von Wisner; but seated in the centre box, gorgeously dressed and displaying many jewels, was Madame Eliza Lynch . . . more resplendent and enticing than I have ever seen her. The Gentlemen in the audience all watched her with definitely respectful admiration. The Ladies gave her hostile looks, the meaning of which was perfectly clear.

More imposing . . . was President López. One rarely sees a more impressive sight than this great tidal wave of human flesh. He is a veritable mastodon, with a pear shaped face, narrow forehead and heavy pendulous jowls. During the entire performance, the President ostentatiously wore an enormous, atrocious hat, quite appropriate to him and equally suitable for either a museum of curiosities or for the Buenos Aires carnival.

During the evening which seemed an eternity, I watched López for a sign of any impression produced upon him witnessing a play for the first time in his life. It was like watching a stone in the field. At the end of the tedious proceedings, without any display of either approval or disapproval, the old monarch of the jungle glared momentarily at Madame Lynch and rose and left, ponderously followed by his wife, his daughters, and the soldiers of the Praetorian Guard.

The performance of the players, as well as Señor Bermejo's epic, can be dismissed with a line:

It was as ridiculous as President López's hat.

It was probably on this occasion that Varela chose to record how he was "struck by the deep dislike and rancor that all Paraguayan Ladies showed toward Madame Lynch because of her handsome physique, superior education, modishness, and elegance. Particularly did they resent as mortifying and humiliating to themselves, her role in Asunción. . . . They dislike to think of the even more prominent position which she [will] occupy when López [succeeds] his father."

3

Shortly after the Bermejo fiasco (the two fled back to Europe in disgust) this "deep dislike and rancor" became transmogrified into abject hatred; it also proved to be but an adumbration of the fear that Eliza was to instill in the hearts of the Paraguayan Ladies.

The transmogrification, which took place aboard a steamboat in the middle of the Paraguay River, can be said to have marked the point of no return along the path whose antipodal termini were

Madame Lynch's determination to win acceptance by the Ladies and her determination to destroy them.

Before leaving for Europe, Francisco had conceived the idea of inviting a group of French agriculturists to colonize an area in the Chaco, to be called Nuevo Burdeos (New Bordeaux, to honor the French port whence came the majority of the immigrants). It was stipulated that the Paraguayan Government would give each family a house, as much land as it could cultivate, and provisions necessary to support the colony for eight months, by which time, it was assumed, the colony would be self-sustaining. Further, the colonists were granted remission from all taxation for ten years and were to be exempt from induction into the military service. The colonists were for their part obliged only to reimburse the Paraguayan Government for the expenses incurred in bringing them over and getting them started.

(The colonists were given the worst possible accommodations for their trip to Paraguay, and the most inhospitable land to cultivate. The upshot was that most of the unfortunates died either of starvation, heat prostration, or hostile Indian attacks, or were put to death if, while attempting to flee the colony, they fell into the hands of López's militiamen. The French Minister at Asunción made violent representations on behalf of his government, but to these Francisco Solano, by then his father's successor, turned a deaf ear. Madame Lynch, who kept abreast of what was happening outside the Río de la Plata region, assured her Friend that *his* friend, Louis Napoleon III, was too involved trying to extricate himself from the complete mess attendant upon his mad scheme to establish the hapless Habsburg prince Maximilian as Emperor of Mexico to bother going to war over a mere five hundred Bordelaises.)

The occasion upon which the aforementioned transmogrification occurred was the great celebration ordered by Francisco Solano to mark the official opening of the colony. On behalf of his father, who was now too ill to partake of the festivities, Francisco invited the entire Diplomatic Corps as well as all high-ranking Paraguayans (that is, merchants, clergymen, and government functionaries) to attend an elaborate *fête champêtre* at the site of the settlement.

The men were to travel out from Asunción by horseback. The Ladies were to follow by river steamer.

As wife of the French envoy, Madame Cochelet was named to be Guest of Honor.

But, as a means of obliging the Ladies of Asunción to be civil to his mistress—and over the strangulated objections of his mother and sisters, not to mention La Cochelet—Francisco named Madame Lynch to be Official Hostess.

As the band on deck played tunes appropriate to the occasion, Madame Lynch—a vision in white lace and again pregnant—stood at the top of the gangway to receive the Ladies as they boarded the gaily decorated steamer.

Eliza realized that hers was a tenuous position. The Ladies would at long last have to at least acknowledge her in her capacity as Official Hostess. But she did not want it to appear obvious that she was being forced upon them.

She was prepared to greet them with a warm smile, a gracious word. She would circulate among them, taking great pains not to patronize them. She would *prove*, once and for all time, that she was not the unmitigated ogress they took her to be.

As the many carriages rode onto the rotting quay at the foot of the Plaza de Palma to discharge their well-dressed cargo, the Official Hostess awaited, perhaps with justified tenseness, the moment she had so long anticipated: formal recognition by her social coequals.

Led by Madame Cochelet, the Ladies all tripped laughingly up the gangway (with the exception of Doña Juana and her slovenly daughters, Doñas Inocencia and Rafaela, who waddled puffingly) —and right past Madame Lynch. The Official Hostess's warm smile froze. When the captain requested orders to get under way, she nodded almost imperceptibly, her face now a mask of violently repressed emotion, and went to sit—by herself.

The steamer pulled away from the quay and out into the river as the sun shone down brilliantly on the crème de la crème of Asunción femininity—all of whom quickly dispersed into small groups and settled down to some fairly animated gossip, all the while pretending elaborately that their Official Hostess did not exist.

Ere long a platoon of servants in white coats set up trestle tables on the deck, which they proceeded to inundate with the finest damask linens, gleaming silver plate, and Limoges and Sèvres china (all on loan from Eliza's private stock). The Ladies paused long enough in their conversations to anticipate, with the appropriate oohs and ahs, the succulent repast that was appearing as if from the bowels of the ship for their delectation and refreshment: baby lambs, roast turkeys, suckling pigs, a riot of fresh fruits and vegetables, the best in imported wines (personally selected by Von Wisner)—even, to herald the occasion, ices molded and dyed in the tricolor of France. Madame Lynch had attended to every detail of the feast's preparation; for the more chauvinistic, she had even provided *yerba maté* and *sopa paraguaya* (said to have been the favorite fare of the López Ladies).

The waiters kept coming, the tables kept filling up, the collective appetite and thirst of the Ladies kept increasing—and Eliza kept to herself, seated off to one side of the deck like a gorgeously draped pariah.

When the waiters signaled that all was ready, Madame Lynch arose and moved toward the table of honor to preside. She was still the Official Hostess, and she was damned well going to fulfill the duties incumbent upon her. But the Ladies were so closely huddled together, she could not even get *near* the table! When Eliza politely requested that some of the more obdurate among them kindly step aside, the Ladies banded even closer together.

Whereupon Madame Lynch stepped back a pace, eyed the scene

a long, severe moment, and then, without moving any muscle below her neck, commanded the waiters in an icy but well-modulated tone, "Throw it all overboard." The horrified gasp that went up from the Ladies gave way to a dead silence, which was broken momentarily with Madame Lynch's reiterated command to the waiters: "I said, throw it all overboard." And then a clipped "*All of it!*"

Eliza then turned and moved slowly toward her isolated chair, where she sat motionless as the food and wines were heaved over the side. Except for sending word to the bridge that the captain was to keep the ship anchored in midstream until further orders, she said not another word for the duration of the "voyage." She merely stared at—and through—the perspiring, parched, famished, and insanely livid Ladies.

By ignoring Madame Lynch from the moment they boarded the ship, the Ladies had made their point.

By the time the captain received permission to weigh anchor and return to Asunción—*ten hours later*—Madame Lynch had made hers.

It was the sort of thing that would appeal to Francisco Solano's sense of the comedic. For days on end he, Eliza, and Von Wisner sat around the quinta at La Recoleta having a good laugh over it.

But Eliza's laughter was more than tinged with bitterness.

In the more than seven years since she had come to Asunción, Eliza had tried to meet the Ladies more than half way.

Knowing her position, she had not been prepared to expect they would welcome her with open arms, or that they would even tolerate her as the social equal of those grotesques, the Doñas Juana, Inocencia and Rafaela—perhaps the worst parvenus of the entire pack.

Conversely, she was not prepared to tolerate the total ostracism she had been forced to endure.

And worse, her maternal instincts having been revived after the tragedy of little Corina Adelaida, the fact that the four sons she had by now given Francisco were considered *bastardos*, their mother openly sneered at as "that Irish Concubine," raised Eliza's contempt for the Ladies of Asunción above the level of the contempt they held for her. (In addition to the aforementioned Pancho and Enrique, the other sons were Federico Noel, born 1860, and Carlos Honorio, 1861. A fifth son, Leopoldo Antonio, was born in 1862; yet another, Miguel Marcial, Eliza's and Francisco's seventh and last child, would be born during the war.)

For more than seven years, during which she had been forced to tolerate social ostracism and abject humiliation, Eliza had sought acceptance, had tried, as best she knew how, to bring culture to this barbarous land.

Now she became utterly ruthless, deviously calculating, and hard as the hardest granite toward those who had rejected her less from a sense of propriety and prudery than outright jealousy and envy.

She became the veritable nemesis of all those—and there were many—who had treated her as a common whore, a social leper.

She also became the First Lady of Paraguay.

The old "monarch of the jungle" finally died.

PART TWO

THE REIGN

The Accession

All reliable sources are in total agreement on two points: Madame Lynch played absolutely no role in her Friend's accession to power (though she undoubtedly gave him what encouragement he needed), and her Friend did not so much inherit the presidency as steal it. For there is strong evidence, of the "trout in the milk variety," that Carlos Antonio López did not intend that his eldest son succeed him.

The old dictator had finally concluded that Francisco's military preparations were not rooted solely in the desire to defend the country against its fractious neighbors. Unfortunately, by the time he arrived at this conclusion he was ill-prepared to stem Francisco's course, suffering as he was from the dropsy that was finally to carry him off after a prolonged siege.

The elder López had wisely decided toward the end of his reign that it was in Paraguay's best interests to maintain a strict neutrality in the chaotic affairs of Argentina and Uruguay, and to settle all border problems with Brazil through diplomatic means. He had even proclaimed on a number of occasions that he would rather lose half his country's territory than to defend it by war (in itself a wise decision, since more than half the country's territory was then, as it remains to this day, uncultivable and not worth defending).

According to Father Maiz, the old dictator's dying words were "There are many pending questions to be settled, but settle them with the pen rather than with the sword, particularly with Brazil. . . ."

Less through prescience than pragmatism, the dying President had come to fear that Francisco Solano would rather wield a sword than a pen.

Too, he feared the consequence of placing under the command of the headstrong Francisco so powerful a military machine as Paraguay now boasted.

And there is little doubt that the López Ladies exploited Carlos Antonio's feelings toward Francisco as regarded Madame Lynch, who had always been a sore spot with the old man. They quite honestly feared the consequences for them should Francisco become President. In this fear they were joined by brother Benigno, who had openly expressed his contempt for Eliza from the moment he met her in Paris, and Father Maiz, who undoubtedly anticipated the revenge he must have known Francisco Solano *and* Eliza would exact for his having refused to baptize young Pancho.

According to the constitution, the President was empowered to appoint a vice president whenever he should so choose. In case of death, resignation, or disability of the President, this appointee was to act as interim President until the Congress could be convened to name a successor.

Though he knew he was dying—he had been dying for four or five years—Carlos Antonio did not name a vice president.

But he did leave a will.

The will was locked away in a vault, the keys of which had been entrusted to Chief Justice Pedro Lescano, described by a contemporary as "a man of about sixty years of age [who had] been selected for the position . . . for nothing but the personal regard of the elder López, for he was an ignorant man, having no knowledge of the law and very little of anything else." On the death of the President, Lescano was to open the vault and read the will in the presence of the Cabinet.

Some sources claim Carlos Antonio added a codicil to the will naming Benigno as his political heir, but that he subsequently annulled the codicil and designated Francisco Solano instead. The inference here is that while he feared the consequences of the nation being ruled over by the bellicose Francisco Solano, he feared more the consequences of being succeeded by the horribly inept Benigno. But if he did in fact intend Francisco Solano as his heir, why did he not name him Vice President while he was still alive?

On the other hand, it is possible, however remote, that the old man decided to pass over both his sons and leave it up to the nation to name a new President, as the constitution demanded. And not to be overlooked is that possibility, again admittedly a remote one, that Carlos Antonio had no political heir in mind—a common practice among egomaniacal dictators who, rather perversely, feel that no mortal is capable of succeeding them. Masterman's claim that "the will of the late President . . . provided that at his death a triumvirate consisting of his eldest son Don Francisco-Solano, Judge Lescano, and Colonel Toledo [otherwise unidentified] should hold office until a new ruler had been elected by the people" is doubtful in the extreme.

The contents of the will were never revealed.

And Francisco Solano's actions more than suggest that, while he had no idea what was in the will, he was not about to take any chances.

In September 1862, on learning that—after a long death watch in which the other members of the First Family were joined by Padre Maiz and Chief Justice Lescano—his father was about to give up the ghost, Francisco Solano made his move. Accompanied by his personal escort cavalry regiment, the "Black Tails," he sped to the presidential deathbed. His arrival there coincided with that of the Angel of Death. No sooner had the old dictator breathed his last than Francisco abruptly demanded the key to the vault.

Lescano demurred, supported by the scandalized Padre Maiz and the frightened López family. Francisco ordered the house surrounded by his "Black Tails," sent word to those military leaders loyal to him to patrol the streets of Asunción—and again demanded that Lescano produce the key. Lescano produced the key, and Francisco went into the vault—alone. A few moments later he emerged to announce to his horrified family that he had been named Vice President and that, in accordance with the constitution, he would summon a national congress.

In the meantime, he would act as interim President.

We have no evidence that anyone asked to see the will. Perhaps they realized that Francisco had no intention of displaying it. This would lead us to conclude—again, admittedly circumstantially—that he had indeed been passed over in the succession.

(In discussing this with one pro-López Paraguayan scholar, the present author was told, "The fact that Francisco Solano did not reveal the contents of the will would not in and of itself lead to the conclusion that he had not been named Vice President and political heir. You must realize that Francisco Solano was a proud man; he must have been extremely hurt that his own family would doubt his claim that he was the legitimate successor. Tell me, Señor Brodsky, what would *you* have done, had you been in Francisco Solano's place?" When Señor Brodsky replied that if he had in fact been named the heir, he would have shown the will as proof that he was not acting in contravention of his father's wishes, the scholar replied, "Ah, my friend, you would not make a good dictator." Señor Brodsky conceded the point.)

After proclaiming himself heir apparent, Francisco ordered the immediate arrest of Father Maiz, Justice Lescano, and all known sympathizers to his late father's policy of neutrality; these he replaced with men loyal to himself.

He also took pains to assure that the upcoming Congress would confirm him in his office.

The constitution had defined the Congress as being truly representative of the people; actually it was truly representative of the leaders of the ninety-two *partidos*. The judge, the police chief, and the parish priest of each *partido* would decide among themselves which of their number would be the district's congressional delegate. To make sure that the forthcoming Congress reflected his will, Francisco demanded that the list of all delegates be submitted in advance for his personal scrutiny. Any name either unknown to López or suspected of being less than 100 percent loyal to him was struck from the list.

(One potential delegate, a wealthy Asunción landowner and merchant, foolishly announced that the coming convention might offer the perfect opportunity for modifying many of the laws of the country which were in dire need of modification. Francisco not only had the man's name struck from the list of delegates, he confiscated the man's estates. Washburn advises that the poor fool "finally perished as a common soldier, in the trenches" during the war.)

The hand-picked Congress convened in the Cabildo on October 16, 1862, Vice President Francisco Solano López presiding. While the delegates sat inside, Francisco's troops marched outside, all around the building—indeed, all around Asunción.

After welcoming the delegates, and making known the late President's wishes, Francisco called upon Don Nicolás Vasques. A former minister of foreign affairs in the old López Government, and the man considered best informed in all of Paraguay on political matters, Don Nicolás had wisely rushed forward to protest his undying loyalty to Francisco even while Carlos Antonio's body was still warm. Now, in a nominating speech that fairly reeked of obsequiousness, Don Nicolás proposed that the delegates "follow the will of the people" and confirm Francisco Solano President by acclamation.

Francisco thanked Don Nicolás for his kind words of adulation and then turned to one of the Asunción delegates to second the motion. Instead of doing so, the delegate suggested that the constitution be re-examined as regarded the entire process of electing the nation's chief magistrate; he professed to find the appropriate constitutional clause "somewhat ambiguous." Francisco, wondering how *this one* had managed to get into the Congress, indignantly allowed as how he would not tolerate such an insult to the memory of his father, the author of the instrument in question. The delegate, as Washburn advises, "in his ignorance and simplicity, sunk back into his seat." (He was subsequently arrested and executed on the grounds of having "conspired to subvert the legal and constitutional process.")

At that point, Don Florencio Varela (no relation to Héctor) asked to be recognized. Don Florencio was the wealthiest man in all of Paraguay with the exception of the López brothers; and there is this to be said for him: he came by his wealth honestly. After expressing the profoundest admiration for the talents and patriotism of the Vice President, and alluding graciously to the debt of gratitude owed by all Paraguayans to the Hero of the Corrientes, Don Florencio admitted to some doubt regarding Francisco's eligibility as President—but on a technical point:

While disposed to support him for the office—Francisco Solano was, in his humble opinion, the only man fit for the job—Don Florencio acknowledged the "confusion" he entertained in light of the constitutional provision that the presidency should never become the property or heritage of any one family. For that reason, he could not support Francisco Solano. However, he added hastily, he would be highly pleased "to hear the views of the other delegates," and if his "confusion" could in some way be resolved, he would be the first to cast his vote for Francisco.

At a nod from Francisco, Don Nicolás Vasques bounced back up and argued that, whereas the constitution did indeed contain such a provision, the Congress "should not be fettered or restricted in their choice." The *proper* interpretation, argued Vasques, was that the clause was aimed at preventing the head of government from transmitting his power in defiance of the people's will, but that the Congress, "as authorized representatives of the Paraguayan citizenry," could in fact elect whomsoever it pleased, familial relationships notwithstanding. Don Florencio then rose, announced that Don Nicolás's interpretation had resolved his "confusion," and seconded the motion that Francisco Solano be named President by acclamation, for a period of ten years.*

Before dismissing the Congress, Francisco Solano, now in an expansive mood, shared with the delegates the good news that Madame Lynch had just presented him with another son (Leopoldo Antonio). After acknowledging the thunderous applause, the President informed the nation, through their representatives, "I would like it known that it is our pleasure and desire that from this day onwards Madame Eliza Lynch should enjoy the same privileges as those usually accorded to the wife of a head of State," and allowed that he had "every confidence that my countrymen as well as the Corps Diplomatique will respect my wishes in this matter."

Up in the Distinguished Visitors' gallery, Doñas Inocencia and Rafaela barely managed to stifle their gasps of horror, Madame Laurent-Cochelet suffered an attack of the vapors, and Doña Juana Carillo López, now the ex-La Presidenta, shrieked, *"Por Dios!"* and collapsed in a swoon. Baron von Wisner smiled benignly in approval of what had transpired on the floor below.

López then turned to the next order of business on his agenda: subjecting Padre Maiz and Chief Justice Lescano to a military trial on charges of conspiring to "deprive" the newly elected President of his "rightful heritage." Lescano was tortured to death; Father Maiz fared better. Having "confessed" to a multiplicity of crimes including "the teaching of heresy," he was sentenced to three years in prison. If, as Washburn seems to imply, Maiz went to prison as a saint, the "series of most cruel tortures and indignities" to which he was subjected would seem to have triggered some metamorphosis. When he eventually won his re-

---

* Some historians claim that the Varela-Vasques "dialogue" had been arranged by López, lest anyone suspect that he had not been elected in accordance with the organic law of the land. It was the sort of trick of which López was capable. But reliable evidence indicates that immediately upon the adjournment of the Congress, Varela was arrested, his property confiscated, and he was thrown into prison—from which he never emerged under his own steam.

lease after making his peace with Francisco Solano, Maiz went on to become López's chief inquisitioner.

Madame Lynch convinced her Friend that he had better justify in the eyes of the foreign envoys the great purge he had undertaken. Heeding her advice, López "admitted" that he had "conclusive proof" that his brother Benigno, in concert with Padre Maiz, and with "the active support" of Chief Justice Lescano, had managed to "bribe" some of the congressional delegates to put either Benigno or Maiz into the presidency. López was unable to ascertain whether the two hoped to share the office or alternate in it; he was "not too sure of the sordid details." In the event, "the heart of one of the many persons [involved in the alleged plot] had failed him about thirty-six hours before the Congress met," and López was able to forestall the attempted "coup."

Professing "great grief," "horrendous surprise," and "total mortification" with the brother whom "I love with all my heart, as only a brother can love," Francisco—over the howling protests of his mother—banished Benigno into the interior, where he was ordered to remain on one of his estancias until further notice. López also broadcast to the diplomatic colony "with profound sorrow" that alleged "confession" of Padre Maiz; and while he was vague about the charges brought against Chief Justice Lescano, he was nevertheless "saddened to announce" that Lescano had "succumbed suddenly to the infirmities of his advanced years." (López seems to have been rather persuasive: Edward Thornton, the newly accredited British Minister, informed his Foreign Office that "His Excellency was not free from anxiety, and in conversation expressed to me that his position was one surrounded with difficulties tho' he hoped to be able to silence his opponents.")

Within a month of his accession, upwards of a thousand men of prominence whose loyalty López suspected were either in prison or in flight. One observer recalled that "immediately on his election, by ones and twos prominent persons besides well-informed foreigners, began to leave the country. Their estimate of the character of the new ruler and the expectation of war were the principal reasons."* United States Secretary of State Seward was advised by Minister Washburn that "the only offense so far as I know that is charged against the prisoners, is that they preferred some one else for President rather than Francisco Solano López and this in most countries would not be considered a capital crime."

Having begun to dispose of his enemies, imagined or otherwise, Francisco now disposed of his father. A great funeral was held at Asunción's Catedral de la Encarnación, and the remains were taken in a stately procession for interment in the church at La Trinidad, the López ancestral estate four miles outside the capital city. The new President then called for the erection of a national monument to his late father's memory. All Paraguayan merchants, plus all foreign residents including the diplomats, were "invited" to subscribe the equivalent of five dollars toward the project. None had any choice but to accept the invitation. A total of $50,000 was collected, but the monument was never built (nor was the money ever accounted for). Was this Francisco's way of striking back at his father for not having named him Vice President? Perhaps. But given the nature of the beast, it is more probable that Francisco was one of those people who feel (not without some justification) that money should be spent for the living rather than for the dead.

López next concentrated on bringing the Church completely under his control, at the same time discharging an outstanding debt. Bishop Urbieta was by now aged and infirm, and though his particular Angel of Death had sent indications of an imminent

---

* By the time war broke out, close to 25 percent of the Paraguayans were living in exile, mostly in neighboring Argentina. A quarter of Paraguay's population has always lived in exile; it is estimated that the same number today live in Argentina, political refugees from the Stroessner dictatorship.

arrival, it seemed to have been delayed. Encouraged by Madame Lynch, who was never one to renege on a promise, her Friend precipitated that Angel's arrival, in a manner of speaking, and named Father Palacios Bishop of Paraguay.

Father Palacios's qualifications for the bishopric as López conceived the office were impeccable. He agreed that López was justified in suborning the priests to turn over to him all secrets garnered in the confessionals. And he concurred wholeheartedly when López told him that many prerogatives enjoyed by all other bishops, such as having the bells rung in their honor whenever they entered or left the Cathedral and using a throne during the celebration of the Mass, were prerogatives that were henceforth to be enjoyed by López alone.

Not only did Bishop Palacios's moral qualifications leave much to be desired, so did his theological qualifications. Masterman recounts in his memoirs a delightful experience illustrative of the new Bishop's lack of acquaintance with Holy Scripture. While walking down an Asunción street one day, Masterman came upon Madame Lynch and one of her sons who was playing with a replica of Noah's Ark and was crying furiously. It seems that one of the puppets representing that patriarch's three sons (Ham, Shem, and Japheth) had disappeared. As Eliza scolded the boy for being so careless with his possessions, Bishop Palacios, who happened to be walking by, raised his hand in benediction and said, "Pray, do not scold the dear child, Madame. There could not have been three figures, for Noah had only two sons, and as all the world knows, their names were Cain and Abel"!

Official notification of López's election as, to quote his formal title, Commanding General of the Armed Forces and President of the Republic of Paraguay (the title is also used by the incumbent dictator, Stroessner) was sent to the heads of state of those countries with which Paraguay maintained diplomatic relations.

The acknowledgments of this earth-shattering news were rather disappointing.

Emperor Dom Pedro II of Brazil and President Bartolomé Mitre of Argentina were too busy rattling sabers at each other to do more than instruct their respective ambassadors to offer congratulations. Victor Emmanuel II of Sardinia was too preoccupied in his new role as the first king of a united Italy to take much notice of the event. Queen Victoria was too grief-stricken over the recent death of "Dear Albert" to think about anything, much less a Paraguayan election. And Abraham Lincoln was concerned less with what was happening in far-off Asunción than with what was transpiring in nearby Virginia where the Union Army was managing, barely, to prevent the Confederate Army from closing in on Washington (the bloody Battle of Antietam).

However, López did receive one acknowledgment, one that more than compensated for the general lack of interest in Paraguayan changes of government. His dear friend the French Emperor somehow managed to take time out from planning his gigantic fiasco in Mexico to send along a letter of congratulations. Though no copy exists of the letter López sent Napoleon III, its contents can be inferred from the response it elicited:

General,
  I have been very touched by your personal letter and its warm recollections of your visit to My Imperial Court.
  Believe me, I assure you, that I too remember them with pleasure. I have had occasion to appreciate your noble qualities [?] which do you honour and therefore it is with that knowledge that I congratulate your country in electing you to safeguard her destiny [!].
  It has filled me with great pleasure to look with admiration at the remarkable progress which Paraguay made under the rule of your illustrious father, may he rest in peace, and I have no doubt that under your wise and patriotic direction, your country will continue her progress along the path of civilization.
  In expressing my cordial best wishes for your personal happiness

and for the dignity of your office, it pleases me to offer you my
personal esteem. In so far as I can, I pray to Almighty God to
bless and preserve you.

   Given by my hand in the Palace of the Tuileries,

Your good friend,

      NAPOLEON   (*January 1st, 1863*)

(Had López's "good friend" enjoyed the gift of prescience, he
would undoubtedly have prayed a little harder to Almighty God
to bless and preserve not only López but himself as well. Both
were destined to fall from power within months of each other.)

2

Francisco was determined that Eliza's rank was to be respected.
Notorious were the prolonged rages into which he launched himself whenever anyone, of high or low station, failed to accord
Madame Lynch her due as the President's Amiga Primera. Even so
eminent a personage as Senhor Viana de Lima, the new Brazilian
Minister, was subjected to public humiliation when, either through
ignorance or determination, he failed to pay his official respects
to Eliza on assuming his Asunción post. López sent only one carriage to fetch the Minister and his entourage for their first official
call to present his credentials, even though the protocol of the
times throughout South America demanded that a fleet of equi-
pages be put at any new envoy's disposal. Relations between
Brazil and Paraguay were strained enough as it was, and Viana de
Lima did not wish to cause a diplomatic incident. Tactfully, he
journeyed out to the quinta at La Recoleta to "call upon" Madame Lynch and congratulate her on the recent birth of the infant
Leopoldo Antonio.

Also subjected to public humiliation was Edward Thornton, the
newly accredited British Minister to Asunción. He had had the au-
dacity to make public his lack of intention to acknowledge "the
Paraguayan Pompadour." (The phrase itself was contained in one
of Thornton's dispatches to Lord Russell at the Foreign Office,

which dispatch was copied by one of Eliza's spies before being transmitted.)

Chances are that López would have sought to humiliate Thornton even if the envoy had kissed the Pompadour's feet. For, with what can only be attributed to Lord Russell's utter lack of tact, the new envoy was the very man who, while British chargé d'affaires at Buenos Aires, had ordered Francisco held as hostage against the release of the aforementioned Canstatt.

At Eliza's suggestion, Francisco commanded that in presenting his credentials the new British Minister was to proceed to the Cabildo on foot. After plodding along the cobblestoned streets to the presidential office, trying as best he could to ignore the jeers of the populace, Thornton was accorded the further humiliation of being asked to remain standing in the Presence instead of being invited to sit. Lord Russell's next dispatch from his man in Asunción contained the sentiments that "though the Government of the elder López was a despotism, that of his son is indescribably worse. The new President has already developed into a tyrant so vain, arrogant and cruel that there [is] no misery, suffering or humiliation to which all within his power [will not be] exposed."

While he still retained his own house in downtown Asunción on the Market Plaza, López lived openly with Eliza, spending many an hour either out at La Recoleta or at the various town houses he had built (or appropriated) for her. The *casa* on the Market Plaza was where he entertained his whores and concubines; though he undoubtedly discussed his "conquests" with Eliza, he respected her too much to flaunt them in her face. Now that he was El Presidente, there was no necessity for López to resort to coy subterfuge. Madame Lynch was the Favorite, his sons by her were the Heirs, and woe be to anyone in Paraguay who did not accept that!

The Ladies of Asunción quickly got the message. Choking on their bile, they all made the pilgrimage out to the quinta to "call upon" the First Lady of Paraguay . . .

. . . who was waiting for them.

Leading the procession was Madame Laurent-Cochelet, in her capacity as doyenne of the Diplomatic Corps. Eliza received her on her balcony (the only one in all of Paraguay at the time) and personally poured the *café con leche*. According to one chronicler, on being ushered onto the balcony La Cochelet observed the formal amenity: "A votre service, Madame," to which Eliza, demonstrating that she was well versed in diplomatic niceties, replied, "C'est notre devoir de travailler ensemble pour le bien du Paraguay." La Cochelet agreed that they must indeed "work together for the good of Paraguay," and then forced herself to declare that the coffee was delicious. Madame Lynch accepted the compliment graciously. La Cochelet then complimented Madame Lynch on her beautiful sons, another compliment which was accepted, probably in the spirit in which it was offered. La Cochelet then launched into a series of small, strained pleasantries with her hostess, for whom the *café con leche* could not possibly have been anywhere near delicious as the sight of this particular *bête noire* squirming miserably. Madame Lynch had the good grace to avoid any references to the countless open snubs which La Cochelet had inflicted upon her. It is hoped that La Cochelet had the equal good grace to be thankful for *that*.

After the wives of the foreign envoys, came the parade of strait-laced women of what passed for Asunción's "nobility": the wives of the merchants, government functionaries, and the military. Some were driven by curiosity; La Cochelet had fairly gagged at the splendor of "Patiño," and had broadcast its wonders in detail. Some came hoping to advance their husbands' careers. Some—most notably his mother and sisters—came simply because El Presidente had informed them in no uncertain terms that they had damned well better.

Her decision to "receive" at the quinta instead of in her town house was precipitated less by Eliza's desire to make the Ladies travel a distance than by her desire to show off what was by now the best-appointed mansion in all of Paraguay. Though her town houses were tastefully decorated, Eliza seems to have lavished her best efforts on the quinta, to which she was partial.

A procedure was established—by Madame Lynch.

Upon awakening in the morning and completing their ablutions, the Ladies would send their servants out to La Recoleta to inquire if "the Señora" would be "at home" that afternoon. On receiving the affirmative reply, they would don their best gowns and baubles and be driven out to the quinta. There they would go into flights of rapture over Madame's furnishings and appointments, fuss over her children, down pots of *café con leche*, offer their apologies for not having come to visit sooner—and flee as hastily as common decency permitted.

When Francisco Solano's mother and sisters, having been prodded into making the journey under threat of dire consequences, expressed their profoundest regrets over not having "had the opportunity to call upon you sooner," Eliza felt secure enough to restrain herself from observing that surely they might have found an hour or two *some time* during the previous eight years to have done so.

The Ladies, one and all, expected to meet a well-dressed but intellectually inferior grisette from the *trottoirs* of Paris; in their delusions, they had ignored the suggestions of their husbands that this was far from the case. Thus it was a little like having salt poured into their wounds when the visitors to La Recoleta realized that the First Lady of Paraguay was in fact a highly polished matron of great beauty and ineffable (certainly by their standards) refinement who could converse fluently in English, French, Spanish, and Guaraní, who was obviously devoted to her children (and adored by her servants)—and who managed at one and the same time to be a charming hostess who made them feel instinctively parochial.

As Eliza had suspected they would, her guests fawned over her parasitically and then tore her to shreds the moment they had made their "official call." To Eliza, it was bad enough that they had waited eight years to pay their respects; worse, they returned to Asunción convinced that they had done all that was expected of them. They no longer need look upon the First Lady, Madame Lynch, as anything more than the President's *puta*—a whore to be *tolerated*, yes, but certainly not to be *accepted*. Eliza had her spies. She knew that the Ladies who fussed over her found her insufferable.

She also knew what the Ladies either could not comprehend or would not acknowledge: that more than being the First Lady of Paraguay, Eliza Lynch was a proud, ambitious woman to whom the very idea of being *tolerated* by these provincials was both insupportable and unforgivable.

Their day of reckoning was coming. But first Eliza must lay the groundwork for the empire over which she would preside as Empress-Consort.

Indubitably, if Francisco had had his way what was in fact a one-man government would have *looked* like a one-man government in the eyes of other nations. But, as Eliza advised him, even his idol Bonaparte had allocated portfolios. Francisco saw the wisdom of presenting to the world the stance of a government that was legitimate in form if not in substance. With her assistance, he formed a shadow court, surrounding himself with men who enjoyed the perquisites and emoluments of high office without having to earn either.

Named to be Vice President of the Republic was Señor Sánchez, "a feeble and decrepit old man of about eighty-two years of age," who was chosen by López, some say at Eliza's explicit suggestion, to give a fillip of *clase* to the Government. He was probably the best-educated man in all of Paraguay. Carlos Sánchez had entered government service as personal scribe to El Supremo, and had been held over by Carlos Antonio López, who "invariably treated him with the greatest rudeness and contempt, which he bore with utmost humility." As one foreign observer noted, Francisco Solano "made him Vice President [because] he was without ambition and was too old to be a rival."

Sánchez's reluctance to join the López "Cabinet" was equaled by that of Dr. José Berges, a sixty-five-year-old "man of good judgment and much astuteness" who had been the elder López's first commissioner to the United States. Around the close of the 1850s, Berges had gone into voluntary retirement on his estancia in the hinterlands, disgusted with the Lópezian concept of "republicanism." He was recalled to Asunción by Francisco and appointed Ministro de las Relaciones Exteriores, in the words of Washburn "an honor he did not covet, but he dared not refuse."

> López knew he was far better qualified for the position than any other of his subjects that he could trust, and Berges was compelled to accept a position that required of him services at which his soul revolted. He knew he must be both the slave and the spy of an imperious, selfish, and brutal master, but he also knew there was but one step from refusal to imprisonment. His position was most trying. He was compelled to treat with the representatives of foreign nations in personal interviews in which questions would arise that he could not even discuss without danger of incurring the anger of his master— . . .

and of, we may add, his "mistress." Madame Lynch involved herself with the nation's Relaciones Exteriores (as well as Interiores) to the point where foreign envoys were soon bypassing Berges and dealing directly with her. This was especially so after the outbreak of the war, when López was, more often than not, at the front in personal command of his armies.

Carrying the portfolio of Minister of War and Marine was brother Venancio, who owed his appointment to the fact that, in addition to not caring for his duties, he was not, unlike Benigno, hostile to Madame Lynch. Named to be Minister of Treasury was Don Saturnino Bedoya. This was in return for his willingness (if not eagerness) to marry Doña Rafaela. Serving as Minister of Government (whatever *that* ministry was supposed to entail) was

Don Mariano Gonzales, a compleat toady whom López enjoyed having around and whose title was in all probabilities a euphemism for Court Jester.

López's favorite military commanders were Vicente Barrios, Antonio Estigarribia, Wenceslao Robles, and a handful of others, all of whom were totally subservient to El Presidente, and all of whom possessed some measure of military talent. (Barrios cemented his position with López by agreeing to marry the other frumpy sister, Doña Inocencia; Robles ingratiated himself by demonstrating his impeccable talents at extracting "confessions" from anti-López "conspirators," though it must be admitted—something López would not admit—that Robles was probably the best tactician in the Paraguayan armed services.)

Rounding out the López "court" was Gumesmindo Benítez, nominally Berges's deputy, who took over the duties of writing the editorials in *Semanario* after the war broke out. Benítez was charged with getting up the patriotic speeches for the "spontaneous assemblies" Madame Lynch organized during the war at which the Ladies of Asunción were compelled to "offer their jewels and their lives in devotion to" the glory of the *patria*. It is said of Benítez that he "was one of the very few who in praising López and Madame Lynch seemed to believe what he said." Sad to relate, his faith and fidelity "availed him no more at the last than did the hypocrisy and submission of the others."

Of the entire court, only Colonel Estigarribia and Vice President Sánchez were destined not to die as "traitors or conspirators" —Sánchez because of his total lack of ambition, Estigarribia because he had the wisdom to surrender himself (along with his army) to the Brazilians in the opening phase of the war.

Serving in the role of Principal Adviser to both Madame Lynch & Friend, as well as Lord Chamberlain and Lord High Everything Else, was Von Wisner—of whom it can be said that he was the only man in all of Paraguay, save for the lowliest soldiers in the trenches, who never once came under the cloud of suspicion that hovered over the entire nation like an omnipresent penumbra. (At war's end, he fled to Buenos Aires, where he died a few years later of natural causes.)

Eliza selected as her Ladies-in-Waiting Señora Juliana Echegaray de Martínez and Doña Dolores Carísimo de Jovellanos; and as Mistress of the Robes (surely a full-time job, considering the extent of Eliza's wardrobe, which was constantly being replenished), Doña Isidora Díaz. Perhaps the best qualifications the three ladies enjoyed, other than a willingness to curry Eliza's favor at an early stage in her career, was that they were without peers when it came to being *au courant* with what was happening around Asunción. Her ladies kept Eliza informed of the latest gossip—and, more important, on the location, extent, and value of the various personal collections of jewelry. (Doña Isidora was the sister of General Díaz, another of López's "favorite generals." Both were fated to be put to death after López's uncovering of the "Great Conspiracy" in the closing years of the war; a like fate awaited Señora Martínez and *her* husband, *also* one of López's commanders. Of the three Ladies closest to Madame Lynch, only Doña Dolores was to survive the war—perhaps because she was not related to any of López's generals.)

Completing the "official family" were Masterman, whose services López had purchased while in England, and who served as Apothecary General to the Paraguayan Army; Colonel George Thompson, also a purchased mercenary, who more than earned his pay by doing so masterful a job in overseeing the construction of the great fortress at Humaitá that bogged down the invading Allied armies for more than two years; and Baron R. von Fischer-Truenfeld, a German adventurer, who built for López the first telegraph line in South America and who was rewarded with the post of Director of Telegraphs and Communications.

Also at Eliza's instigation, a great dinner was given in the Cabildo to launch the reign. All members of the Diplomatic Corps and the "official family" were commanded to appear. Eliza took charge of the arrangements, which included the planning of a

ten-course epicurean delight based on French cuisine. The fact
that many of the Paraguayans attending found themselves unable
to do more than dabble at the delicacies was of little concern to
Eliza: she need no longer attempt to court the opposition by
serving such *affreux* items as *sopa paraguaya* and *chipás*. For all
Eliza cared, if the peasants among her courtiers could not ingest
nourriture fit for her concept of an imperial court, they could
damn well starve.

Henry Lyon Young has painted an amusing word portrait of
that occasion which bears quoting:

> The guests drove their carriages to the bottom of the orna-
> mental steps, which arose in stately zigzags to the balustraded
> terrace overlooking the orange groves. They were received by
> the Lord Chamberlain, the members of the household and the
> ladies in waiting. The Baron von Wisner was dressed in the uni-
> form of a Colonel in the Hungarian Hussars. His doublet was
> embroidered in silk frogs, and, in spite of the heat, he wore
> an astrakhan collar. . . . López's sisters Inocencia and Rafaela
> were prominent among the notabilities assembled.* They
> wore identical dresses of black corded silk, a colour that did
> not suit their sallow complexions. Their husbands don Saturnino
> Bedoya and don Vincente Barrios stood awkwardly holding
> glasses of spirits to their lips to give them strength to go on
> bullying their wives who otherwise would get the better of
> them. . . .
>
> Once the guests were assembled they were herded by the
> members of the household towards a miniature Galerie de
> Glace overlooking the main courtyard where a table [covered
> with the finest in linens and china, all on loan from Madame
> Lynch's private stock] had been set for fifty people.
>
> Presently the double doors at the far end of the Gallery were
> flung open by a couple of flunkeys and Eliza and Francisco made
> their entrance hand in hand. . . . López was in evening dress

---

* It is said that López's mother Doña Juana had screamed, "I will not
attend! I will not attend!" until she learned that her presence was not
solicited, whereupon she screamed even louder, "I was not invited! I was
not invited!"

and wore the Presidential band across his chest, while Eliza was attired in white satin and crowned with a diadem of brilliants. It can only be regretted that there was no Winterhalter [the fashionable portraitist of the time who captured for posterity many of the crowned heads of Europe] at the Court of Asunción to do justice to Madame Lynch's starlike beauty. Eliza and Francisco sat at the center of the long table on either side of the bishop [Palacios] in his black soutane as if wishing to bask under his cloak of respectability [a cloak, we might add, that was as respectable as the proverbial "emperor's clothes"]. . . .

A certain consternation was caused at the end of [this] first state dinner party when Eliza got up from the table and none of the ladies present could find their shoes. They were obliged to walk out of the dining room barefooted and send their slaves to retrieve their slippers from a tangled heap under the banqueting table.

Taking a leaf from the Roman emperors, Francisco and Eliza offered the masses circuses and bread, albeit with a variation: The "circuses" were actually balls and fiestas, and the "bread" was withheld. Another Lynch-Lópezian deviation from the Caesarian concept of keeping the masses happy: Funding for the balls and fiestas came not from the imperial treasuries but from the pockets of the people. Even foreign diplomats were compelled to buy "subscriptions" to the various fetes, none of which they dared refuse to attend. As for the masses, "being happy" soon became not so much an invitation from their new President and First Lady as an imperial ukase. Masterman reports on how "a series of sumptuous feasts, balls, and spectacles followed [López's] election, and for more than a month endless processions and felicitations, until the merchants and shopkeepers were half ruined, and everybody was heartily tired of them!"

Eliza paid particular attention to the balls, the arrangements of which she oversaw down to the last detail. Now, with her Friend the nation's Chief Executive (as well as its Chief Executioner), Madame Lynch had an ironclad guarantee that her costume balls would be well attended (and oversubscribed: Eliza never failed to realize a rather tidy profit from these entertainments). Invitations were tantamount to command appearances. Even the foreign envoys (and their livid wives) dared not decline an invitation—or express, except among themselves, any lack of willingness to purchase a "subscription."

Eliza was now not only the leader of fashion, but its arbitress as well; and here arbitress is used in its purest sense. It was she who decided just exactly how the Ladies were to dress at the balls, which followed one on top of another. All were to wear new gowns; the gowns were to conform to Parisian *haute couture;* and *all* were to wear shoes. Madame Lynch had no intention of presiding over a society that preferred to wear the native *tupoi* and whose Ladies, in the words of one contemporary, "danced much more at their ease barefoot." (One wonders whether any of López's courtiers had the temerity to point out that Madame Lynch's insistence on new gowns for every event imposed a great hardship on those Paraguayans of limited means.)

When announcing that a *bal masqué* (her favorite social indulgence) was to be held, Madame Lynch would also announce what particular costume was to be worn, and by whom. Her sense of the aesthetic precluded her risking the possibility that twenty Marie Antoinettes or thirty Aphrodites might spoil the overall ambience. Even the gentlemen were not excused from being dictated to sartorially on these occasions: after all, there was always the risk that many of them, perhaps either lacking imagination or suffering financial straits, might turn up masquerading either as Simón Bolívar or an Asunción ragpicker.

At the masked ball she threw to celebrate López's election to the presidency, Eliza "prescribed the dress for all—assigning the garb of a Swiss shepherdess for one, an Italian fruit seller for another, and prescribing for each some peculiar style of costume." Madame herself came arrayed "in the gorgeous style of Queen Elizabeth." Madame Laurent-Cochelet was commanded to appear in the "ungorgeous style" of Queen Victoria. This was a bit of whimsey on Eliza's part, matched by her "decision" that the

López sisters, Rafaela and Inocencia, should attempt to pass themselves off as "two emaciated Guaraní Indian maidens," and Mother
López should masquerade as the goddess Diana, replete with bow
and arrow. Francisco Solano came—of course—as Napoleon Bonaparte "on the day of his coronation as Emperor of the French."
Von Wisner was Lorenzo de Medici. Father Palacios was the
Apostle Paul.

The Ladies of Asunción fairly howled as they climbed into their
prescribed attire (it is said that Mother López swore she would
shoot one of her arrows directly into "the *puta's*" heart). But as
the Ladies howled, Eliza smiled. After having had her face rubbed
in the mud of social ostracism for more than eight years, she was
eager—nay, frantic—to demonstrate that the slipper was now on
the other foot.

However, it was not too long before Madame Lynch began to
wonder just how long that slipper would stay on.

Thornton's dismissal of Eliza as "the Paraguayan Pompadour"
was, though the British envoy had no way of knowing it at the
time, a fair estimate of what her Friend had in mind for Madame
Lynch. Construction was moving along rapidly on the great Palacio, and Francisco Solano was on the verge of proclaiming himself
"Emperor Francisco Primero."

He was also on the verge of attempting to legitimize his imperial aspirations by marrying a young lady who would be his
empress.

His candidate for the honors was not to be Madame Lynch.

Prelude to Disaster

What was common gossip in the capitals with which Paraguay maintained diplomatic relations—that Francisco Solano López hoped to marry the youngest daughter of Emperor Dom Pedro II of Brazil—could hardly have been much of a secret to the one person who most enjoyed the intended bridegroom's confidence. Thus it is extremely doubtful, the claims of many chroniclers to the contrary, that Madame Lynch learned of her Friend's marital plans only through her spies. The spies—little more than an aggregation of gaggling female courtiers whose total loyalty would prove to be nonreciprocal on the part of their mistress—were charged with keeping tabs on who talked about Madame behind her back. Anything Eliza wanted to know from Francisco, she had merely to ask him; and if she did not ask him, eventually he would tell her anyway.

Construction was moving ahead on the new Palace down by the waterfront. (Though forced to depend for his labor force on a battalion of slaves whose average age was eleven, the designer, Alonzo Taylor, achieved about 70 percent completion on the magnificent limestone and stucco-covered brick edifice that remains to this day the most imposing government building in all of Paraguay.) In some of the remote districts of the country, López was having his name hailed as Francisco Primero, instead of Excelentísimo Presidente. Eliza assumed she would soon be hailed as Eliza Primera, that *she* would be moving into the Palace. There is little doubt that Francisco shattered Eliza's illusions shortly after he had gotten his government organized, and no doubt but that his dream of an imperial alliance probably predated his alliance with Eliza.

The elder López had always regarded all Brazilians with the utmost aversion and contempt; to Carlos Antonio, they were all *macacos*, monkeys. So great was his enmity toward them that at the time of the old dictator's demise the only *macaco* at Asunción was the Brazilian Minister. But all that had changed with the advent of Francisco Solano. According to a contemporary, even as his father lay dying, Francisco spoke of the Brazilians (behind his father's back) with respect; and while indulging, through *Semanario*, "in the most unstinted abuse of his Argentine neighbors, he allowed nothing to appear in it inimical or disrespectful towards Brazil." While enroute to Europe in 1853, López had stopped off at Rio de Janeiro, where he was treated to a display of handsome hospitality by Dom Pedro II. (But then, Dom Pedro, who was Francisco's contemporary in years, was the sort of egalitarian who would give a meal even to Attila the Hun.)* As a result of the attention showered upon him, López seems to have received a "signal" of sorts which many doubt his imperial host had transmitted.

---

* When Napoleon Bonaparte invaded Lisbon in 1807, King John VI fled with his family to the Portuguese colony of Brazil. Following Bonaparte's downfall, John was recalled by his parliament, leaving behind as regent his son Pedro, who declared Brazil an independent empire in 1822. A thorough reactionary, Pedro was forced to abdicate (1831) in favor of his five-year-old son, who after a ten-year regency was proclaimed Emperor Dom Pedro II in 1841. The young Emperor is alleged to have remarked, "Were I not a monarch, I should be a Republican." And when he himself was overthrown in 1889, thus ending the last empire in the Western Hemisphere, no less a personage than the dictator of Venezuela commented, "The only Republic in South America is ended—the Empire of Brazil."

Were Dom Pedro a reactionary, or López a liberal, an alliance between their two countries would have been mutually advantageous. López was logical in assuming that no European power would accept him as an emperor unless he won the acceptance of the only legitimate emperor in South America, an acceptance that would surely have been his were that emperor to consent to the honor of being Francisco's father-in-law. As for Brazil itself, that sprawling giant feared a resurrection of the old Spanish Viceroyalty, a threat they saw should Argentina ever become unified. For despite its great size and great wealth, the Portuguese nation was in many respects at the mercy of its smaller neighboring states. The Government, which was centered in coastal Rio de Janeiro, was easily cut off from its interior provinces by the rivers which Paraguay controlled. And compounding Dom Pedro's problems, the largest and wealthiest of these provinces, Rio Grande do Sul, was ideologically as well as geographically closer to Paraguay.

Given the philosophical orientation of the two, López's coy claim to Washburn that Dom Pedro would support an autocratic empire on his southern flank, much less give his daughter in marriage to the reactionary Paraguayan dictator, must be weighed judiciously. For if, as López broadly hinted to the American envoy, the Emperor was "encouraging a marital alliance," such "encouragement" could have been predicated only on Dom Pedro's fervent hope that such a step would lead to López's ultimate destruction; that the neighboring states, having finally thrown off Spanish imperialism, would never accept another empire in their midst, especially one whose war machine was rapidly becoming the most powerful on the continent. (That the states of the Río de la Plata region were having difficulty accepting a Portuguese empire in their midst would account for the fact that Rio de Janeiro quickly became the breeding ground of the best diplomats to be found in all of South America.)

Dom Pedro considered López to be "licentious, dissolute, and cruel," and knew that for years he had been living with Madame Lynch, "who had great influence over him and was as ambitious, as false, and as cruel as himself; that by her he had many children, and that for them alone had he ever shown any affection; and that any person whom for state or ambitious purposes he might take to share his throne would hold but second place in his regard, and be in reality but the servant and captive of his mistress." Thus it is quite probable that the "projected marriage" was nothing more than a gigantic aspiration on López's part that somehow got out of hand. But for a time it appeared to Eliza that the alliance might go through, so persuasive (and self-deluding) was Francisco.

Francisco tried to convince Eliza that her status would not be altered: she would still be the Favorite. (The parallel between herself and the Empress Josephine cannot have been lost on Eliza, who knew that Josephine had had no choice but to step aside when Bonaparte married a daughter of the Austrian Emperor in order to legitimize his own dynasty.) But what would become of her sons? Since Francisco claimed he was marrying strictly for dynastic reasons, surely any son Isabella might give him would take precedence over young Pancho and the others. So desperate was her situation, it is possible, as some commentators claim, that Eliza offered to marry López. But this would have been a futile gesture. Madame Lynch was many things to her Friend, but she was not to the purple born. And if she threatened to return to Europe (which is doubtful) Francisco could easily have stopped her (though we can assume the López Ladies would have moved heaven and earth to help her pack and get her on her way).

She was now at López's mercy. And as the "secret negotiations" continued between Asunción and Rio de Janeiro (it should be noted that many responsible historians suspect that the correspondence was a one-way affair), even Von Wisner, her closest confidant, advised Eliza that there was little she could do but play things Francisco Primero's way: settle for being the Pompadour.

It would be convenient to report, as have some of her more imaginative biographers, that Madame Lynch single-handedly thwarted her Friend's marital plans by heaping contempt upon him for even considering an alliance with the hated *macacos*. The fact remains that it was Dom Pedro himself who "thwarted" the plans simply by ignoring "the pretensions of this upstart who would aspire to the hands of a Braganza!" Thus we can imagine Eliza's relief, not to mention López's fury commingled with his embarrassment in the eyes of the foreign envoys, when it was announced in the Brazilian press that Princess Isabella was being married off to a scion of the old French Royal Family.

By refusing to consider López as a son-in-law (it is said that he did not even consider López a member of the human race), Dom Pedro not only incurred an implacable enemy, he unwittingly strengthened Madame Lynch's hold over her Friend. According to one foreign observer, "López seemed to surrender completely to the counsels of his Irish mistress. . . . She purchased the houses and lots on a square adjoining the new palace, and openly talked of her purpose of building another, of almost equal importance, for herself." (It was never built.) The implication here is that Eliza convinced Francisco that the only kind of empire for Paraguay was one in which the emperor and empress were coequals—a coequality in which he seems to have concurred.

Much in the manner of a contrite husband, López sought to make amends. Some chroniclers claim he went so far as to seek papal dispensation that would allow him to marry Eliza "on the grounds that her first marriage had not been consummated." López definitely wanted Pancho and the other boys to be declared legitimate, and thus recognized in the eyes of the Christian world as the natural heirs of the López dynasty. But a man who was not above expropriating Church funds, suborning priests, and staffing the local hierarchy with his own flunkies would hardly have considered papal feelings as regarded his personal life. It is questionable whether López communicated with the Pope in this regard; it is doubtful that Eliza would have encouraged such a correspondence. (The Vatican, as is its wont, has maintained a discreet silence on the entire matter.) Suffice it to say, the boys, who had been given the baptismal surname Lynch, now became Lópezes. (It is said that the young Lópezes' paternal grandmother, Doña Juana, took to her bed for a month when the official announcement was proclaimed by Bishop Palacios from the high altar of the still uncompleted Cathedral.)

Eliza now realized that she had been spending too much time out at the quinta at La Recoleta arranging balls, gathering information on the various jewelry collections, and otherwise playing the Lady of the Manor, while López had of late been spending more and more time in the half-finished Palace playing at his own weird brand of diplomacy. The time had come to move closer to the action—in fact, into the Palace itself.

She would still handle all arrangements for the public spectacles. Francisco was too busy allowing himself to become unwittingly the tool of wily Uruguayan diplomats to concern himself with such mundane matters as who was to wear what to which particular *bal masqué*. Eliza was blessed with a capacity for extending herself that exceeded even her capacity for greed. While serving as López's social directress, fund raiser, part-time paramour and part-time procuress, she would manage to find quite a few hours to function as his quotidian sounding board.

Simply stated, Madame Lynch quickly assumed a direct role in the political affairs of state. As one contemporary Paraguayan scholar remarked ruefully to the present writer, "It was bad enough that López was making so unmitigated a mess of things in the Plata area. But now that Madame Lynch decided to assume the position of 'court adviser' and 'minister without portfolio,' along with her other somewhat dubious responsibilities, not even divine intervention could have steered Paraguay from the course it was pursuing: a rendezvous with tragedy."

2

The "brilliant truce" López had worked out in 1859 between the liberal Mitre and the conservative Urquiza had proved to be little more than a temporary cease-fire. On September 17, 1861, at Pavón, Mitre and his Buenos Aires Unitarians defeated Urquiza and his provincial Confederationists; eight weeks before López became President of Paraguay, Bartolomé Mitre became President of Argentina. His hold on the nation was exiguous: though the liberals had defeated the conservatives, they had yet to win their cooperation toward total political unification.

The struggle between the Unitarians and the Confederationists now shifted to Uruguay; there the factions dividing that small country were politically as well as ideologically allied to those in Argentina. The conservative Blancos were in power, the liberal Colorados were in exile. Since Mitre owed his victory over Urquiza to help from Venancio Flores, leader of the Colorados, he was obligated to allow Argentinians to assist Flores when the latter led his gaucho followers into Uruguay (April 1863) in an attempt to topple the incumbent Blanco government and thus, as has always been *de rigueur* in Latin American politics, replace one dictatorship with another.

Mitre had to move cautiously, going so far as to swear openly that none of his *porteños* was in any way involved in what was shaping up as yet another Uruguayan civil war; he feared that Urquiza and his provincials, whose sympathies were all for the Blancos, would get into the act, thus turning the Uruguayan civil war into yet another Argentinian civil war. In hopes that this was exactly what would happen, Brazil, despite its vested interest in Uruguay as a buffer state against a strong Argentina, decided for the moment to maintain a strict neutrality.

Uruguay had for years been seeking an alliance with Paraguay. Francia had maintained an isolationist policy. Carlos Antonio López, while sympathetic to the conservatives at Montevideo, had backed off from involving himself in their problems. But Francisco Solano was a thoroughly unpredictable quantity. Should he unite with the Blancos, whose obsessive desire (after defeating the Colorados, that is) was to bring down the liberal Buenos Aires government, he would have had the support of the powerful Urquiza faction; this would have spelled disaster not only for Argentinian unification but for Mitre as well.

Such would have been the logical move for López. But López was not logical; megalomaniacs rarely are. Encouraged by Madame Lynch, he decided to play the role of power broker, hoping to maneuver the various factions into calling upon him to arbitrate an overall settlement for the Río de la Plata region.

Fearing an alliance of López-led conservatives, Mitre initiated a correspondence aimed at pacifying the Paraguayan dictator. But López was impossible to pacify. He resented that Mitre permitted a revolutionary committee of Paraguayan exiles to flourish in Buenos Aires. (These exiles, who but for the Lópezes would have undoubtedly controlled Paraguay's economic and political life, were never a threat, in main because they were totally unable to achieve any sense of cohesion.) And he resented the constant attacks on himself and Madame Lynch in the Buenos Aires press. (One rather amusing article, denigrating his Guaraní ancestry, referred to López as "an Indian chief," to Asunción as "a dismal collection of wigwams," and to Eliza as "a ridiculous Indian squaw." Name-calling was nothing new: indeed, Carlos Antonio López had been called much worse, and had managed to shrug it off. But Francisco Solano was more sensitive in this respect, though he was not too sensitive when it came to writing attacks on Mitre in the *Semanario* that ran the gamut from the tasteless to the obscene.)

Mitre was so anxious, as the correspondence reveals, he went so far as to accede to López's demand that their differences be negotiated at Asunción instead of on neutral ground, realizing this would give López the prestige of playing host at an "international conference which would thus magnify the importance of Paraguay." But, as Pelham Box notes, "On every point raised by López, [though] Mitre had given way [there] is nothing in the correspondence to indicate that López wanted a conference or a settlement." While Mitre was trying to appease him, López had "privately expressed his fears" to a visiting British diplomat "that Mitre would attack him to occupy a portion of territory which Paraguay holds and claims on her south eastern boundary." Since this was the *last* thing the Argentinian leader had in mind, it is questionable whether López actually entertained such "fears," or was simply attempting to justify his stalling Mitre's attempt to work out their differences, including a bilateral agreement not to intervene in the affairs of Uruguay.

López's diplomatic position was tenable—in Paraguay. From a "Confidential Despatch of Edward Thornton to Lord Russell [head of the British Foreign Office] On The Conditions of Paraguay," we learn that with the "prisons . . . filled with so called political prisoners, many of them of the best families," the dictator's hold on the nation was viselike: "The President looks into and directs everything . . . not a man in the Republic, from the ministers downwards, would refuse to perjure himself at the order of the President. No one is allowed to marry without His Excellency's permission . . . His Excellency's system seems to be to depress and humiliate; if a man shows a little more talent, liberality, or independence of character, some paltry excuse is immediately found for throwing him into prison . . . the Judges are unpaid and are the most servile instruments of the President."

Thornton goes on to speculate that while "it might be supposed that such a tyrant . . . could not long be endured," he does not "think however that any change is imminent. The great majority of the people are ignorant enough to believe . . . that they are blessed with a President who is worthy of all adoration. The rule of the Jesuits, of the Dictator Francia, and of the Lópezes father and son, have imbued them with the deepest veneration for the authorities. There may be three or four thousand who know better and to whom life is a burthen under such a Government," but among these "there is such an utter want of confidence in each other that . . . I do not believe that there is any one man who would dare to confide his feelings with regard to the Government to his Brother or his dearest friend, lest he be denounced," so pervasive was López's spy system.

Though by now more of Asunción's streets had been cobble-stoned, new country roads laid down, and old ones improved, especially in the provincial cities, López allocated most of his funds for military preparedness. Under the supervision of for-eign technicians, telegraphic and railroad systems connected the capital city with the vital fortresses, and the Asunción Arsenal was working full time. Among the old fortresses that were improved, and the new ones built, López's pride and joy was the complex at Humaitá; constructed under the direction of Colonel Thompson, with an able assist from Von Wisner, it was being hailed abroad as the "Sebastopol of South America." The Paraguayan Navy consisted of less than a dozen gunboats, for the most part converted wooden mercantile paddle-wheelers. Nevertheless, this flotilla, through cooperation with cleverly situated shore batteries along the Río Paraná, made it all but impossible for any enemy ships to force a passage past Humaitá and through to Asunción, which was now all but impregnable.

The extent to which priorities were allocated was evident to Sir Richard Burton, who, when visiting Asunción on the eve of the war's outbreak, observed that

> public conveniences are nowhere; the streets are wretched; drainage [has] not been dreamed of; and every third building, from the chapel to the theatre, is unfinished. The shops [are] miserable stores. . . . The barracks and churches, the dungeons, and the squares for review, are preposterous. . . . The lieges [that is, the masses] must content themselves with the vilest

ranchos, lean-tos, and tiled roofs supported, not by walls, but by posts . . . A large and expensively-built arsenal, riverside docks, a tramway, and a railway, have thrown over the whole affair a thin varnish of civilization; but . . . the pretensions to progress are simply skin-deep.

López's fealty from his troops was unequivocal—this despite the fact that the recruits received no pay and were compelled to depend for food either on stealing, requisitioning from the provincial farmers with government-backed (and unredeemable) IOU's, or receiving gift packages from home. They knew that El Presidente was a great statesman, a great military tactician, an unmitigated genius; they had read it in *Semanario* (indeed, they read it in just about every issue that came off the press). And had not their beloved Hero of the Corrientes, who drank with them and joked with them in their own Guaraní language, and wenched with them—had he not promised to "liberate" them from the Asunción aristocrats who had always treated them as little more than *basura*, trash?

López had no desire to keep happy those aristocrats—the Spanish and mestizo merchants and minor government functionaries—who grumbled into their *maté bombillas* and wondered where and how it would all end. But he did wish to keep the masses happy. (Thornton: "Anxious as the President is that his fellow Citizens should not trouble themselves with Political matters, he cares little how much they may be addicted to vices of all kinds, and the immorality that pervades the Country is extreme . . .".) The program to keep the masses happy was, López felt, best left to his Favorite. He would foot the bills (rather, he would force the aristocrats and foreigners to foot the bills), she would make all the arrangements.

The extent to which Eliza "arranged things" can be gauged from a confidential report which Minister Washburn sent to U.S. Secretary of State Seward on August 5, 1863: "The President's birthday had been made the occasion of such festivities as were never known before. [For two weeks] it has been a continual series of balls, excursions by river, excursions by railroad, bull-fights, fire-works, and everything that is calculated to dazzle and please the multitude. The lower classes have been indulged in a manner they never dreamed of before."

The lower classes reveled in being so indulged. But the more astute among the merchants, in addition to resenting having to buy those "subscriptions" to finance the great celebration and pay outrageous taxes on everything from importing *and* exporting their wares to carrying a portmanteau from one village to another, were "full of doubt and apprehension in regard to the future. I trust that what they now fear will never be realized, but from what I have observed, I must say that they have reasons for their anxiety and uneasiness, and I fear lest I may have occasion to write another dispatch ere long that will be a dark chapter in the history of Paraguay."

3

Washburn's "fear" was to be realized "ere long," that "dark chapter" was about to become absolutely stygian. Among the honored dignitaries in attendance at a lavish banquet Madame Lynch threw in the Palace to toast her Friend on his thirty-seventh birthday was Dr. Octavio Lapido, who had been sent by López's ideological brother, Uruguayan President Bernardo P. Berro, on a mission of extreme urgency.

Montevideo had broken off relations with the Buenos Aires Government only days before, because of Mitre's tacit support of the invading Colorados. Lapido's mission was to get López to enter into a formal alliance with Berro aimed at bringing down the liberal Buenos Aires Government. (Had Lapido been gifted with prescience, he might well have stayed home; for, thanks to what *Semanario* proclaimed to be López's "Supreme gift for statesmanship," Lapido's efforts were to bring down, not the Mitre Government but, eventually, his own!)

Uruguay's geographical location—as a buffer state between

two powerful antagonists, Brazil and Argentina—and military weakness justified her efforts to find allies; and who better to ally herself with than Paraguay, whose government shared Berro's conservative ideology, whose nation was in no way threatened by a civil war, and whose army was rapidly becoming the most respected in the entire Río de la Plata region.

But whether Paraguay needed any allies is debatable. For more than a half-century, she had managed to ward off any threats to her independence by Brazil or Argentina simply by staying out of Plata affairs, and by maintaining an army strong enough to discourage armed aggression. The only thing López had to gain by involving himself in Uruguayan affairs was a bit of prestige. However, prestige is exactly what López craved.

López refused to enter into a formal alliance, though he did commit Paraguay to assisting Uruguay "in case her independence were threatened." Such a commitment cost him little. The Flores revolt was not going well, and Uruguay's independence was hardly threatened at this point. Too, López could not risk war with Buenos Aires: the port must be kept open to ships bringing in tons of materiel from Europe. Working like a demon, flattering both Francisco and Eliza and imbuing them both with a gift for statesmanship that was hardly consonant with reality, Lapido finally prevailed upon López to make public his intention to "guarantee" Uruguay's independence, and to send a protocol to Mitre (September 1863) demanding an "explanation" of Mitre's implied violation of Uruguayan neutrality through his aid to Flores and the Colorados.

Lapido was beside himself when it was learned, a few days later, that López had included in the protocol copies of highly secret Uruguayan correspondence in which an anti-Mitre alliance and certain specific actions planned by the Berro Government against Buenos Aires were more than suggested. While a number of historians have seen in this action an ineptitude at diplomacy approaching lunacy, it is more logical to argue, as do many historians, that López's ulterior motive in "leaking" the confidential memos was to see Argentinian-Uruguayan relations deterioriate to the point where he would be called in to arbitrate. Convinced that he had brought off a brilliant diplomatic coup, and assuming that it would not be long before Mitre (whom he loathed) and Berro (whom he admired) would be begging him to mediate their differences (which were, in fact, irreconcilable), López now directed his attention to the Great Circus which Eliza had arranged to celebrate the first anniversary of his accession to the presidency.

This time, Eliza really outdid herself. Though "the expense was principally borne by the State" (taxes were upped 25 percent on the export of *yerba maté*), many of the aristocrats and foreigners were invited to "contribute heavily." Down by the waterfront an immense open-air hippodrome was built where bullfights alternated with dancing and general mummery. Butts of wine were broached, and a veritable river of *caña*, the native rum, flowed freely.

One of Eliza's more novel touches was to arrange for the multitudes, who were now roaring drunk (and, in the words of one observer, "actively engaged in raising the birth rate"), to be "amused" by the *camba rangas*, grotesque masked buffoons who mingled with the crowds and "danced and played absurd antics in the ring." The *camba rangas* were in reality members of López's secret police, who on this occasion chose to be not so secret, which led one foreign observer to "fancy the money the people threw was more to propitiate than reward." (It is said that Madame Lynch was in for 10 percent of the money tossed by the "amused" multitudes.)

The bullfights must have been rather uninspiring: "The *picadores* and *matadores* were but herdsmen in their usual dress [hat brims and ankle spurs] . . . the bulls were very tame, and showed only blind terror." Equally dull must have been the horse races which Madame Lynch had arranged. (It was her intention, once Paraguay had assumed leadership of the Río de la Plata region, to have built a great track on the outskirts of Asunción, along the lines of Paris's Longchamps; she had even selected the site.) Masterman reports that the races were run in such a manner that "an hour or more was lost in wrangling and mutual abuse" between the contestants "before one race could be decided," and adds laconically, "There was little betting or excitement amongst the crowd."

In addition to the hippodrome, Madame Lynch had ordered constructed two enormous gaily festooned marquees in the plaza to handle the overflow of the "lower classes" who flocked into the capital from the outlying districts. For two days, to the heavy throb of the *gomba* (the immense Indian drum which Masterman "could never hear without a shudder"), "beaten in turns by hundreds of willing hands," the people danced ceaselessly "as only savages can dance; swirling, shrieking, and wildly gesticulating, till at last they staggered out, trembling in every limb from exhaustion and fierce excitement, only to make room for other inebriates eager to take their places."

Even the López Ladies begrudgingly admitted that when it came to throwing a celebration, Madame Lynch had few peers. Like the rest of the Ladies of Asunción, they were still upset with La Irlandesa's presence in their midst. Though they could never bring themselves to "accept" her as an equal, they had managed, with a bit of prodding from Francisco Solano, to bring themselves to "accept" that she was there to stay. All the Ladies, including the Lópezes, made a pretense at being more than civil to Eliza, whose influence with López they knew to be a pronounced one; some, in fact, went out of their way to fawn over her (this was especially true of those whose husbands occupied high positions in the Government and military).

But, thanks to her loyal Ladies in Waiting, Madame Lynch knew that behind her back she was being referred to sneeringly by all the Ladies as "Madame Lavincha."

Eliza was going to settle their hash; but first she must help

Francisco settle the hash of his Brazilian and Argentinian antagonists.

After thanking Eliza for giving him so magnificent a celebration, Francisco Solano returned to his desk at the Palace to await that call from Mitre and Berro to arbitrate their differences. Much to Francisco's chagrin, the call did not come. The Uruguayan envoy at Buenos Aires had managed to overcome the "misunderstanding" precipitated by López's release of those confidential Blanco memoranda; though the Berro Government wanted war with Buenos Aires, they were afraid to move without a firm commitment from López. Mitre proposed, in view of the "misunderstanding," that Dom Pedro of Brazil be called upon to arbitrate all differences between Argentina and Uruguay. To this, Berro agreed—provided López was named co-arbiter. But Mitre refused, irritated beyond measure by López's having turned their months-long correspondence into an exercise in futility, the Paraguayan's avowals notwithstanding.

Indignant at being ignored, López now demanded to know Mitre's "intentions in Uruguay." The Argentine President disclaimed any responsibility in the Flores invasion, and informed him that Buenos Aires was adhering to a strict neutrality in Uruguay—and fervently hoped that López would follow suit. Goaded by Lapido, who was still working desperately to get him to join the Blancos in declaring war on Buenos Aires, López broke off his correspondence with Mitre and ordered general mobilization.

A month later (March 1864), he established his headquarters at Cerro León, a well-fortified encampment about fifty kilometers from Asunción, and began to conduct maneuvers (Colonel Thompson: "He drilled his troops so hard, that many of them died from overtraining"). Within five months, López would be able to field an army of 30,000 trained men, with a reserve of 34,000 partially trained boys aged fourteen to eighteen; and by conscripting younger boys, old men, merchants, and cripples, he would have a standing army exceeding 100,000—surely a formidable military strength for a nation whose population was little more than half a million!

López also convoked Congress and "requested" a grant of $25 million for more armaments and supplies. He needed more uniforms from France and machine guns, bayonets, and cartridges from Prussia—and unlike the Blyth Brothers, the French and Prussian merchants wanted cash on the line. With the "request" granted him unanimously, López sent his agents rushing off to Europe. (One agent was ordered to purchase, in addition to a supply of bayonets and cartridges, "a new landau and many yards of muslin for Madame Lynch.") The agents were ordered to hurry: López realized that once war came he would be cut off from Europe; Mitre could easily close the Buenos Aires ports to Paraguayan shipping.

While López's agents were shopping in Europe, and Lapido was knocking his head against the wall trying to get Paraguay to join with Berro in a war to the death against Buenos Aires, Brazil was being slowly sucked, most reluctantly, into the Uruguayan vortex.

The Flores revolt, after making little headway in the west of Uruguay, had moved up toward the Brazilian border. There the Colorado chieftain sought assistance from the Riograndenses whose caudillo leader, General Antonio do Souza Netto, though an anti-monarchist and an ideological conservative, was a personal friend of Flores. Netto galloped off to Rio de Janeiro, where he prevailed upon the Emperor to intervene in Uruguay to "protect the interests of the people of the province of Rio Grande do Sol who are suffering as a result of the Uruguayan civil war." (Netto conveniently failed to advise Dom Pedro that just as many Uruguayans were suffering at the hands of his Riograndenses.) Dom Pedro openly demanded that Uruguay agree to an immediate settlement of all Brazilian claims, and guarantee that Brazilian subjects would not be further endangered.

But José Antonio Saraiva, the Emperor's most astute diplomat, saw that the only way to protect Brazil's interests was to end the Uruguayan civil war first and *then* worry about claims and reparations. Saraiva called for immediate negotiations with the Berro Government aimed at settling the Blanco-Colorado imbroglio. Berro, still relying on an open commitment from López, refused to enter into negotiations; concurrently, a new Uruguayan minister was rushed to Asunción, with orders to succeed where Lapido had failed. José Vásquez Sagastume, "a polished diplomat with a veneer of culture who liked to air his English [and who] never missed an opportunity to flatter López and send costly gifts to Madame Lynch," sought desperately to get López to ally himself with Berro.

Had López joined with the Blancos, liberalism could well have been expunged from the Río de la Plata region. Urquiza, who had given López permission to move Paraguayan troops through the relatively unpopulated Misiones region in order to strike at Buenos Aires, would have brought the Argentine Confederationists into the coalition, which would have brought down the Mitre Government, eliminated Flores and the Colorados in Uruguay, and forced Brazil to resume her neutral posture. In essence, if there was one point in time when López could have maneuvered himself into leadership of the Río de la Plata region and thus bring closer by light-years his dreams of empire, it was now.

But López missed the point completely.

Try as Sagastume did to get him to move, the Paraguayan dictator was still intent on playing things *his* way: sending out bombastic notes to all governments (and factions) involved, demanding to know what was going on and why his good services as mediator were being rejected. In this, he had the support of Eliza, whose indignation was equal to Francisco's when an article appeared in the Buenos Aires press advising him "not to interfere in matters concerning countries far better civilized than Paraguay!"

In July 1864, Saraiva delivered an ultimatum to the Berro Government: either Uruguay must accept international mediation or face a Brazilian invasion to protect those Riograndenses. Berro knew full well—as did Saraiva—that Brazil was playing a dangerous game. If Brazil did in fact invade Uruguay, Berro, with the aid of the Urquiza-led Argentinian provinces, would knock off Brazil and stamp out the Mitre Government, thereby extirpating liberalism in the Río de la Plata region and putting Brazil in a precarious position—*provided* López made a move.

When López stood pat, Berro had no choice but to submit to Saraiva's demand. Led by the Brazilian diplomat, the mediators—who included the British Minister at Buenos Aires—sat down in an honest attempt to end the Uruguayan civil war. At that point, Sagastume, having ingratiated himself with Madame Lynch, convinced her that if the Saraiva negotiations succeeded, Paraguay would never again be handed a golden opportunity to "lead the Continent." Without authorization from his government, Sagastume prevailed upon Madame to assist him in getting her Friend to offer his services as mediator between Uruguay and Brazil. Seeing the wisdom, as advanced by Sagastume, that if he did not act immediately he would be left out of things completely, López sent a protocol to Dom Pedro along the lines Sagastume suggested.

But the Saraiva negotiations were showing signs of a settlement. Thus López's "services" were turned down not only by the Emperor but by the Uruguayan President as well.

The indigant López then ordered an ultimatum delivered to Dom Pedro (August 30, 1864) to the effect that "Paraguay could not stand by indifferently" and allow Brazil to "swallow Uruguay"—the last thing Brazil had in mind. Concomitantly, López had his agent at Montevideo make it known that while he still favored the Blanco cause, *he was violently opposed to the incumbent Blanco Government.* He had not forgiven Berro for turning him down as a mediator!

López's next move—having alienated just about everybody,

including his powerful quondam *compadre,* Berro—was to launch himself into a glorious fit when his agent at Rio de Janeiro reported that Dom Pedro's response to the ultimatum had been little more than a patronizing smirk, and then to climb into his lushest Bonapartesque uniform. It was time to join his Favorite in the gigantic celebration she had organized to mark his thirty-eighth birthday, a celebration that was now in its fifth week. That the Favorite was a superb organizer, and was without peer when it came to making her and her lover's enemies pay—both for the festivities and for their attitude toward her—should be apparent from a dispatch which Thornton sent to Lord Russell at the Foreign Office.

Dated September 6, 1864, it notes that for more than six weeks the populace had been "forced to devote themselves to banquets, balls, and other festivities" which the Diplomatic Corps and other foreigners were asked to believe were "spontaneous effusions." A Mass, "celebrated at the expense of the ladies of the town" for López's "prosperity and welfare," featured a sermon preached by Bishop Palacios "in which an amount of eulogium and adulation was heaped upon the President amounting almost to blasphemy; indeed the adoration due His Excellency is the principal, if not almost the only, topic of the preaching of the Clergy." All classes were called upon to "subscribe" in order to defray the costs of the festivities. Even the political prisoners "were not forgotten, and these unhappy men hoping that by this means their release might be hastened, put down their names for large sums." (At one Mass, the congregants included a group of political prisoners who had to endure the mockery of "praying for the happiness of the Chief Magistrate who had condemned them to perpetual misery.")

In addition to the Masses, there were the balls, from which "no Ladies had the courage to absent themselves." (One of Eliza's detractors claims that when a young girl whose father had just passed on petitioned to be excused from one particular *bal masqué,* Madame Lynch replied coolly, "That is no novelty;

everyone's father dies eventually." If the charge is true, it demonstrates that although Madame might have been heartless, she was nevertheless pragmatic philosophically.)

Since Eliza had decreed that, in honor of López's natal day, all the people were to enjoy themselves, and since she did not permit ankle spur-toting riffraff within the Palace precincts, a large colorfully festooned pavilion was erected in one of the public squares "where the lower classes were made to dance; sentries were stationed to prevent the women from going away, even when they were tired." (One pathetic creature, on being overheard to comment that it was difficult to dance on an empty stomach, was hauled off to the police office "and punished by a hundred blows given with a cane; several others were banished to the interior for similar offenses.")

Commenting that this "Englishwoman, calling herself Mrs. Lynch . . . possesses considerable influence with the President," Thornton also advised his superiors at the Foreign Office that "her Orders, which are given imperiously, are obeyed as implicitly and with as much servility as those of his Excellency himself." Then, speculating on the possibility—and it must be borne in mind that Thornton was not one of Eliza's admirers—that "as years creep on, she feels that her influence diminishes, and to this feeling may be partly attributed her exertions" that honor be done to López, the British envoy adds that "I need hardly tell your Lordship with what profound and bitter hatred she is looked upon by the native Ladies."

While López had been enjoying the festivities, there had been a drastic change in Uruguayan leadership. On the basis of López's claim that while he still favored the Blanco cause he was now anti-Berro, a more intransigent conservative, Atanasio Cruz Aguirre, had been swept into office. Assuming that the Paraguayan leader would now march south to his aid, Aguirre abruptly broke off negotiations with Saraiva. López's armies did not cross down into Uruguay.

Dom Pedro's forces did, however, on October 16.
Uruguay had wanted war with Buenos Aires. Brazil had wanted
war with nobody.

Now, thanks in large measure to López's "great statesmanship,"
Uruguay and Brazil were at war with each other!

Sagastume was frantic to bring Paraguay into the war on the
side of the Blancos, who were now fighting Brazilians as well as
Colorados; toward that end, he presented a memorandum to
López that smacked, in equal measure, of obsequiousness and
logic. Prefacing his thesis with the most abject attempt at appealing to the dictator's vanity—"to Paraguay falls the enviable
glory of carrying its power and its arms into the theatre of deeds
to liberate the great principle and the future of these countries"—
Sagastume ticked off some convincing arguments for López following through on his August 30 ultimatum to Dom Pedro:
not only was Rio de Janeiro cut off from its interior provinces,
which in the event were closer ideologically to López than to
their own emperor, the imperial army numbered barely fifteen
thousand men and was hardly in a position to fight a two-front
war. Too, Mitre would not come to the aid of his beleaguered
fellow liberals in Brazil. He had his hands full trying to cut
the ground from under Urquiza, who was only waiting for
López to make a move, which would probably result in the
downfall of the Buenos Aires Government and put an end once
and for all time to Mitre and his Unitarian *porteños.*

López's response to the Sagastume memorandum was to return
to his headquarters at Cerro León and, as announced in *Semanario,*
"inform the various combatants in the Plata region that they
accept the good offices of Su Excelentísimo El Presidente El
Señor Don Francisco Solano López in arbitrating the various differences which plague us all."

For Eliza, who had remained behind at Asunción, this was
absolutely too much! She was now approaching thirty, and the
royal diadem had yet to be placed on her head. Indeed, it would
never be placed on her head, reasoned Eliza, were Francisco to

limit his actions to bombast and rhetoric. The time had come to push Francisco into the war.

In her fierce determination, Eliza was aided by the wily Sagastume, who convinced her that hers and Francisco's dreams might well be achieved, were Paraguay to go to war against the militarily weak Brazil, whose troops were now bogged down in Uruguay. As Henry Young has noted, "With a complete lack of logic, she wanted war with Brazil to punish them for having slighted Francisco yet knowing that if matters had gone otherwise she would have been the first to be sacrificed. Her ambitions drove her on. She would not rest until she had seen López the Napoleon of South America and herself standing by his side."

Eliza's (as well as Sagastume's) efforts to get López to move *north into Brazil* instead of *south into Uruguay* were not only totally naïve, but, over the long haul, thoroughly disastrous. It is said that some of López's more rational military commanders were all pushing for an invasion of Uruguay, to come to the aid of the beleaguered Blancos, but were overruled by Eliza, who wanted nothing less than an invasion of Brazil proper. If so, then more's the pity. Perhaps a suitable analogy would be General Cornwallis's decision (purely hypothetical) to give sustenance to the Loyalists in New York City by invading Mexico. As one pro-López historian admitted to the present writer, ruefully, "Perhaps things might have turned out differently had Madame Lynch confined herself to arranging balls and bullfights."

4

Early in the morning of November 9, 1864, Sagastume appeared at the Palace and requested an immediate audience with Madame Lynch. The Uruguayan envoy had just been informed through one of his agents that the *Marquez de Olinda*, the largest steamer in the Brazilian merchant marine, was about to enter Paraguayan waters enroute to Corumbá, capital of the province of Matto Grosso; aboard were, in addition to the new provincial governor, a large contraband shipment of ammunition and gold. After hearing Sagastume out, Madame Lynch ordered him to depart immediately for Cerro León, and to carry along her insistence that her Friend *strike now.*

Coming directly to the point, Sagastume told López that "the status of South America" was in his hands; that if, as Madame Lynch urgently suggested, he retaliated swiftly against the militarily weak Brazil for "having violated Paraguayan waters," he could "dictate your own terms, Sir." (The great Brazilian statesman and historian, José Maria da Silva Paranhos, writing after the war, believed that Sagastume went so far as to "warn" López that a "secret treaty" existed between Argentina and Brazil whereby the latter was to take Uruguay, the former was to take Paraguay.) Suddenly adopting the attitude that "war with Brazil is inevitable," and seeing an opportunity to "punish" Dom Pedro for having refused him as a son-in-law—and perhaps even believing Sagastume's ridiculous "warning"—Lopez dispatched immediate orders for the *Tacuarí*, the fastest ship in his minuscule navy, to overtake the *Marquez de Olinda.*

Three days later, the Brazilian Minister at Asunción was advised that the ship had been captured and towed back to Asunción, and that "in view of the Brazilian invasion of the Banda Oriental [Uruguay] all friendly relations hitherto existing between Brazil and Paraguay will now cease." (According to Washburn, the new governor of Matto Grosso "was kept a close prisoner, and so was the military engineer and the commander and crew of the steamer. Not one of them was destined to see his friends or country again . . . they were to rot in prison. The [Brazilian] Minister was not allowed to hold any communications with them. After a few days' detention . . . they were all, with the exception of the engineers, who were Englishmen, and some other passengers who were foreigners, transferred to some barracks . . . and a few weeks later were sent into the interior [where] they all died [eventually] of starvation and torture.") Though handed his passport, the Brazilian envoy was prohibited from leaving Asunción for more than a month —and then only through Washburn's intervention. López later admitted to Washburn that several Paraguayan ships were still within reach of the Brazilian Navy, and had Brazil known of his one-sided declaration of war, the ships would have been captured.

On December 14, 1864, "amidst general rejoicing and salvos," a force of five thousand troops under the command of López's brother-in-law, General Vicente Barrios, sailed from Asunción for Corumbá, their ears ringing with Francisco Solano's manifesto: "Soldiers! My endeavors to keep the peace have been fruitless [surely a Freudian slip here!]. The Empire of Brazil, not knowing our valor and enthusiasm, provokes us to war, which challenge we are bound by our honor and dignity to accept in protection of our dearest rights!"

No word had reached Matto Grosso of the breach in Brazilian-Paraguayan relations. At any rate, the Brazilians were unable to offer any appreciable resistance. Their forts, designed strictly for defense against marauding Indians, were aimed toward the Chaco in fixed positions and could not be turned around to fire on the Paraguayan invaders sailing up the Paraná. Within fifteen days, all territory claimed by Paraguay in Brazilian hands was now occupied by Barrios's troops; in addition, the retreating Brazilian soldiers left behind enough gunpowder to supply López's army for a year.

Among the few to escape was the Baron de Villa Maria, the province's richest landowner. Traveling on foot, and guided only by the stars, it took the old Baron a month to reach Rio de Janeiro. It was only then that Dom Pedro learned that Brazil was at war with Paraguay and had lost its wealthiest province.

So intoxicated was López by this success, he ordered the equally ecstatic Madame Lynch to stage a massive celebration —and did not solicit any "subscriptions" to foot the bills. Pennants waved from every housetop and hovel; the wild dancing of the multitudes in the streets led one Buenos Aires correspondent to describe the demonstration scathingly as "an outbreak of St. Vitus's dance." On the Campo Grande, a vast plain in the outskirts of Asunción, Francisco Solano, astride a horse and accompanied by a radiant Madame Lynch and their eldest sons (dressed as cadets), held a four-hour military review. At the conclusion, a brief ceremony took place during the course of which Madame Lynch was given the patent of nobility looted from the *fazenda* of Baron de Villa Maria, and López was presented with a necklace that was draped ceremoniously over his shoulders—a necklace of Brazilian ears that his thoughtful brother-in-law had dispatched by fast messenger.

Writing after the war, the Austrian observer Major Max von Versen advanced the convincing thesis that, had López now marched directly to the aid of the Uruguayans "the final result of the war would have been different." The Blancos were suffering a series of setbacks at the hands of the invading Brazilians and their Colorado allies. Urquiza and his Confederationists shouted encouragement from the sidelines, assuring the besieged Blancos that the armies of López would soon arrive. Mitre was frantic that a move by López into the maelstrom would signal a move by Urquiza against Buenos Aires. Whether out of fear or out of hope, depending on which side of the issue one stood, everyone in the Río de la Plata region was waiting for López.

But waiting for López was like waiting for Godot.

López could not move. He was too busy enjoying the encomiums being heaped upon him by his adoring public and presiding over the banquets, balls, and fiestas Madame Lynch arranged in his honor to mark "the conquest of Brazil." The general hoopla at Asunción went on for two months.

And in that two months, López's fate was sealed.

On January 2, 1865, the Uruguayan stronghold at Paysandú fell to the Brazilians, who then executed summarily the defeated general and many of his staff officers—after they had surrendered honorably. When news of this slaughter spread to the Argentinian province of Entre Ríos, which was across the river from Paysandú, Urquiza was barely able to restrain his people from joining the Blancos. And though the slaughtered victims of Paysandú were conservatives, even the liberal press at Buenos Aires was appalled by the Brazilian massacre. Now presented with an opportunity—a truly golden one—to capitalize on this Brazilian gaffe (the Empire seldom committed such errors, either diplomatically or militarily), López continued to waste time in witless diplomatic maneuvers that alienated the friends Paraguay still had (that is, the Urquiza-led Argentine Confederationists).

(Meanwhile the Favorite cooked up another delicious little surprise for the great diplomat. She "suggested" that the Ladies of Asunción "beg" López to accept from them a "magnificent flag embroidered in gold, with diamonds and rubies, and a silver staff, with mountings to correspond.")

Had he marched his army across the thinly populated Misiones region, as Urquiza had already invited him to do, López would have met only with Argentinian protests. Mitre could not have brought his people to fight Paraguay: Public opinion in Buenos Aires, fiercely anti-Brazilian to begin with and now exacerbated by the atrocities committed at Paysandú, was overwhelmingly in favor of Paraguay and Uruguay joining in common cause against the Empire. They would have strewn garlands in López's path, had he moved through the Misiones to consolidate his hold on the Matto Grosso.

Also militating in López's favor was Brazil's position, which was tenuous in the extreme, so much so that Dom Pedro rushed a bevy of his ablest diplomats to bring Mitre into an alliance against Paraguay. Though in concentration of power, and in size, wealth, and population it led the continent, Brazil knew it could not possibly defeat Paraguay without Argentinian assistance. Brazilian troops needed food from Argentina's rich cattle lands; too, with the Brazilian Navy bottled up in Uruguay, and Paraguay controlling the rivers, there was no way for Dom Pedro to get his troops to Paraguay except across Argentina; also, the Empire lacked enough ships to keep an army supplied from its source of supply, which was along the coast.

Brazil offered Mitre every inducement to come into the war on its side, including the payment of all costs, but to no avail. Much as he mistrusted López, Mitre feared that if López accepted Urquiza's offer to move his armies through the Misiones region Buenos Aires could well find itself at war against its fellow Argentinians. For the relatively defenseless Brazil and the dangerously divided Argentina, not to mention the war-ravaged Uruguay—each nation loathing the other two, besides being divided internally—the situation had degenerated to the point where nothing less than a miracle could bring a semblance of order out of the overall regional chaos.

López provided the miracle.

At the end of January—some say at the express suggestion of Madame Lynch—López sent a message to Mitre. The message, which made about as much sense as Canute's command that the waves recede, formally requested permission for transit of the Paraguayan Army through the province of Corrientes to occupy the neighboring Brazilian province of Rio Grande do Sul. When Mitre refused, on the grounds that Argentina was not at war with Brazil, López convoked the Congress (March 18) and, after making the delegates realize that he had gone as far as *he* could go "in order to maintain the peace and stability of the Plata region," solicited—and was promptly and unanimously granted—a declaration of war against Argentina.

As he had done following his Brazilian maneuver, López made sure that the declaration was not delivered to the enemy until he received word that his invasion of Corrientes (commenced April 13) had succeeded. When the declaration finally reached

Mitre—thirty-five days later—López refuted the charge that he had "acted beyond the laws of civilized nations" in not making public a declaration of war by claiming blandly that he had in fact sent an envoy to Mitre with the declaration, but that the envoy, after having reached Buenos Aires, "instead of being treated with chivalry and sent back under a flag of truce . . . had been thrown into a common jail."

(Actually, López, having interned the Argentinian Minister, had ordered his messenger to delay his arrival as long as possible, in order to allow time for the *Esmeralda*, a ship loaded with incoming munitions and Madame Lynch's new landau and muslin, to pass through Buenos Aires unmolested, and to give his agent at Buenos Aires, who had been secretly advised of López's intentions, time to withdraw all Paraguayan gold reserves invested in Argentina.)

Urquiza was thoroughly disgusted with López, and succumbed to Mitre's appeals to the conservative caudillo's sense of patriotism. Thus, as a direct result of López's invasion of Corrientes, Argentina achieved total unification, Brazil achieved total unification (Netto and the conservative Brazilian provincials feared López more than they disliked their own emperor), and Argentina and Brazil, traditional enemies, achieved unity in a common purpose, a "purpose" in which they were now joined by Flores, whose Colorados had by now overthrown the Blancos with Brazilian assistance.

On May 1, 1865, the three powers signed the secret Treaty of the Triple Alliance—a secret that soon became public knowledge when a Uruguayan official showed a copy to Queen Victoria's envoy at Montevideo, who in turn sent it along to London, where it was read to a closed session of Parliament, which promptly had it published in the British press.

López had initially enjoyed the sympathies of many foreign countries, including the United States, because of his claim to be helping a small country (Uruguay) against a menacing power (Brazil) when he issued his original ultimatum to Dom Pedro. Then, by moving aggressively and displaying a disregard for international law, he had caused world opinion to swing away from him. Now, with the publication of the "secret treaty," the pendulum had swung back in López's favor.

The treaty revealed that while the cosignatories had publicly proclaimed that they entertained no designs on Paraguayan territory or wealth, they had in fact agreed that Paraguay was to bear all costs of the war to the Allies, future boundaries were to be established in such a manner as to give Argentina and Brazil all territory they had ever claimed against Paraguay, and the country was to be deprived of all power to make future wars, its arms and munitions to be divided among the victors. The Allies had bound themselves "to respect the independence and sovereignty of Paraguay" and to permit its people to elect their own government; it was stipulated that the war was directed not against the Paraguayan people but against the López Government, and provision was made for the formation of a legion of Paraguayans who might wish to assist in deposing López.

But the fact remains that the Allies were determined to destroy Paraguay. And when this became known, López gained a scattering of moral support throughout the hemisphere. Unfortunately, wars are not fought with moral support. And if, as some chroniclers claim, Madame Lynch encouraged her Friend in believing that *his* friend, Louis Napoleon III, and "the esteemed El Presidente Señor Abraham Lincoln," a champion of the underdog, would send troops, then surely her naïveté was commensurate with López's. Not only was "Señor Abraham Lincoln" dead, but the United States, now in the process of becoming truly united, was in no position to involve itself in any foreign wars (though this did not inhibit López from trying to whip up some support for his cause in the American press).

And as for Louis Napoleon, he was too involved in trying to get his armies out of the Western Hemisphere, his "Mexican adventure" having failed dismally, to consider sending them back in, regardless of the "great affection" in which he professed to hold "the esteemed President of Paraguay."

López had committed himself originally to a Uruguayan government which by his vacillating had been driven from office, and had wound up in a war against his three most powerful neighbors. His "assistance" to Uruguay had been limited to little more than vehement protestations that he was being ignored; threatening Argentina and Brazil; and unwittingly helping into power at Montevideo a government whose intransigence was manifest. Then, having created such a mess, and finally deciding to "defend Uruguay" by taking up arms against the Brazilian invaders, he had attacked in the opposite direction from his beleaguered Blanco allies' position. He had justified his invasion of Brazil on the grounds that only through a war—a war against a major power that could never have defeated Paraguay by itself, given the geographical factors which obtained—could Paraguay gain the "respect and attention" (his words) López felt it deserved, that it would remain isolated and barely known beyond South America until, by force of arms, it had compelled other nations to "treat us with more consideration."

In view of all the original advantages López enjoyed—the disunity in Argentina, the geographical and political factors inhibiting Brazil, the long-standing mutual distrust between Argentina and Brazil, the control of Uruguay by fellow-thinking conservatives, the potential assistance of the contiguous Argentinian provinces, and the magnitude of his war machine—it boggles the imagination to conceive that López could have committed so many inanities in the name of "great diplomacy and foresight."

Had López listened to the dictates of reason, he might well have achieved his goal of being the arbiter of the Río de la Plata region chaos, and won his isolated country "the attention and respect it deserves." His consummate hero, Napoleon, could have brought it off beautifully.

But far from being the reincarnation of Napoleon, his claims to the contrary, Francisco Solano López was an egomaniacal idiot who preferred to listen to the dictates of his own twisted concept of Machiavellism—and to the advice of Madame Lynch.

Madame Lynch & Friend Go to War

The Byzantine-like concatenation of diplomatic disasters which resulted in the War of the Triple Alliance was only preposterous; the prosecution of the war itself was quite beyond the pale of intellectual comprehension. Mitre—who was named overall commander of the Allied forces and who went on to prove the old dictum that great statesmen do not great generals make—had boasted it would all be over within three months. It should have been over within four weeks. It dragged on for five years. It was a grotesque admixture of comedy and error, of tragedy and farce. The overabundance of ignorance, overconfidence, and downright stupidity that existed on both sides defied credibility. The contempt with which the Allies looked upon the Paraguayans was returned in kind. Neither side was able to appreciate fully the other side's capabilities. Because they had overrun the Matto Grosso so easily, the Paraguayans assumed that the rest of the Río de la Plata region would fall without too much effort on their part. The fact that López had the country behind him was to the Allies incomprehensible.

While Paraguay, in the person of López, must bear responsibility for precipitating the war's outbreak, the Allies must bear responsibility for not precipitating its hasty conclusion. Mitre's lack of expertise was almost matched by that of L. A. de Lima e Silva, the Duke of Caxias, commander of the Brazilian forces, a man less concerned with winning battles than winning glory. Since Brazil was bearing the burden of the Allied cause both in men and armaments, her commanders (most notably Vice-Admiral J. M. Lisboa, the Baron of Tamandaré, commander of the Allied fleet, which was in fact an all-Brazilian fleet) resented taking orders from an Argentinian—especially an Argentinian who refused to attack, once he had won an immediate objective.

And while the Allied chieftains failed to achieve even a modicum of harmony, powerful opposition parties in their respective countries were carrying on bitter attacks against President Mitre and Dom Pedro II. (Uruguay's contribution to the war effort was minimal, and soon dissipated: Flores was given a separate but subordinate command, but he preferred, more often than not, to operate as a guerrilla leader, with one eye on the war and two eyes on consolidating his own position back in Montevideo.) To complicate matters, the Allies, in *stalling* instead of *moving*, committed perhaps the gravest of tactical errors: allowing the enemy to fight on the ground of his choice. López's talents as an offensive strategist were on a par with his talents as a diplomat—but when it came to fighting a defensive war he had few peers.

Though López had few chances to defeat his enemies, they were blessed with a number of opportunities to crush the Paraguayans, opportunities which they allowed to slip by. The ineptitude of the Allied commanders was not only an affront to the science of the martial arts, it was a crime against humanity: a war they might have ended quickly was allowed to drag on until both sides had sustained staggering losses (50,000 people, troops as well as civilians, succumbed to disease before the first major land battle was fought!) and a nation lay in complete ruin. If it is true, as some believe, that the god Ares roars with delight when nations go to war, it must be assumed that when these four South American nations went to war Ares bellowed with disgust.

On May 5, within hours after the "secret alliance" was made public, López convoked the Congress, which granted him full authority to prosecute the war as he saw fit. Along with that authority went the title Marshal (Mariscal) of Paraguay, a title that carried with it a $30,000 marshal's baton; a gold-hilted sword; and "a wreath of gold oak leaves similar to Napoleon's crown." Madame Lynch had already begun to rally the women by "suggesting" that they give a tithe of their jewelry toward the cost of the war (although, as Warren suspects, "most of the baubles found their way into if not on Madame's chest") and had already organized a series of fiestas, parades, balls, harangues, "and general synthetic enthusiasm" aimed at confirming the belief that Brazil and Argentina—countries which to the average Paraguayan were little more than names—"must bow before the Mariscal's genius." And if there remained any doubt in the mind of his soldiers that their marshal was, in fact, a genius, they need only pick up the latest copy of *Semanario* and all doubts were removed.

When López casually suggested that the Congress might care to demonstrate its appreciation of how assiduously Madame Lynch was overworking herself in coordinating the war effort on the home front, the Congress dispatched an agent to Paris, by way of Bolivia, to purchase "a coronet of brilliants studded with pear shaped diamonds reminiscent of Empress Josephine's crown." (The coronet, along with a plaster cast of Bonaparte's crown which had been sent on from Paris for López's inspection, was last seen ten years later in a warehouse on the Buenos Aires waterfront.) Also, the Congress unanimously adopted Madame Lynch's "suggestion," as transmitted through her Friend, that all government employees kick in to present him with "an album of solid gold covers, ornamented with precious stones, in a gold box atop which stood an equestrienne statue of solid gold."

Then, having done its duty, the Congress was adjourned sine die, and López went off to war.

Whether Paraguay's war machine was superior to that of the Allies at the war's outbreak is a matter of interpretation. Against an army of 40,000 (25,000 Brazilians, 12,000 Argentinians, 3,000

Uruguayans), López could field an army twice that number; however, the Allies boasted of grown men in fighting shape, whereas López's ranks were filled with an alarming number of fourteen-year-old boys, fifty-year-old men, and partial cripples.* The Paraguayan Army must have been more *attractive* than their opponents, thanks to those magnificent uniforms López had ordered from Paris (only command officers wore boots); however, logic (and common decency) demands that a man go into battle with more than a spiffy uniform. Only two in five Paraguayan soldiers had firearms; the others had to make do with lances and knives, more often than not of the homemade variety.

Militating in López's favor was his artillery, of which he was particularly fond; indeed, except for the first months of the war, he had to depend more on his artillery than on his infantry, mainly because the fighting was of a defensive nature. But it must be admitted that the artillery varied so in caliber and type, and consisted of so many outmoded pieces, Sir Richard Burton was moved to suspect "López had acquired all the old smoothbores which had previously decorated Montevideo street corners as trash receptacles!"

Also militating in López's favor was the morale and esprit de corps among his troops, and the ability to raise more levies. Voluntary enlistments practically dropped to zero in the Allied capitals when it became known that periodic epidemics of smallpox, cholera, pneumonia, and measles were carrying off more troops than actual combat. True, the Paraguayan soldiers were also dropping off like flies from such nonmartial causes.

However, the Paraguayan soldier was a man to be feared, holding both a contempt for death and a conviction that he was the equal to eight of his enemies. He was most effective in patrol

---

* Paraguay would probably have withstood the subsequent Allied invasion far better if its army had been smaller, since so many workers were taken from the fields, as the casualties piled up, that agricultural production suffered disastrously. Worse, because the Guaranís were essentially vegetarians they had a hard go of it on the heavy diet of meat made necessary by the lack of manpower to till the manioc crops.

work, especially in those swamps which he knew so much better than did his adversary, and he relished the *mano-a-mano* form of combat. (Colonel Thompson: "A Paraguayan soldier never complained of an injustice and was perfectly contented with whatever his superior demanded. If he was flogged, he consoled himself by saying, 'If my father did not flog me, who would?' Everyone called his superior officer his father, and subordinate, his son.")

If the Paraguayan soldier suffered a weakness, it was a lack of intelligent initiative commingled with an unthinking dependence upon officers who were, for the most part, totally unreliable. And as for what motivated the officers, their reliability as tacticians notwithstanding, to commit acts of bravery, well, perhaps the answer lies in their awareness that if they retreated—or even if they were overwhelmed into surrendering—their wives, mothers, sweethearts, and daughters would be called to account. The idea of surrender, much less the possibility of suffering defeat in battle, was alien to enlisted man and officer alike. (As an added precaution, López sent his men into battle in such a way that each was "responsible for the good conduct of at least five others." If a man showed signs of willingness to surrender, there was always a companion nearby to kill him on the spot.)

The average Paraguayan infantryman—a Guaraní Indian—was possessed of a will or willingness that transcended comprehension by foreign observers of a more civilized bent. Despite demoralizing conditions as the war progressed, especially among the wounded, who were forced to lie unattended on the floors of the stinking hospitals that were disastrously constructed and deplorably utilized; despite epidemics that accounted for more casualties than enemy fire; despite officers who were thoroughly incompetent; despite conditions that approached indescribable horror, the Guaranís suffered and fought and perished in stoic, heroic silence. Paraguay today takes immense pride in the performance of its soldiers during the Lópezian holocaust, a pride that is equaled only by the glory in which López himself is held today. The pride in those Guaraní Indians is understandable and completely justified; but how *any* Paraguayan can be proud of Francisco Solano López defies logic.

2

It is the considered opinion of the present writer that the only thing more boring than reading about battles is writing about them; and since this is, after all, the story of two individuals and not a chronicle of the disastrous war they precipitated, it is not within the scope of this book to examine the campaigns. Which is probably just as well, considering that in the entire war no more than a handful were fought. There are, however, two compelling reasons why it is incumbent upon us to give some scrutiny to what might be termed López's Grand Strategy:

1) Had it succeeded, Paraguay might well have won the war before the Allies could have even got themselves organized. As Masterman notes, "López would have been victorious for he would have instantly appeared before Buenos Ayres or Monte Video, and, by threatening a bombardment, compelled them to make terms with him" (in which event Brazil would have dropped out of the war). Lacking access by land into Paraguay—there were no railways or highways, and the Allies were loath to march their divisions through swamps—the Allies had only two avenues of attack: across the Río Paraná between its confluence with the Río Paraguay and the fortress at Encarnación, or up the Río Paraguay itself. Compounding Mitre's problems, the route up the Paraguay —the most efficacious route—was dotted with strongly fortified positions, behind which stood that imposing fortress of Humaitá. Also militating in López's favor, the Allies had to transport men, munitions, and supplies over long distances.

2) López was so sure his Grand Strategy would succeed, he had not bothered to work out any other plan.

López's master plan was a twofold one. General Wenceslao

Robles, who had led the 25,000-man invasion of Corrientes, was to continue the attack southward, while Colonel Antonio de la Cruz Estigarribia was to lead a task force of 12,000 men across the Paraná at Encarnación and invade the southernmost Brazilian province of Rio Grande do Sul; the two armies were to meet on the Brazilian-Uruguayan frontier and, enjoying the tactical advantage of logistical superiority over the stretched-out enemy, destroy the Allied Army. Meanwhile, the Paraguayan fleet—nine converted merchant paddle-wheelers and a few dozen barges—was to clear the Paraná of the Brazilian flotilla, which had by now blockaded the river from a rather safe position some ten miles below Corrientes.

López was positive he would be dictating the terms of peace within a month.

Late in the afternoon of June 10, 1865, five hundred men of the crack Sixth Battalion under the command of Captain Pedro Ignacio Meza set out with his nine-boat fleet and many *chatas* (barges) to break the Brazilian bottleneck. The fleet was to steam downriver from Asunción during the night, reach a point below the Brazilian armada at dawn's break, turn and attack upstream, and thus catch the enemy by surprise. Each of the ships was to throw a grappling iron onto a Brazilian vessel and speed back to Asunción with its prize in tow. Meza's flotilla was well armed: thirty-four guns were mounted on the gunboats, and six sixty-eight-pounders were towed on those *chatas*.

The fleet was given a glorious sendoff. López was attired in one of his gaudiest uniforms; surrounding him were Von Wisner, Madame Lynch, the eleven-year-old Pancho (meretriciously attired in his uniform of aide-de-camp to his father), and all high-ranking government and military dignitaries. So confident was the nation of victory, even the López Ladies deigned to nod—barely —to Madame Lynch as they waddled to their seats in the reviewing stand. Raising his hands imperiously, thus cutting off the din of all of Asunción who had crowded down by the waterfront to speed the victors on their way, López delivered a magnificent speech of anticipated success, to which Captain Meza, speaking on behalf of his men, swore before the heavens that they would bring back the Brazilian ironclads to Asunción on the morrow.

An hour after the Paraguayan fleet sailed, one of the gunboats —the one towing those *chatas*—ran aground on a mud flat through a navigational error. Though no one realized it at the time, this proved to be a malign omen. Meza failed to time his arrival properly, and when dawn broke the next morning the Paraguayan flotilla sailed smack into the startled Brazilian fleet. Instead of turning at once and heading back toward the safety of Humaitá, Meza continued downstream to Riachuelo (where one of his gunboats was put out of action by an Allied shore battery, and still another ran aground on the mud flats). Meza's decision to move downriver, instead of retiring *up*river, gave the enemy enough time to weigh anchor and move into a more favorable position. Now, with the Brazilian ironclads bearing down on them, three of the Paraguayan gunboats (including the *Tacuarí* and the expropriated *Marquez de Olinda*) trained their guns on the lead enemy vessel, the *Paranahyba*. The fire that the *Paranahyba* took from the three Paraguayan ships was not as severe as the fire the three Paraguayan ships took from each other.

But all was not lost—yet. Though superior in weaponry, and enjoying the advantage of ironclads over wooden ships, the Brazilians were having their own problems: their admiral, for reasons which have never been ascertained, was unable to give intelligible commands. The Brazilian ships were now maneuvering into total confusion, and but for a subordinate Italian engineer who overcame the language barrier by screaming and gesticulating wildly, the Allied fleet might well have rammed itself to death.

During the confusion, the *Tacuarí* and its sister ship the *Salto* found themselves alongside the *Paranahyba*, and while no one was looking, thirty Paraguayan soldiers jumped on board and captured the Brazilian ship—momentarily. The *Tacuarí* and *Salto* prepared to throw the grappling irons to their compatriots on the *Parana-hyba* and tow it away in the confusion.

It was at that point that the Paraguayans realized the grappling irons had been left behind at Asunción!

According to one version of what next occurred, the Brazilian soldiers on board the *Paranahyba* either rushed below deck or jumped overboard, and the Paraguayan sergeant in charge of the boarding party, instead of ordering the fastening of the hatches on the by now floundering ship, marched up and down the deck beating a reveille on his drum, which "brought Brazilians pouring out of the hold, and Paraguayans took their turn at jumping overboard."

What in fact probably happened, is that the Brazilian flagship *Amazonas* hove to alongside and swept the *Paranahyba*'s deck with grapeshot, thus eliminating the Paraguayan boarding party. Thanks to that aforementioned Italian engineer, the *Amazonas* managed to ram Meza's flagship the *Paraguayí* and thus break up the bottleneck.

Within an hour, the four surviving Paraguayan vessels had managed to escape, and Brazilian control of the Paraguay and Paraná rivers became a *fait accompli*. (The *Marquez de Olinda* keeled over on its side and drifted downstream with the current until it finally came aground off the Chaco coast; the *Salto* sank immediately, quite possibly from wounds inflicted by the departing Meza's flagship, though this has yet to be verified.)

López had returned to his headquarters at Cerro León to await news of the naval victory; when a canoe came upriver bringing word that the Brazilians had been routed, López was so ecstatic that he telegraphed the news to Madame Lynch at Asunción, whereupon word was sent out to the foreign colony and government dignitaries that the dinner she had planned to celebrate the elimination of the Allied Navy had now been upgraded to a masked ball, to be held the following evening at the Palace.

(Madame planned to attend in one of her favorite costumes, a replica of the coronation robes of Queen Elizabeth I.)*

As López was preparing to leave for Asunción the following morning to be with Madame Lynch in this hour of triumph, he learned not only of the disaster at Riachuelo but of the magnitude of the disaster. His arrival at the capital city coincided with the arrival of the four maimed surviving ships straggling into home port, minus their captain. Meza, whose lung had been penetrated by a musket ball (it has not been determined whether the musket ball was Paraguayan or Brazilian), had been left off at Humaitá to receive medical attention. López's first reaction was to send a message to Meza advising the captain that if he did not die immediately he would be shot for incompetence. Meza accommodated López (and saved himself much grief) by expiring immediately upon receipt of the message.

López then summoned his command officers to a *beso mano* (literally, "kiss the hand," that is, a levee) and expended his wrath: "I am working for my country, for the good and honor of all of you, and no one helps me! I stand alone! I have confidence in none of you; I cannot trust one amongst you!" He then clenched his fists, and screamed, "*Cuidado!* Take care! Hitherto I have pardoned offenses, taken pleasure in pardoning, but now from this day on, I pardon no one!" Masterman, who was present at the levee, reports that "As I looked around on the wide circle of Officers bowing as [López] left the room, I saw many a blanched face amongst them for they knew that he would keep his word."

Madame Lynch had been fanning public morale by organizing a series of balls the attendance at which was required of "all citi-

---

* It is probable that the messenger who announced the "victory" had been observing the chaos from a safe distance, and had assumed that when the Brazilian fleet started maneuvering in circles, until that Italian engineer got them straightened out, it was apparent that the Paraguayans had succeeded in their mission.

zens of substance." (In the first two years of the war, only the peasants were under arms; it was not until their numbers were completely decimated that the "citizens of substance" were dragged into the fray—along with their wives, their sisters, and their mothers.) Even the foreigners were "permitted" to demonstrate "their loyalty, their patriotism, and their devotion" to Marshal López—so much so, that Washburn complained to Secretary of State Seward on one occasion that "these abominations [are being] repeated so often, that at last they [have become] absolutely disgusting!"*

Also, Madame had begun the process of getting her hands on "the incredible amount of jewelry" owned by "the Paraguayan women of all classes." Her method here was not too subtle; but then, no one ever accused Madame Lynch of subtlety.

Notices would be published regularly in *Semanario* that a public meeting was to be held at the Palace on a given day, "at which time a formal proposition would be made that the Ladies should all unite in contributing some testimonial of gratitude for the protection that the Great López had afforded them, and of admiration for his heroic services in the field, in defending his country against the invasion of a barbarous foe." Simultaneously, similar "demonstrations" would be made throughout the towns and districts of the interior, "and from all the partidos in the country there came letters for publication in the *Semanario* that the women had no sooner heard of this proposition than they had come together in great enthusiasm, and demanded that they should be permitted to join in this offering."

The manner in which the jewels and money could be used for the nation's defense is questionable. They could not be sent out of the country to establish credit against debts incurred abroad.

---

* Washburn adds, "Some of the foreigners who [keep] their money and valuables in my house for safekeeping, whenever anything of this kind [has been resolved upon] come and take away sufficient to pay their assessment; for though called by another name, they [have] no hesitation in telling me that it [is] an assessment, and that they must either pay or go to prison."

Nor was there any necessity for purchasing goods from the interior: all provisions and clothing for the armed forces had, in the words of one observer, "been ruthlessly taken from the outset, without question." Thus, the women knew that all their contributions would go toward swelling the private fortunes of Madame Lynch & Friend—although they were compelled to pretend that they "contributed everything willingly, in the full belief that it was to enable the Marshal-President to defend their country."

Even prior to the war's outbreak, the Ladies had gotten wise to Madame Lynch. They were now loath to advertise the jewelry they owned (although under ordinary circumstances the Ladies were in the habit of wearing just about everything they owned whenever the occasion to do so arose—and such occasions could be anything from a fiesta to a visit to the local market).

Madame circumvented this minor problem by canceling the masked ball planned to celebrate the naval "victory" at Riachuelo, and tossing instead a Great Victory Ball to celebrate the anticipated forthcoming victory of Estigarribia, who had by now invaded Brazil. The Ladies were "requested" to wear their most elaborate ball gowns—and to arrange themselves in their finest baubles. *All* of them.

This put the Ladies in a quandary. They knew that Madame Lynch would take notes as they paraded their inventory at the Great Victory Ball. Conversely, they had read in *Semanario* that Estigarribia was "waging a titanic struggle against the enemy."

The Ladies compromised. They would wear only *some* of their jewelry.

Whatever Estigarribia was "waging," it was not much of a struggle and it was hardly titanic. And while the Ladies were in a quandary over how many jewels to parade at the Great Victory Ball, López was in a greater quandary over how many of his 37,000 men would survive the Army's role in his two-pronged Grand Strategy.

When news of the disaster at Riachuelo reached Robles, instead of pushing on southward with his 25,000 troops he instead "hurried back to a point near Corrientes, where he wasted his time in futile marching up and down the river bank." On learning of this, López had sent his brother-in-law, General Barrios, to arrest Robles on charges of "insubordination" and send the miscreant back to Asunción for trial, and then continue with the plan to team up with Estigarribia's forces and destroy the Allied armies on land.

Barrios would have teamed up with Estigarribia—but he had no idea where Estigarribia was. To compound matters, Estigarribia had no idea where Robles was. Since no one had bothered to inform him of the Riachuelo fiasco, Estigarribia had moved forward into Brazil and, against minor opposition, had scored a number of successes in the province of Rio Grande do Sul—successes which are attributable less to his military genius than to the fact that the Brazilian Army was on the verge of mutiny, a mutiny that was forestalled when Dom Pedro II hastily sped up from Rio de Janeiro and mollified the men.

Estigarribia had unwisely split his army, leaving 4,000 men to march down the opposite bank of the river; these were attacked and cut to shreds by a task force under the command of Flores. By the time Estigarribia knew what was happening, the Allies had gone on the offensive, and Barrios's army of 25,000 was in full retreat out of Argentina. Realizing that he was hopelessly outnumbered, Estigarribia agreed to surrender himself and his surviving 6,000 men.*

While López was enroute from his headquarters at Cerro León

---

* Though Estigarribia and his officers were taken to Rio de Janeiro and treated honorably, the bulk of his "army," despite assurances from the Brazilians that they would be held as prisoners of war, were either butchered to death, sold as slaves, or forced to fight on the Allied side against their own countrymen. Many of these later escaped and made their way back to their own lines, where they told of the uncivilized treatment Paraguayans could expect to receive as prisoners of war. As Warren notes: "If there had been any previous inclination on the part of the Paraguayans to surrender, little if any inducement remained after the fugitives made their way back home and told their stories."

to attend the Estigarribia Victory Ball, Estigarribia was enroute to Rio de Janeiro. The Marshal-President was, in fact, climbing into his uniform at the Palace when he received news of the surrender and of Barrios's retreat back from Argentina. After announcing that he would not attend the ball, López went into one of his monumental rages. His overall strategy to end the war before it could get properly started had resulted in a loss of thirteen thousand troops, five gunboats, ten barges, and forty-two pieces of artillery. Worse yet, as has been indicated, he had been so confident that his plan would succeed, López had not even bothered to conceive a back-up plan.

López's problem—how to end the war—could easily have been resolved for him by the Allies, had they merely forced their way upriver past Humaitá and pushed on to Asunción, while their brethren who were chasing Barrios and his army back into Paraguay simply continued the offensive. The casualties would have been rather staggering; but they would have been comparatively minimal, considering the incredible losses they were to suffer as a result of close to four years of warfare that would have been obviated had Mitre, Caxias, Tamandaré, Flores, et al. agreed to fight López instead of each other.

Madame Lynch issued orders that news of Estigarribia's "victory" was to be withheld until after the ball was over. Then, escorted by Von Wisner, she set out for the affair, where, after leading in the toasts to Estigarribia, she offered López's apologies to the guests on the grounds that he was "too preoccupied with affairs of state" to attend in person. His absence notwithstanding, López was enabled to receive the homage of his people. A gigantic idealized oil painting of the Marshal-President was placed above the empty throne in which he usually slouched while presiding over court functions; and to this portrait, as one chronicler reports, "the women genuflected and the men were obliged to bow."

Amidst the general festivities marking Estigarribia's "victory" and the conviction of all present that the war would soon be over,

Madame Lynch enjoyed a moment in which to demonstrate her total loyalty to her adopted nation. On noticing that Señora Jovellanos, one of her Ladies in Waiting, was standing off in a corner crying hysterically, and being informed that she had "just received news that my husband has been killed on the battlefront," Eliza looked at her "coldly" and replied, "You should rejoice. It is a privilege to die for one's country."

As the aristocrats and foreigners frolicked and gamboled the length and breadth of the ballroom, Madame Lynch, the ever-present Von Wisner at her side, moved about through the throng, extending her hand graciously to be kissed by the eager caballeros, complimenting the Ladies on their gowns, agreeing with them that, yes, Estigarribia was indeed the Man of the Hour, and taking mental notes on the jewels.

Eliza knew that the Ladies who now fawned over her looked down on her from their pathetic aristocratic heights as so much trash. Very well, she would really give them something to be upset about. She had prepared a little surprise. At midnight, having finished their rounds of the city, the *peinetas de oro*, the whores of Asunción, appeared at the ballroom demanding admission. Madame Lynch, who had invited them, personally opened the door and bade them welcome. The Ladies of Asunción were scandalized; they had *never* deigned to be in the same room with *putas!*

Madame Lynch justified the admittance of the social outcasts on the grounds that the ball was a patriotic gathering and that "all classes should mingle on so festive an occasion." As their hostess circulated throughout the ballroom, the Ladies were reduced to murmuring behind their fluttering fans, "Madame Lavincha is only defending her own!" In fact, Madame Lavincha was practicing egalitarianism; too, she had learned that the *peinetas de oro* also possessed some trinkets worthy of her appraisal.

Estigarribia's "victory" could not be kept a secret. At Eliza's suggestion, Francisco had *Semanario* print a diatribe to the effect that the colonel had "sold himself to the Allies for ten thousand pesos." This "revelation" led to a demonstration, organized by Eliza, at which the defector was burnt at the stake in effigy. (His family estates were, of course, confiscated, and all his relatives in the first degree banished to the interior, where they died either of malnutrition, disease, or overwork while digging fortifications and trenches.) López then reconvened the Congress and demanded that the entire nation place their lives and property in his hands —an academic demand that was approved unanimously by the cringing delegates.

Before thanking the Congress and sending its members home, López announced that "the course of the war no longer allows me to continue the self sacrifice of absenting myself from the theater of operations. I feel the necessity of personally participating in the fatigues of the brave and loyal defenders of our fatherland, thus leaving the public administration duly provided for. I depart for the seat of war to assume the duties of General in Chief of the Armies of Paraguay." The General in Chief then left for his headquarters at Humaitá.

Madame Lynch was left behind as Regent of Paraguay.

3

Eliza's first act as Regent was to have an announcement run in *Semanario* to the effect that "the women of Paraguay propose to contribute all their jewelry to the state, in order to furnish His Excellency the President the means of carrying on the war, and defending the loyal Paraguayan people from the barbarous enemy." Concomitantly, a meeting was called at the Palace, presided over by the Regent, at which the Ladies were moved "to express their desire to lay at the feet of their great Defender all their treasures, even, if necessary, to take up arms, if he would permit them, and allow them the privilege of entering the ranks as soldiers."

Their treasures would suffice for the moment, the Ladies were assured graciously by Madame Lynch, who promised that perhaps they would be permitted "even to take up arms" at a latter date. The jewels were turned over.

Eliza was enraged. The Ladies were obviously holding out on her: all the jewels collected did not amount to a tenth of what she had seen at the Estigarribia "Victory Ball"; worse, her spies informed her that the Ladies had worn to the ball much less than half of what they actually owned.

But more pressing matters precluded Madame Lynch taking further steps for the nonce; there could (and would) be more announcements in *Semanario*, more meetings at the Palace. Her immediate priority was to discharge her duties as Regent.

Examples must be set; so Eliza, herself a fierce anti-papist, attended services regularly at the still-unfinished Cathedral, accompanied by her boys (save for Pancho, who was with his father at Humaitá), by members of her court, and, when he could get away from his military responsibilities, Von Wisner. (It is said that every time Eliza entered the Cathedral tears streamed from the statue of the Virgin behind the altar, which is doubtful; and that Mother López, considering that God's House had been desecrated, installed a private chapel in her quinta at Trinidad, which is probable.)

She received members of the Diplomatic Corps regularly, both in her office at the Palace, and at her table, which, in the words of one chronicler, "was the only place in all of Paraguay where one could receive a civilized meal, properly served." (The only ones who never received an invitation to dine with Eliza were the Laurent-Cochelets, but the French Minister and his wife failed to take umbrage, having had it bruited about Asunción that they would "as soon break bread with a nigger as accept a morsel from that devious Irish slut.")

She received reports regularly from her spies, reports that allegedly included the news that the López family was conspiring to replace Francisco with brother Benigno, who had been recalled from his exile at the insistence of Doña Juana, and to sue for peace with the Allies.

She was many things to many people. Washburn found her charming and cultivated, Masterman considered her a superb hostess, Dr. William Stewart wrote to his family in Edinburgh that "nobody felt at ease in her presence, despite her great beauty."

She played, to the hilt, the role of Lady Bountiful to her faithful Guaranís. On those mornings when the wind was in her favor, Eliza would wade through the horripilating stench emanating from the hospital run by Masterman and a pair of English assistants, and present the pathetic patients with a cup of *yerba maté*, a cigar or two, an encouraging word. (Warren: "Disease ran wild in the stinking hospitals where, as the war progressed, a few fortunate victims lay by twos on rough beds. Others were consigned to the floors and suffered under open colonnades. At one time 1,000 wounded men were crowded into the general hospital at Asunción in a space intended for 300.")

She even managed to find time in her hectic schedule to oversee the ongoing construction of the Palace, the Opera House, and the National Library—or so some of her chroniclers would have us believe.

Eliza was no fool. Though the Allies were unable to agree on much of anything, she realized that now, with López having lost half his army and most of his navy, it would take nothing less than a miracle from on high for Paraguay to come out of this war intact, much less victorious. And Eliza Lynch was one of those pragmatic people who do not believe in miracles, whether they come from on high or from any other direction. She dared not suggest to López the possibility of defeat, the fear that their dream of empire was not going to be realized. It is quite possible that Madame Lynch was at this point in time laughing discreetly behind her fan whenever her Friend, as was his wont, strutted his Napoleonic airs.

López had asked her to take the pulse of the nation.

The pulse was weak—but highly revealing.

If López were to fall in battle, Eliza and her sons would be at the complete mercy of the López family, who could in turn count on the support of the aristocrats; none had a sense of loyalty to López's cause, all would indeed welcome an Allied victory. Eliza could not, *in extremis*, depend on any support from the Guaranís. These indigents were easily led by whoever controlled the country; besides, at the rate López was managing things, it was doubtful that many Guaranís would survive.

Opportunities still abounded for Eliza to flee Paraguay, especially with Francisco out at Humaitá. She was popular with some of the accredited envoys, through whose services, had it been her desire, she could get through the Allied blockade.

But she would stay. She would be loyal to López. Was it out of some perverse sense of obligation? Or was it out of some sense of greed? She had already been sending money and jewels to a Monsieur Antoine Gelot in Paris, to be held in trust for her. But her "collections" thus far amounted to less than a fraction of what was available in this primitive albeit rather lucrative adopted land of hers.

And there was this to be considered, in Eliza's favor: If Francisco eventually came to realize that all was lost, if he decided to retire to Europe, funds must be available to support him in the style to which he had become accustomed; her loyalty to López demanded that he be provided for too. Eliza realized that eventually *she* must return to Europe, with or without Francisco. She had sons to educate. Besides, she had no intention whatsoever of spending the rest of her days in, of all places, *Paraguay*. Funds must be set aside against the day when she returned home, with or without her Friend. God only knew she could not possibly resort to again being an "instructress in languages" in order to support herself and her sons.

Having taken the pulse of the country, Madame Lynch decided the time had come to take the treasury of the country as well. Not all of it; López conducted periodic audits. But enough to serve as an insurance policy against the future. She wanted only four cases of gold coins—a handsome sum, yet a sum that would not bankrupt the treasury. Four cases of gold coins would stand her and her sons in good stead when the time came to flee; besides, if López decided to flee with her, he would bring along the rest of the hoard.

Both Lópezes had established the practice of exacting payment on anything coming into the country in hard gold; thanks to these dictators' old-fashioned ideas on international finance, the Tesorería del Paraguay contained more gold than those of all the other South American nations combined. The keys to the vaults had been entrusted by López to his toadying brother-in-law, Don Saturnino Bedoya; the Marshal-President knew that he enjoyed the complete trust of his Treasurer-General, a trust that was rooted less in abject loyalty than abject fear.

Eliza had been informed that Don Saturnino was spending practically every afternoon at his mother-in-law's quinta, in company with the rest of the López family. Even if it were true that a conspiracy was being hatched, Eliza had no proof; and without proof, she could not make an accusation to Francisco; she knew that among Latins blood (even of the contaminated variety, as was the Lópezes') was thicker than water.

Resorting to what may well have been an outrageous bluff, Eliza called at the office of Don Saturnino one morning and ordered him to release to her the four cases of gold coins. When the request was refused, Eliza coolly informed the quaking Don Saturnino that she "knew" of what had been going on behind Francisco Solano's back: that Mitre had been corresponding secretly with the López family, inviting them to replace Francisco with the gross Benigno (through assassination, if necessary), after which the Allies would call a halt to the war. She "knew" that the correspondence was being carried on through the good offices of Monsieur Cochelet, who had made available his diplomatic pouch. And she had "no doubt" that if Francisco were told of the plot, the entire family would be eradicated.

Don Saturnino could have challenged Eliza to prove her claims; perhaps the fear of such a challenge was what prompted her, after delivering that veiled threat, to preclude any further discussion of the matter by turning on her heels and sweeping dramatically out of the Treasurer-General's office.

Historians are divided on whether Eliza had actually stumbled onto a conspiracy—or whether the López family (including sons-in-law) feared that her hold on Francisco was such that she could get him to believe *anything*. At any rate, two dozen slaves appeared at the Palace that very night bearing four crates of gold coins.

The following morning, accompanied by a retinue of children, servants, bush beaters, and slaves bearing crates of china, linens, jewelry, gowns, gold, and, of course, her Pleyel piano, Madame Lynch set out for Humaitá.

On arriving at the fortress complex she was pleased to see a few neutral ships which had run the blockade to deliver arms and munitions to López and diplomatic pouches to the accredited envoys. Among the ships was the Italian trading corvette *La Ardita*, which was just weighing anchor. Eliza consigned the shipment of gold coins and jewels to her agent in Paris, Gelot, and then led her caravan to Paso Pucú, López's headquarters in the Humaitá compound.

It is said that when López demanded to know why she had joined him, instead of remaining behind in Asunción, Eliza replied, "But I have discovered that the seat of government is wherever you are, dear Francisco."

Eliza had also made another interesting discovery.

She was pregnant again.

4

The seat of government was indeed at Paso Pucú. Set in the midst of an orange grove, far from the heavily fortified outer defenses, was a large building (made of bamboo and thatch, as were all the other buildings in the complex) which served as the nerve center of the Paraguayan Army. López's house was immediately behind the headquarters building. To the rear of the Casa del Presidente, completely hidden by trees, was the house of Madame Lynch and her children. It is interesting to note that Eliza and Francisco maintained separate establishments. Was López still striving to keep up "appearances"? Hardly. He insisted that they keep separate establishments lest Eliza be offended by the comings and goings of his various concubines.

In the immediate vicinity were houses for Colonel Thompson, Von Wisner, brother-in-law Barrios (who had by now been promoted to Minister of War), and all senior officers who still enjoyed López's confidence, in addition to Bishop Palacios, whose ostensible function was to serve as the presidential chaplain but whose actual duties consisted for the most part of offering daily masses for the preservation of the Marshal-President and diurnal reminders to one and all that El Mariscal was on the side of the angels.

Also included in the elaborate encampment was the military court, where could be heard prisoners "dragging themselves back and forth with heavy iron rings and chains fastened to their legs" and where, usually at sundown, the flogged and tortured were put out of their misery before firing squads. A newspaper was published, in the Guaraní language—the *Semanario* was still being published at Asunción for the Spanish-reading audience—devoted largely to cartoons and scatological verse ridiculing the *macacos* (even the non-Brazilian Allies had earned that particular Paraguayan epithet).

With the Allies still undecisive about making a move, the entire ambience was similar to that period of "phony war" that immediately followed the outbreak of World War II in England.

Though he still enjoyed total command of his mental faculties, López was by now beginning to show the first signs of the psychosis that was to overtake him. It is true that the Allies lobbed shells in from their ironclads nesting below Humaitá, but since the complex was protected by concentric rings of outer defense works, and Paso Pucú was far outside enemy range, the shells were less a threat than a damnable nuisance. And even though his headquarters, far from the outer defenses, was surrounded on all sides by a stockade and a mountainous wall guarded by his elite troops, López's house was piled about so thickly with earth as to render it virtually bombproof.

Washburn, who visited the encampment, noted that when López, "at the first sound of a gun from the allied lines, would hasten to gain the shelter of his cave," Madame Lynch would move about unconscious of danger, "as danger she knew there was none." At the same time, she would counsel López "not to expose to a chance shot his valuable life—a life on which the hopes, the fortunes, and the liberty of all Paraguayans depended." Speculating on the probability that "her object in playing on his fears was to increase her influence over him," the American Minister went on to report that Eliza was constantly reiterating to López that he was a martyr surrounded by a swarm of enemies. With the Favorite ever at his side trying to make him realize that he was "too good, too credulous, too kind-hearted, and too indifferent to danger for his own safety," that "he was in great danger, that his enemies were plotting his destruction," it is small wonder that López was "constantly haunted with fear of treachery and assassination."

Eliza established a semblance of normality at Paso Pucú—or at least what would pass for normality in those somewhat abnormal times. As Dr. Stewart, López's personal physician, noted, "Even in this backwater Madame Lynch's house exuded an air of Europe." Every evening she would preside with Francisco over elaborately served gourmet meals, to which had been bidden such court pets as Von Wisner, Thompson, and whoever happened to be in her favor at the time; after dinner there would be a round or two of whist. Washburn, who enjoyed a few of those evenings, was appalled to discover that Madame's epicurean efforts were totally lost on her Friend. A gourmand as opposed to a gourmet, López, who dined both irregularly and uncouthly, consumed enormous quantities of "rank and greasy food." Such habits, along with his excessive drinking, "were constantly bringing on ill-turns." Washburn speculates that if López had not died on the battlefield, he would probably have died in bed from "a chronic infirmity" brought on by his overindulgences.

Eliza always kept on hand a large stock of the best in foreign wines, liquors, and, for her English visitors, ale; however, López's favorite liquid was brandy, which he swilled constantly. The addiction to brandy was less out of some aspiration to prove Doctor Johnson's contention that "Claret is the liquor for boys, port for men; but he who aspires to be a hero must drink brandy," than out of a frantic attempt to ease the constant pain caused by his rotted teeth and infected gums. Instead of swallowing the brandy, López would usually spit it out—all over whoever happened to be standing within range.

But, there must have been times when he swallowed more than he spat, for one foreign observer noticed that occasions arose when López "often exceeded his own free limits," his capacity for holding spirits notwithstanding. On such occasions, he was "liable to break out in the most furious abuse of all who were about him" and "would then indulge in the most barbarous acts," such as ordering the execution of some unfortunate. Upon recovering from such debauches, "he would stay the execution of his orders, if they had not been already enforced." But, since his subordinates fearfully carried out all orders with rapidity, when López "came out of his drunken fits" it would be too late, "the victim would be already executed."

The Brazilians were now firing upwards of four thousand shells a day on Humaitá, yet the damage was still minimal. The Paraguayans were unable to return in kind; what with the Allied blockade, the loss of those forty-two pieces in López's initial Grand Strategy, and the fact that with the death of Mr. Whytehead, its English superintendent, the Arsenal at Asunción was in a bit of a shambles, artillery was in short supply. Therefore, as the Allied shells kept coming in, the Guaranís did little more than blow short blasts on their hornlike *turututús*, which, though they failed to inflict any damage on the Brazilian ironclads, at least showed what the Paraguayans thought of the *macacos*.

Ere long—perhaps, as some claim, at the suggestion of Madame Lynch—the Paraguayans turned the daily bombardments to their own two-pronged advantage. Though Madame Lynch set a lavish table, and the senior officers were eating fairly well, the soldiers and their camp followers were suffering a severe food shortage. Thus it was announced by López that a reward of a small pot of corn would be offered for every undetonated shell recovered behind Paraguayan lines. The women in the camp were thereafter to be seen scurrying around like frantic mice, falling on every incoming shell that did not explode; these were turned in to the quartermaster, who doled out the promised pots of corn and turned the shells over to the artillerymen, who sent them back to the Allies in Paraguayan guns. (Unfortunately, there were times when the women throwing themselves on the shells were blown to bits if detonation occurred some time after landing. But, as Madame Lynch is alleged to have remarked, such are the fortunes of war.)

López's army was now on the defensive, with offensive action limited to occasional raids into the Allied lines to harass the enemy, to reconnoiter for information, and to loot. "Even the terribly wounded," according to one source, "would rather die in their tracks than drop a piece of cloth, a garment, or a bit of food which they had captured. The precincts where the wounded lay took on the appearance of a busy market place, with everybody trying to exchange booty."

The Allied blockade led to a veritable explosion of ingenuity on the Paraguayan side as native and foreigner alike sought to overcome serious shortages. The arts of spinning and weaving cotton and wool for clothing were revived by the Guaraní women (who were offered prizes by López in order to stimulate production, although, as Cecilio Báez has written, "those prizes were never paid to anyone, and all war work . . . was [thus] given free by

the people"). One of the foreign technicians built a crude factory
that turned out paper made from cotton and wild pineapple fibers,
which ensured enough stock to keep *Semanario* going; for López's
official documents, there was excellent parchment from sheep-
skins; ink was made from a black bean treated with ashes. The
soldiers made their own soap and salt (the latter commodity was
derived partly from river mud, partly from one of an indigenous
variety of thick-leaved trees which abounded in the swamps).
Gunpowder—admittedly of an inferior quality—was created from
the sulphur extracted from iron pyrites and saltpeter "manufac-
tured from urine and decomposed animal substances." And at the
Asunción Arsenal, as Warren notes, foreign engineers "designed
and cast guns, changed rifling and breeches to accommodate recovered enemy ammunition, and displayed rare ingenuity in solving a succession of difficult problems."

  That López still had a sense of humor, albeit a slightly macabre
one, is apparent from his decision to send a little paddle-wheeler,
the *Gualeguay*, downstream every afternoon "to defy the whole
of the Brazilian navy." As the *Gualeguay*, like a yapping Pekingese,
would fire 12-pounders into the midst of the enemy fleet while
somehow managing to evade the 68- to 150-pounders lobbed at it
from all directions, Francisco, Eliza, Von Wisner, and invited
guests would look down from the heights of Humaitá and roar
with laughter. López was furious when, after three weeks of making a nuisance of itself, the *Gualeguay* was finally destroyed: he
had nothing to amuse him of an afternoon. For days he walked
about in a pout—a pout which soon gave way to unmitigated fury
when his plan to torpedo the Brazilian fleet came to grief.

  The torpedoes had been fashioned by those ingenious Englishmen at the Asunción Arsenal, and were delivered to Humaitá.
Jaime Corbalan, a scion of one of the old families of Asunción
who had been drafted into the Army and who was not too happy
about it all, was given the task of carrying the missiles downstream
in a canoe and releasing them in the midst of the enemy armada.
Some historians claim that López acted foolishly in sending out a

canoe to do an ironclad's job. The fact remains that the grounded *Marquez de Olinda* blocked any attempt by a gunboat to sail downriver from Humaitá. (López had tried to have the *Marquez de Olinda* refloated and retrieved, but the attempt had proved impossible.) Also, in defense of López's decision, it was undoubtedly easier for a canoe to sneak up on the enemy fleet than an old converted paddle-wheeler. No, López was wise to send the canoe; where he was not wise was in sending along Jaime Corbalan—who on reaching his destination, surrendered to the Brazilians.

While Jaime cannot be condemned for having used the occasion to, in his words, "escape the tyranny of López," he is to be condemned for not having taken his family along on the mission. His widowed mother, Doña Oliva Corbalan, one of the leading Ladies of Asunción, after writing (under duress) an article for *Semanario* denouncing her son, was stripped of all her possessions, including her clothes, and exiled with Jaime's four sisters to an Indian settlement in the Chaco; there Doña Oliva eventually died, three daughters were reduced to slavery, and the fourth—perhaps the luckiest of the lot—went mad.

In addition to those troops lost either in the Robles retreat from Argentina or the Estigarribia surrender in Brazil, López had lost devastating numbers to various diseases which swept through the swamps with an infuriating regularity. By now there was not a single able-bodied man in the entire country between the ages of fourteen and fifty, save for the men of good family, who was not either in the Army, in López's secret police, or in jail. López had wisely held off drafting the scions of the aristocratic families, suspecting they would either make poor soldiers or would constitute what amounted to a fifth column within the ranks.

At the suggestion, some say, of Madame Lynch—though it is doubtful López could not have conceived the idea all by himself —the age requirements for armed service were both lowered and raised. In addition to ordering the induction of all males between the ages of eleven and sixty, López decided to take his chances and induct the aristocrats; he assumed, quite logically, that should any of them attempt to sabotage the war effort in any way, they would forfeit their lives to the Guaranís, who hated them atavistically. As an added precaution, the scions were organized into a specific battalion, the Fortieth, so that López could keep his eyes on them. It should go without saying that they were sent to the front without training, without shoes, and without weapons.

Even the farmers were caught up in the big draft, leaving the women to plow the fields and plant the maize and manioc, which when harvested was taken off for use by the troops. And, as Washburn observed, even "the butchering at the slaughter-yards near the capital was performed by women, and in the market-place of Asunción none but women were to be seen, except the police, who were always present to overhear and report any remark of discontent or impatience at the hardships to which they were subjected. An expression of a wish that the war might end, if overheard, would surely send a woman to prison."

Regardless of how he did it, there can be no denying that López was improving his defenses—for which he can have been thankful to the Allies. Mitre, whose army was now composed of 40,000 Brazilians, 18,000 Argentinians, and 4,000 Uruguayans, had refused to move, though it was more than five months since the last Paraguayans had been chased back into Paraguay. The question remains: Was it the stronghold at Humaitá that prevented an invasion, which would have had to come up the river and which would have ended the war? Or was it the fact that the Allies, now enjoying an overwhelming superiority in men and materiel, were unable to settle their differences? Both factors should be considered.

As was to be soon demonstrated, when the Allies finally drew up across the Paraná from Paso de la Patria, not far from Humaitá, they waited for more than three months before crossing over into Paraguay proper. Colonel Thompson had constructed a Potemkin-village-like fortification of dummy guns which, manned by a handful of Guaranís, held off more than 40,000 Allied troops plus the Brazilian squadron accompanying them. But it was not only the dummy guns which delayed the Allied advance. The Brazilians, who were furnishing the majority of the land forces, plus the entire naval force, resented having surrendered overall leadership to an Argentinian. Too, the Allied troops had made known their unwillingness to fight through the swamps, where more men had fallen victim to cholera and malaria than to Paraguayan knives and lances.

Also to be considered was Mitre's hope that López would come to his senses and agree to end the war on Allied terms: unconditional surrender.

By the end of March 1866, however, the Allies had more or less straightened out their differences, and Mitre had received a brace of refusals on López's part to abdicate and go into European exile. On the sixteenth of the following month the Allied armies, led by a vanguard of 15,000, crossed over into Paraguayan soil. The "invasion of the fatherland by the barbarous foe" that *Semanario* had been touting since the day the war began was now an accomplished fact.

Having long since demonstrated his ineptiude as a diplomat, Francisco Solano López now commenced to display his extraordinary ineptitude as a military tactician. Instead of pulling in his defenses (thereby conserving what strength he had) and giving some serious consideration to Mitre's repeated pleas that a truce be called in hopes of arriving at a settlement of the war, López sent a poorly equipped force of 3,000 into the breach to meet the oncoming invaders; worse, he provided no backup support. After destroying most of the 3,000 Guaranís, the Allies began to pour into Paraguay en masse.

A month later, two events occurred of personal importance to the Marshal-President: his Favorite gave birth to her seventh and last child—and he lost the war.* For if one can fix upon a specific moment in time as the turning point in the War of the Triple Alliance, it was May 24, 1866—the Battle of Estero Bellaco (also known as the Battle of Tuyutí).

López had decided that one concerted attack would send the Allies reeling back across the border. He had been urged by Von Wisner—who was about the only one of his advisers to whom López ever listened—*not* to attack, but to maintain a defensive posture. If he allowed the enemy to be drawn in toward the Humaitá complex, most of the fighting would have to be done in the swamps; and when it came to swamp fighting the Guaranís, as was their boast, were each of them the equivalent of eight *macacos.* Too, it was known that the Allies were averse to fighting in the swamps; had López taken Von Wisner's advice, he might well have worn down the enemy through attrition.

Mitre had planned his attack for May 25, Argentina's Independence Day. López struck a day earlier, hurling an army of 24,000 at the invaders. Considering the complexion of those 24,000, one is tempted to suspect that López hoped to accomplish a twofold purpose: destroy the invading army and destroy the aristocratic scions whose mothers and wives had treated his beloved Eliza so contemptuously. For in the vanguard was that aforementioned Fortieth Battalion. Foreign observers to the carnage were unanimous in their conclusion that if the Marshal-President was not verging on insanity, he was showing every promise of moving in that direction.

Semanario was able to boast that the valiant Paraguayan soldiers killed 971 of the enemy and accounted for 3,000 severely wounded—but was not able to admit that Paraguayan losses amounted to 8,000 wounded, 350 captured, and 5,000 dead.

---

* The ultimate fate of the child, Miguel Marcial, remains a mystery even to the Lynch-López descendants; some claim he died in childbirth, others that he died shortly thereafter. It is known that the child did not survive the war. Indeed, the existence of the child is not mentioned in any of the Lynch-López biographies.

(One biographer claims that some of those 8,000 wounded "came home wearing looted uniforms and with their pockets full of gold, which they were later made to change into [worthless] paper currency by Madame Lynch." One would like to doubt strenuously that Eliza had stooped *that* low.)

One result of the Battle of Estero Bellaco that seems to have escaped the attention of most historians is that, with the loss of the Fortieth Battalion, the Spanish race in Paraguay was annihilated. Those of their wives, daughters, or sisters who survived the war would intermarry with, in addition to the surviving Guaranís, the conquering Allies and the speculators and colonists who flooded into the country in the succeeding generation, thus producing the Paraguayan people as we know them today.

An even more grisly aspect of the calamity at Estero Bellaco was noted by Colonel Thompson, who commented on the problem faced by both sides when it came to the disposal of the corpses: "The Allies buried some of their own dead, but they heaped up the Paraguayan corpses in alternate layers, with wood, in piles of from 50 to 100, and burnt them. They complained that the Paraguayans were so lean that they would not burn." (Visiting the site six weeks later, Thompson observed that "the woods and the spaces between them were still full of the corpses from the Battle of May 24. These bodies were not decomposed, but completely mummified, the skin having dried on the bones, and the bodies looking tawny and thin.")*

5

Predictably, the Allies held back from launching an assault on Humaitá, preferring instead to remain in their positions, licking their wounds. Thus López was given time to levy more troops (the hospitals were emptied of the walking wounded)

---

* López's brother-in-law Barrios, who had led the charge at Estero Bellaco, was relieved of his command and carted off to the stockades to await trial on charges of "insubordination."

and to have Colonel Thompson build a strong line of defense at Curupaity, a short distance downriver before Humaitá. By the end of June, the Marshal-President managed to get 20,000 males into the field.

In the following month, Mitre sent a signal to López requesting a truce; López's reply came on July 16, in the form of a major attack on the Brazilian positions. Having assumed that by now the Paraguayans had nobody left to hurl into battle, the Allies were caught completely off guard, to the tune of 5,000 casualties. *Semanario* boasted that the "glorious Army of Paraguay" lost "only 2,500" in this "resounding victory over the invaders." Resounding or otherwise, it was the last "victory" López would enjoy.

Now convinced that López would not give up, Mitre went on the offensive, which brings us to September 1—the Battle of Curuzú (a point on the Río Paraná midway between its junction with the Río Paraguay and the fortress at Humaitá). Allied casualties numbered in the thousands but, as testimony either to the grit of the Guaranís or to the fact that few of them were anywhere near the area, López's losses were minimal. When the lone battalion holding out at Curuzú saw that they were overwhelmingly outmanned and outgunned, they wisely picked up their lances and *turututús* and withdrew back to the safety of Humaitá. On the following morning, Lopez proved it is not difficult for a commander to sustain heavy losses *after* a battle has been fought, once he sets his mind to it: Every tenth officer and man was executed "for cowardice under fire."

A week later, with the blessings of Madame Lynch, El Mariscal sent a signal to Mitre proposing that they call a truce and discuss things face to face. On receiving a favorable reply, López gussied himself up in his most meretricious full-dress uniform "complete with gold spurs and patent leather boots. A high collar of gold lace stood up stiffly from the slit of his scarlet poncho."

Because of the obesity to which he had now fallen victim as a result of overindulgence, the Marshal-President set out for the

Allied camp in an American buggy, accompanied by young
Pancho (in the uniform of a colonel of the Paraguayan Army)
and his personal bodyguard. When the party was within two
hundred yards of the enemy lines, López alighted from the carriage and struggled onto his favorite cream mare. Some historians claim that as he approached the parley site he felt faint
and had to be given brandy; perhaps his guns were bothering
him.

The contrast between the two Presidents as they met must
have been startling: López caparisoned as if he were on his way
to a masquerade ball, Mitre in the old baggy suit and battered
hat he always favored. After greeting each other ceremoniously
with unsheathed swords, the two dismounted, shook hands, and
moved toward a clearing in the jungle where chairs had been
placed.

The meeting lasted five hours. For all it accomplished, it
should have lasted five minutes. Mitre demanded as a precondition to any cessation of hostilities that López abdicate and go
into European exile (a ship and escort would be provided for
him; the Allies did not necessarily want him dead—they just
wanted him to go away). López agreed to entertain the possibility of exile—but only for two years, and with the understanding that he be permitted to return. When each realized the
other would not give in, the two Presidents ceremoniously
exchanged riding crops, toasted each other in brandy, and bade
farewell.

So far as Mitre was concerned, he had just spent the better
part of an afternoon in the company of a lunatic, who in turn
convinced himself that he had been confronted with the antichrist. López's hatred for Mitre as a result of the parley drove
him to fits of near apoplexy; at the very mention of the Argentine leader's name, he would simply run amok. Item: On one
occasion, a patrol of Guaranís who had somehow managed to
make their way back to Paraguayan lines after having been
captured were put on the rack because they could not honestly

claim to have seen Mitre's corpse on the field. Item: Two Argentine deserters stumbled by accident into the Paraguayan camp, and were tortured until they "confessed" to López that Mitre had sent them through the lines to introduce smallpox into the Paraguayan ranks. Item: *Semanario* ran daily articles attacking Mitre (articles that run the gamut from scatological libel to hysterical drivel) and weekly announcements of the Argentinian's death. (For the record, he survived López by thirty-six years.)

López had already, as heretofore noted, cried out that he would pardon no one. It was less a demoniacal threat than a surrealistic promise—a promise that was kept. As Philip Raine has phrased it, "Before the war was over, on practically any, every and no pretext, his generals, colonels, captains, ministers, bishops, priests, men and women, old and young, people of all classes, and nearly every member of his family were tortured, starved, outraged, flogged and executed. The common soldiers were sacrificed in enterprises that patently had no chance of success; they were never rewarded or encouraged, no matter how great the hardships or risks they endured."

To this melancholy list we may add noncombatant non-Paraguayans. In López's tortured mind, Mitre became synonymous with all foreigners. In addition to the various afflictions to which he was rapidly succumbing, the Marshall-President fell victim to a terminal case of total xenophobia.

The War Comes to Madame Lynch
& Friend

Like Agamemnon at the gates of Troy, Mitre and his armies
stood for eighteen months before the fortress at Curupaity, the
outer perimeter of the entire Humaitá complex, marking time.
Colonel Thompson had established a system of trenches that practically enclosed the Paraguayan position—but to the east lay an
expansive and completely undefended area through which a
flanking movement by the Allies could have successfully pushed
and put an end to this madness once and for all. Yet, Allied offensive action was limited to little more than maintaining their
blockade of the rivers, lobbing shells onto the Paraguayan positions (many that failed to detonate were collected and returned
by the loyal defenders), and debating fiercely among themselves
as to the next move.

Mitre hoped to build up his depleted strength before moving
on, in itself a formidable task. Though at the outbreak of the
war Dom Pedro's call for volunteers had seen Brazilians flock-
ing to the colors by the thousands, the fact that Mitre's guarantee that the war would be over in three months had failed to
materialize tarnished much of the romantic aura; and when news
reached Rio de Janeiro that the latest cholera epidemic had laid
low more than 13,000 Brazilians alone, enlistments practically

ground to a halt. The Uruguayans had just about seceded from active participation in the hostilities, and the Argentinians would soon be following suit.

It was probably a blessing in disguise for Eliza and Francisco that the enemy did not prosecute the war more aggressively during those eighteen months; otherwise the two would not have had the time to devote themselves to such tangential endeavors as looting the nation and tracking down those allegedly involved in the so-called Great Conspiracy.

The Marshal-President and his Favorite were not the only ones who put in what must have seemed like twenty-five-hour days. The American Minister to Paraguay was also quite busy. Indeed, now is probably as good a time as any to take a closer look at this rather controversial figure who was to loom largely in the saga of Madame Lynch & Friend.

Charles Ames Washburn, a native of Maine, was a somewhat peripatetic individual who was admitted to the bar in Wisconsin and prospected for gold in California before becoming a newspaper editor back in the East. As a youth, he was more often than not dependent upon his three brothers for support—three brothers who, likewise peripatetic, managed to wind up representing three states in the House of Representatives (Elihu from Illinois, Cadwallader from Wisconsin, and Israel from Maine).*

In 1861, President Lincoln discharged a political debt he owed the Washburn family by sending Charles Ames to Asunción as Commissioner (the rank was upgraded to Minister Plenipotentiary a year later). On taking up his duties, Washburn acquired a large house near the Catedral de la Encarnación (its owner charged that he failed to pay rent) and cultivated the friendship of the aristocrats who loathed (and were in turn loathed by) López, as well as of the López family, who were ever ready to confide to the Minister their woes. While managing to keep

---

* Collectors of historical minutiae might be interested in noting that it was brother Elihu who led the fight in the House of Representatives to impeach President Andrew Johnson.

Washington well informed on events at Asunción, Washburn pursued a literary career of sorts. He wrote two novels (one bore the rather intriguing title *Gomery of Montgomery*) and gathered material for his *History of Paraguay* (1871) which, its occasional prejudices notwithstanding, is probably the definitive history of Paraguay from the colonial period through the late nineteenth century.

Washburn's relations with López got off to a rather strained start when the Minister refused to appear in costume at the masked ball which marked Francisco's accession to the presidency, but Eliza managed to settle her Friend's ruffled feathers. Her encouraging of Francisco to "be nice" to a diplomat for whom he did not particularly care was predicated on the hope that the United States would come into the war on Paraguay's side.

When it became known that Washburn was being seen frequently in the company of the López family, that Washburn was agreeing with the aristocrats in their criticism of López, and worse, that Washburn was being undiplomatically vocal about Francisco and Eliza (whose children he contemptuously referred to as "brats"), López was all for demanding his recall. Again Madame Lynch intervened, arguing that if the American Minister were booted out, Washington would hardly consider sending a detachment of troops. There matters stood when, in March of 1867, Washburn appeared at Paso Pucú and, without instructions from his government, offered his services as negotiator in a peace settlement. López agreed—provided Washburn made it explicitly clear that he would never abdicate.

Flitting back and forth between the Allied camp and Paso Pucú, Washburn suggested to the Allies that, in view of López's obduracy, a basis for any settlement must "include the retention of López himself as the head of the government of Paraguay." When the Allies refused to give in on this point, Washburn undiplomatically wrote a letter to the Duke of Caxias (who was about to replace Mitre as overall commander of the Allied forces) that said, in so many words, Why not ask Emperor Dom

Pedro to abdicate as a precondition to peace; the letter also allowed that Paraguay had been treated shabbily by the Allies, that it was they who had refused "an honourable peace." Washburn had already irked the Allies when, following his return from home leave in September 1865, he had succeeded in reaching his post only with the assistance of the U.S. South Atlantic Squadron, which barreled its way through the Brazilian blockade.*

Allied irritation surpassed all bounds when Washburn tactlessly had his diplomatically tactless letter to Caxias published in *Semanario*. This won him López's gratitude, and both Francisco and Eliza resumed the cultivation of the American Minister— through whose good offices, it was hoped, the South Atlantic Squadron would clear the river of the Brazilian blockade. (Had Eliza and Francisco only known that Washburn earned himself the enmity of the commander of the South Atlantic Squadron because of his high-handed insistence that it run the blockade in order to get him back to his post, they would not have entertained such hopes. The difficulties between Washburn and the commander reached back to Washington and precipitated a contretemps between the State and Navy departments that led ultimately to a prolonged and inconclusive Congressional investigation.)

By now, the Brazilian flotilla had been joined by gunboats from, in addition to the United States, France, Italy, and Great Britain. Word had gotten out that López was not doing right by the foreign nationals in Paraguay, many of whom were already in, or enroute to, jail.

Thanks to Madame Lynch, who could disarm even her severest

---

* The Allies had been unwilling for the American envoy to re-enter Paraguay, since it was felt that his presence would lend moral support to López. Reasoned the Allies: If Washington had no representation at Asunción, perhaps those nations with whom López maintained relations might withdraw their ministers, thus isolating Paraguay diplomatically. Indeed it was because of his antagonism of the Allies that Washburn suffered irreparable damage to his reputation in the immediate postwar years.

critic—provided said critic was a male—and to López's talents
for deception and dissimulation, Paraguay seized the opportunity
to enter upon a magnificent propaganda war aimed at bringing
the foreign powers in on their side. The envoys, most notably
Cochelet, were sending back reports to their governments which
reflected the truth concerning conditions that obtained in Paraguay—reports which Eliza and Francisco finessed the foreign
governments into disbelieving.

All foreign naval officers were invited to come visit Paso
Pucú and see for themselves the *truth*. Washburn writes that
"it is a singular fact that every naval officer who went through
to [López's] encampment came away a friend, apologist, and
defender of the tyrant, while all who went in a diplomatic
capacity afterwards represented him to their governments as a
monster without parallel. Hence it was that, on the return to
these gunboats, two reports invariably got into circulation in regard to the condition of affairs in Paraguay."

On arriving at the camp, the naval officers were permitted to
interview their compatriots—but only in the presence of López's
secret police, "who would report all that had passed; and under
those circumstances, the very men who would gladly have given
anything they had in the world to get away from Paraguay would
not dare to express a word of discontent, or hint a wish to return to their native land."

Suffice it to say, López took pains that the prisoners in the
stockades were not to be seen by the officers; and those who
were permitted an interview were put in a comfortable house,
fattened up and properly clothed. It was the sort of tactic that
Hitler was to raise to perfection whenever he wished to demonstrate to the world "the great lie" about how his political antagonists were being maltreated.

After interviewing the "happy prisoners," the naval officers
would then be treated to a sumptuous meal at which Madame
Lynch flashed her charm; and, on departing, they would be given
"some trifling presents, so that they would go away impressed

with the idea that López and the Madame were much abused and slandered people, and on reaching Buenos Aires would report that they saw no signs of want or suffering in Paraguay, and that, among all the foreigners they had seen, not one had expressed a desire to go away. These reports being sent to Europe and the United States by the agents of López . . . the newspapers throughout Christendom would publish them as proof that López was a wise and just ruler, and all the stories of his cruelties but falsehoods invented and circulated by the allies."

(Two in particular who were anxious to leave Paraguay were Eliza's old *bête noire* Madame Cochelet and her husband, the French Minister, who in the words of Washburn "López so longed to arrest, torture, and execute." Concerned lest they should never leave the country alive, Cochelet asked his government to be recalled, but the man sent out to relieve him took sick at Buenos Aires and was obliged to return to Europe. At long last, another replacement arrived—Monsieur Cuberville, described by Washburn as "a man who at once became the apologist and flatterer of López and Madame Lynch, and [who] made use of his official character [that is, the diplomatic pouch] to assist them in securing the spoil which they had stolen from people whom they afterwards murdered." When the Cochelets were safely back in Paris, they lost no time in reporting to Emperor Louis Napoleon III that many French citizens in Paraguay would be killed if prompt measures were not taken for their removal. But Louis had already received the reports of his naval officers; at any rate, he refused to believe that his "Good Friend" López was as bad as Cochelet portrayed him. For the record, of the more than one hundred French nationals in Paraguay at the outbreak of the war, only three survived—including, of course, Cuberville, who was not only responsible for getting many of Madame Lynch's funds through the Allied blockade and on to a Paris bank, but who probably received a commission for his services.)

Now convinced that it was but a matter of time before the

United States as well as the major European powers came into the war on his side, López, after a brief bout with cholera, returned to Asunción, where on his forty-first birthday a great Te Deum was staged to celebrate his recovery. The High Mass was officiated over by Bishop Palacios at the Catedral de la Encarnación, and attended by all high-ranking officials—and by the peasants, who still regarded López as their Carai Guzú. The Ladies of Asunción abstained from attending, which was probably just as well, since there was a limit to how many the still uncompleted church could accommodate. (One chronicler reports that "the worm-eaten Cathedral looked as if it was about to cave in with the weight of the throng which included stray dogs and baskets of live chickens.")

As he was walking out of the Cathedral following the Te Deum, López ordered the arrest, on the spot, of his brother-in-law, Treasurer-General Bedoya, on charges of looting the national treasury. López had taken a count and had noted that four cases of gold coins were missing. Doña Rafaela threw herself at Eliza's feet, imploring her to "Save him, save him," whereupon Eliza replied icily, "Your brother knows what he is about"; and when Bedoya pleaded with "Señora Eliza" to tell who had actually taken the coins, Eliza "stared haughtily at him until he lowered his gaze. 'Nobody, Don Saturnino, likes to hear the truth,' " she added as she turned abruptly and walked out of the Cathedral.

At least, that is the sequence of events as dramatized by one biographer.

It is known that Bedoya was dragged away and subjected to torture, during the course of which his spine was dislodged and he died—which further infuriated López, who was now denied the pleasure of watching his brother-in-law suffer. And it is suspected that there may well have been a conspiracy of sorts. But to claim, as do her more ardent defenders as well as detractors, that it was Eliza who personally uncovered the presumed plot to assassinate Francisco and put Benigno in the presidency is, on balance, probably farfetched.

There is no gainsaying that Madame Lynch managed not to shed many tears when the López Ladies were subsequently subjected to brutal torture; and it is quite conceivable that she encouraged her Friend when he began to see assassins behind every bush. But the "discovery" of the plot (provided there *was* a plot afoot, which has yet to be proved conclusively) must be attributed to López himself. Eliza's involvement was probably limited to urging Francisco—who was now alternating between depression and optimism, and was slowly slipping into paranoia —to take extraordinary measures when it came to prosecuting the war and persecuting his "enemies." Nevertheless, the fact that Eliza encouraged Francisco in his depravity—a depravity that was about to bloom into abject madness—would make her, if only from a moralist's point of view, an accessory both before and after the fact.

López had by now instituted a rather fascinating espionage system. Every third man was charged to spy upon his neighbor and was given authority to shoot at sight if the individual for whom he was "responsible" showed any signs of "treachery." Since the term "treachery" was never properly defined, since everyone's nerves were on edge wondering if his "neighbor" had misinterpreted a word or a gesture, and since it was deemed wisest to shoot one's "neighbor" before one's "neighbor" shot him, the alleys of Asunción soon began to pile up with "traitors," and the walls of the already overcrowded prisons began to expand as more and more "suspected traitors" were immured on the slightest of pretexts.

Thus, Lópezian logic dictated that since there were so many "traitors," then *obviously* there had to be a conspiracy. (Colonel Thompson has written that "Lopez was continually in fear of being assassinated and at night had a double cordon of sentinels round his house. This was afterwards increased to a treble one." Describing an incident which exemplifies the atmosphere of the times, Thompson tells how one evening, while waiting to see López on official business, he exchanged a few words with the Sergeant of the Guard. On returning to his camp, Thompson received word from the Marshal-President "to write all conversation you have had with the Sergeant of the Guard and bring it tomorrow." Thompson did as he was told—and on arriving at López's headquarters the next day was informed that the sergeant had been put to death and the entire guard given a hundred lashes each because the observed conversation had devolved upon "a plot to murder López." In fact, all that the sergeant and Thompson had discussed was whether or not "Queen Victoria wears her crown when she goes out.")

López could not move against the masterminds behind the "conspiracy" until he knew who they were; while waiting for hardcore "evidence" to surface, he resumed the day-to-day mismanagement of the country.

2

In August of that year, 1867, G. Z. Gould, Secretary of the British Legation at Buenos Aires, arrived at Humaitá aboard H.M.S. *Dotterel,* which had been allowed to pass through the Allied blockade. Gould's mission: to investigate reports that a number of British subjects were being interned (they were) and wished to be escorted out of Paraguay (they did). Gould was not permitted to see any of his countrymen "except the three or four who were in the camp" (he was not allowed to go to Asunción), from whom he "learned that all were very anxious to get away, but that it would be dangerous to say so. No one of them dared make any complaint." Even those in the camp with whom Gould spoke begged him not to tell López that they wished to get away, "as they knew he would not permit them to go," and that as soon as the Secretary was gone "they would be made to suffer for their expressions of discontent." When Gould left Humaitá three weeks later, he was "allowed, however, to take away the widows and children of three English mechanics who had died in the Paraguayan service."

While negotiating with López—who made sure that Gould spoke with Colonel Thompson and Dr. Stewart, both of whom had no complaints about López and were possibly unaware that so many of their compatriots did—Gould managed to travel around the complex and get a fairly accurate picture of conditions; from a letter he sent (August 22) to his superior in Buenos Aires, and which is now in the British archives, we learn that, López's claims to the contrary,

the whole country is ruined, and all but depopulated. Everything is seized for the use of the Government. The cattle on most of the estates have entirely disappeared. All the horses and even the mares have disappeared. The slaves, of whom there were 40,000 to 50,000, have been emancipated, the males sent to the army and the females, with other women, forced to work in gangs for the Government.

Many estates have been altogether abandoned. The scanty crops raised by the women are monopolized to supply the troops. The women have been obliged to part with their jewels and gold ornaments, though this extreme measure has been called a patriotic offering on their part.

Three epidemics, measles, smallpox and cholera, besides privations of all sorts, have reduced the population . . . by more than a third . . . the mortality amongst the children has been dreadful, and both scurvy and itch are very prevalent . . .

The men are worn out with exposure, fatigue and privations. They are actually dropping down from inanition. They have been reduced for the last six months to meat alone and that of a very inferior quality. They may once in a while get a little Indian corn; mandioca and salt are so scarce that I fully believe they are only served out to the hospitals. . . . There must be, from what I saw, a great scarcity of drugs and medicines, if not a total want of them for the sick, whose number is rapidly increasing. . . . The horses have nearly all died off, and the few hundreds which yet remain are so weak and emaciated they can scarcely carry their riders. . . . The draught oxen are in a

dreadful state and cannot last much longer. The cattle . . .
are dying very fast from want of pasture. . . . Many of the
soldiers are in a state bordering on nudity, having only a piece
of tanned leather round their loins, a ragged shirt, and a
poncho made of vegetable fibre.

While being wined and dined by his host and hostess (one
chronicler claims that Madame Lynch personally "won him over"
with a plum pudding "made by her own hands"), Gould became
so "imposed upon by the protestations of López that he was
anxious for peace, and would accept any honorable terms that
might be proposed," he undertook to negotiate with the Allies on
the Marshal's behalf. According to most reliable sources, a pack-
age was drawn up, to be presented to the Duke of Caxias, that
included: formal recognition of Paraguay's independence and
integrity; either reservation "for future consideration" or submission "to the arbitration of neutral powers" all territorial disputes; the retirement of all forces from each side's territory; no
demand that Paraguay pay any indemnity; the immediate release of all prisoners; the disbanding of the Paraguayan Army
(such as it was), "with the exception of the number necessary
for the maintenance of order in the interior of the Republic"
—and the proviso that "His Excellency the Marshal President, at
the conclusion of peace, or the preliminaries thereof, will retire
to Europe, leaving the government in the hands of his Excellency the Vice-President [the antediluvian Sánchez]."

At this point, the saga of the peace proposals becomes somewhat murky. Most sources, including Washburn, claim that it
was Gould who drew up the terms; others claim López himself did so, but without Eliza's knowledge. All agree, however,
that "the allied generals believed they would be acceptable to
their respective governments, and despatched a messenger to
them for authority to negotiate on such bases."

At that point, while awaiting word from the Allied leaders,
Gould had the rug pulled from under him; he was told by the
Marshal-President's secretary that the abdication article "had

never been assented to by López, and that he had previously repudiated all and every proposition for his withdrawal from the country. Disgusted with such falsehood and duplicity, Mr. Gould withdrew from the country without condescending to answer the letter of Caminos [López's secretary], which was but a tissue of audacious falsehoods." (*Semanario*, in giving the Government's account of Gould's attempted mediation, claimed that the abdication article had been added by the Allies.)

Did López actually want peace? Did he or did he not assent to the abdication clause prior to the transmittal of the proposals to the Allies? And is it true, as so many claim, that López was indeed prepared to go into exile but was halted by Madame Lynch, who on learning of the negotiations refused to allow her Friend "to abandon his people, his nation, his sacred destiny"?

Colonel Thompson writes that "the real reason why López . . . refused the terms which he had previously accepted [including the condition that he go into exile] was that, while Mr. Gould was in the allied camp offering them, he received news of a revolt in the Argentine Confederation, which he expected would force the allies to make peace with him on any terms." (One result of the "revolt," which was contained, was Mitre's surrender of overall command of the Allied forces to the Duke of Caxias; this was only just, since Caxias was a professional soldier—albeit a dismal one—and the Brazilians were by now providing most of the men and materiel.)

Washburn, on the other hand, claims that López refused "any terms that would oblige him to leave the country. He knew [or thought he knew] that there were scores of men whose families and friends he had treated so atrociously that only by keeping an army between him and them could he hope for a life lease of a single month. Many of the brothers, sons, and husbands of women whom he had persecuted had sent letters to him telling him that wherever or whenever they might meet him they would kill him at sight. Indeed, as he had told me six months before, there was no future for him beyond the limits of Paraguay."

If López knew that his life was endangered by those seeking vengeance, keeping an *ocean* "between him and them" would guarantee him "a life lease" of decidedly more than a month. And the claim that Madame Lynch would have interfered in any plan that would have gotten her out of Paraguay is palpably ludicrous. Though she would not be leaving as an empress, by now she would certainly be leaving as a very rich mistress.

It is probable that the well-meaning Gould drew up the proposals and that López acceded to the abdication clause (by now convinced that the Allies would not have it any other way) but then changed his mind, suspecting that the change in the Allied command might signal a more favorable conclusion to a war which had become very unpopular in Rio de Janeiro and Buenos Aires. But not to be entirely discounted is the possibility, a strong one, that López, who was enjoying a sympathetic press "throughout Christendom," sought to have it appear in the eyes of the world that it was the Allies and their obdurate insistence on his abdication that were keeping the war from being terminated.

3

Legend has it that in the closing days of the war, Madame Lynch, an accomplished equestrienne, led a battalion of eager Amazons into battle. The legend, which has been fostered by a number of her more imaginative biographers and which is dismissed by even her direct descendants, is quite simply preposterous. Eliza can be accused of having been many things, but being suicidal was not one of them. And while many women were indeed thrown into battle (in some cases literally), it was decidedly against their will. True, they volunteered for field service, thanks to the Favorite's recruiting drive; but it must be conceded that they volunteered their lives with the same enthusiasm that saw them "volunteer" their jewels.

With the collapse of the Gould negotiations, and with the soldiers dying off at an incredible rate, Eliza realized that the time had come to accept the previous "offer" made by the women that they "donate" their services "to the fatherland." (As one woman complained to Washburn, "The tyrant and his whore have taken our husbands, our sons, our fathers, our jewels, our money, our possessions—what else is there left for them to take but ourselves.")

Journeying to Asunción from Paso Pucú, Madame sent out invitations for another of her celebrated "patriotic offerings" to be held at the Palace. (It is said that for those who felt disposed, in one way or another, to decline the invitation, Madame thoughtfully provided police escorts.) After a rather tortuous speech extolling the great sacrifices and heroism of the "Father of the Country, and of the many blessings he [has] conferred upon [you], which it would never be possible for [you] to repay by any services which [you] could render it," Eliza suggested that a committee be appointed "to request one more signal favor from His Excellency—that we be permitted to take up arms and enter the ranks as soldiers."

Professing himself to be profoundly moved upon hearing of this pathetic appeal, López found himself unable to deny the "request." Throughout the country, companies were organized; all hospitalized Army officers who could manage to ambulate, if only barely (and if only on one leg), were "assigned to the duty of teaching them the military evolutions." The "volunteers" were taught the use of the lance; fire-arms were never put into their hands—whether because of the arms shortage or out of fear that not a few of those arms might be aimed in Madame Lynch's direction has never been ascertained.

All women between the ages of sixteen and forty were conscripted, although for some reason, the so-called *alta categoría* were denied the honor of serving. Perhaps Madame Lynch felt that if these aristocratic Ladies were dragged off to war, they would bury what treasures they still possessed, or perhaps wear them into battle. But there were no such exemptions in the interior communities, probably because the suburban and exurban Ladies had already been stripped clean of their possessions. Though few of the female conscriptees ever fought as soldiers—that legend of the eager Amazons notwithstanding—thousands were sent to the front lines as laborers, "where they were required to do all kinds of menial labor, to keep the camps in order, to cut and bring wood, and even, towards war's end, to work in the trenches."

The draft of the women was followed, on September 8, 1867, by a rather extraordinary letter that was published in *Semanario* over López's signature (a letter which some sources claim was actually written by the Favorite):

> The national resources, and those that the patriotism of my citizens has placed in my hands, have been until now sufficient to meet our necessities, and I expect that they will be. *However*, in order to put a climax to the great strife, and that we may sustain and save the country with its honor and its rights (God protecting us and the valorous legions that fight at my orders), these considerations that I am pleased to offer to the deputation of the signers [of the above-mentioned "national subscription" offered López on his forty-first birththday] have decided me to accept but a twentieth part of their patriotic offerings . . . having in this the object of exhibiting to posterity the sublime virtue with which the daughters of the country have distinguished themselves in a time of trial.

Immediately upon publication of the letter, agents were appointed to receive "but a twentieth part of their patriotic offerings." Whichever women had anything left in the way of valuables were obliged to take these to the agents and have them weighed. Where it was suspected that some of the less cringing "daughters of the country" (for the most part, the aristocratic Ladies) might be holding back, the secret police were given permission by Madame Lynch to search the houses and compile their own inventories.

After taking the "twentieth part," the collectors waited a few days—and then went back for the other nineteen parts.

There was, however, one Lady whose collection of jewels was not only one of the finest in the entire country but who was endowed with a religiosity that transcended the miraculous. Because of the very special nature of this Lady (*and* of her collection), Madame Lynch decided to extract it personally and—a switch in tactics—to offer compensation.

That Lady was the Virgin of Caacupé.

Approximately a century prior to Eliza's introduction into Paraguay, a wealthy woman of the interior village of Caacupé had vowed that if her desperately sick daughter should recover, she would adorn the local church's statue of the Virgin with a valuable bracelet. The frantic mother's prayers were answered, the debt was honored; when word got out concerning this miracle, all mothers of sick children made similar vows. What with the prevalence of illness among the children, especially in the interior of the country, the statue was soon engulfed in votive offerings. In time, news of the miraculous cures came to the attention of the authorities, and to test the matter, the Bishop of Paraguay made a pilgrimage to Caacupé to see if the Virgin would work a miracle for him. She graciously complied, and the Bishop formally inaugurated the worship at Caacupé. For more than eighty years multitudes of people had been in the habit of visiting Nuestra Señora de Caacupé and swamping her with jewels in recompense for her divine intercession.

Eliza was aware of the several well-authenticated cases of persons whose offerings were of inferior quality being overtaken, soon after making them, with some terrible calamity. She realized, therefore, that there would be little if any "paste" in the immediate vicinity of the statue.

On returning to the compound at Paso Pucú following her latest "collection" at Asunción, Madame Lynch engaged Bishop Palacios in a theological discussion. Curious as to whether, in the eyes of the Lord, glass has the same value as diamonds, she was assured by Palacios that the Lord is not concerned with "temporal things of this nature." Then, according to this thesis, in Eliza's opinion, the substitution of glass for jewels at the Caacupé shrine would make no difference to the Lord. When Palacios reminded her that the people had sacrificed their jewels as a symbol of faith, Eliza shrewdly countered that since, in the Kingdom of Heaven, it is not the materialistic but the spiritual that matters, the Bishop had to concede that the value of the articles in question, whether genuine or paste, was intrinsically the same. Two days later, accompanied by Palacios, Madame Lynch made a pilgrimage to Caacupé.

One can only imagine Madame's reaction on approaching the statue whose "diadem alone . . . was worth a King's ransom. Pendants hung from her ears, her fingers were stiff with rings and row after row of priceless pearls had been placed around her slender neck by devout pilgrims who, when unable to attach another pearl to her person or ornament to her dress, had laid offerings at her feet so that she stood in a sea of jewels."

Barely able to suppress the excitement she felt, Madame Lynch quickly denuded the figure of its treasures, and just as quickly readorned it with the collection of beads and costume jewelry she had brought along for the purpose. She had also brought along one of her discarded ball gowns, having been advised by the complaisant Palacios that the Virgin's dress was embossed with precious gems—which would explain why more knowledgeable visitors at the shrine to this day are perplexed by the fact that Nuestra Señora de Caacupé readily summons to mind a vision of Queen Elizabeth I frozen in her tracks while fleeing one of her burning palaces.

After stripping the Virgin of her jewels, Madame Lynch returned to Asunción and began to strip the Virgin's petitioners of their property. Washburn reports that for a year previous to the evacuation of Asunción by the government in 1868, "Madame Lynch, foreseeing that López must finally be overthrown, had been engaged in buying up a large part of the most valuable property . . . The people who owned it had no alternative, when she offered to purchase it, but to accept her terms. She invariably paid in the paper money of the country, which would be of little, if any, value should López be overthrown, and of which she had an unlimited supply by order of her paramour. When she made an offer for a house or other building, the owner dared not refuse it, for he knew she had both the power and the will to punish him for a refusal; and hence all those bargains were in fact nothing more than a confiscation of the property for the benefit of Madame Lynch, for which in turn she gave them, in charity, just what she pleased."

4

The Allied Army had finally decided to move, and by November 1867, Brazilian ironclads managed to push past Curupaity and put Humaitá under siege. It was, at best, a desultory siege. The Brazilian ships anchored at a comparatively safe distance "and occasionally bombarded a church, the only structure visible to the gunners." No significant number of troops could be landed along the river; thus the Allies were faced with the choice of fighting through the outer ring of Paraguayan defenses—or changing the direction of their attack: executing a flanking movement through that aforementioned exposed area to the east.

Instead of taking the logical choice, especially since they controlled the river and were guaranteed an essential line of supply, the Allies—inexplicably yet predictably—elected to bog down their armies in the swamps and periodically flooded lowlands on the lower reaches of the Río Paraguay. Which is to say, faced with a choice between doing things the easy way and the hard way, Caxias elected to take the hard way.

Now forced to evacuate Curupaity, López decided to take one last shot at his enemies. At dawn on November 3, more than 8,000 Paraguayans attacked the main Allied camp with such force that the Allies were thrown into total confusion: "Some of the [Allied] troops fled back to the Paraná, where they competed with officers and camp followers for transportation across the stream."

López had ordered his men to loot the Allied stores for much needed materiel; the attacking Guaranís practically disbanded in order to do so. And as Warren notes, "This disorganization saved the Allies from a major defeat. Reinforcements rushed up and forced the [Guaranís] to retreat. . . . Allied losses were about 1,700 killed, wounded and captured, in addition to a heavy destruction and capture of stores, munitions, and artillery. A well-organized attack would have disrupted most of the Allied camp, but López was blind to the opportunity." López was also "blind" to the fact that his strategic attack was, in effect, little more than a maniacal suicide mission; though many of the Guaranís succeeded in garnering enemy loot, they did not succeed in making it back to their own lines.

Having decided to retreat with his "government" into the Chaco, López left the defense of Humaitá to Colonel Paulino Alen, who had at his disposal a mere 3,000 half-starved and practically naked soldiers to man 15,000 yards of trenches. Alen erected a series of torpedo-loaded chains across the river. This was actually a clever gambit—but unfortunately, Alen failed to take into consideration the tides. On February 18, 1868, Brazilian ironclads overran the chains at high tide and moved upriver to bombard Asunción four days later. Predictably, it was only a token gesture. Thanks to a clever deployment of dummy guns, desultory fire, and "marching and countermarching on the part of the Paraguayans," the Allies had no idea that Curupaity was in fact being guarded by little more than a ragged skeleton force. (Perhaps it never dawned on Caxias to send out a reconnoitering mission; had he done so, he would have realized that instead of sending only a few ironclads to harass Asunción, he could have moved an invasion army up the river and into the capital city.)

Before retiring to his new headquarters in the Chaco, López returned to Asunción to collect the Church and national treasuries and government records, and to order the evacuation of the city. It was then that he discovered the mastermind behind the alleged conspiracy aimed at putting him to death and ending the war.

The mastermind was, as López saw it, none other than—the American Minister, Washburn!

5

Actually, López had been suspicious of Washburn all along. The American envoy had been openly consorting with the López family; he was in the habit of playing *malilla* (a form of whist) weekly with such "suspected traitors" as brothers Benigno and Venancio, Foreign Minister Berges, and the Portuguese Consul, José Maria Leite-Pereira (whom López believed had been supplying Brazilian prisoners with food and money, which was true). He was on particularly close terms with the French Minister, Cochelet, whom López loathed as Eliza loathed the Minister's wife, and who had been allowing the use of his diplomatic pouch to Dr. Masterman and Eliza's Lady in Waiting, Señora Martínez. Indeed, both had been arrested and charged with using the diplomatic pouch "to consort with the enemy." (Actually, Señora Martínez was anxious to advise her relatives in Buenos Aires that she was still alive; Masterman was anxious to allay the fears of his family back in Europe.)

López's suspicions regarding Washburn had increased when the latter asked for the release of Masterman so that he could attend Mrs. Washburn in the birth of their first child; and he had, after the *accouchement*, attached Masterman to the American Legation, thus granting him diplomatic immunity.*

Then López's suspicions began to become even more inflamed when he learned that Washburn had taken under his pro-

---

* Poor Señora Martínez was not entitled to diplomatic immunity, nor could she count on Madame Lynch, whom she had served so loyally. After being tortured, she was granted a merciful release in death.

tection two Americans who were near the top of the Marshal-President's most-wanted list: Porter Bliss and Major James Manlove.

Bliss, a brilliant young scholar, had come to Paraguay to write a book on Indian languages, and had wound up being commissioned by López to write a history of Paraguay based on archival research. Since the nation's archives were closed to examination, Bliss was forced to work from secondary materials and from interviews with those still alive who had known Francia. The history extended only to 1810 in manuscript form, and while Francisco Solano played no part in the events of the colonial period, he nevertheless took it as a personal slight that he was not even mentioned in the Bliss manuscript. (It was this manuscript which served as the basis of Washburn's own two-volume *History of Paraguay.*) López had planned to incarcerate Bliss for so heinous an omission, but when the dictator's back was turned, Washburn hired Bliss as his personal secretary.

Manlove was a rather picaresque former Confederate officer who had suddenly appeared at López's headquarters one day with a weird plan to assemble a fleet of privateersmen that would roam the seas in search of Argentinian and Brazilian vessels. Even López had laughed away the idea. *But,* since Manlove had somehow managed to get into Paraguay without a passport, and had so easily slipped through the enemy lines, López became suspicious of something (though he knew not what) and had Manlove put under surveillance—whereupon Washburn had invited *him* to move into the Legation too.

López also knew that the American Legation had become a refuge for all foreigners who feared for their lives, and that Washburn had broadcast that all who wished to might deposit their valuables at the Legation for safekeeping. Among those who accepted the offer was Eliza Lynch, though this was probably unbeknownst to Francisco.

Matters came to a head when Washburn flatly refused to move

the Legation to the new capital López was preparing in the Chaco (and it should be noted that López had made no preparations for receiving the foreign envoys at the new "seat of government"). To López's twisted way of thinking, the refusal was a clear sign that Washburn was determined to protect that Legation full of "enemies" and await the Brazilian invasions of the city. (The Brazilian bombardment of the city had led everyone to believe that an invasion was imminent.)

López arrested his brother Benigno, who after being tortured mercilessly "confessed" that Washburn had masterminded the whole plot; Benigno also "named accomplices, who in turn named others." Instead of ignoring the inane charges against him, Washburn responded to them, chapter and verse; by replying to them in detail, instead of dismissing the whole business as yet another manifestation of López's paranoia, he thus increased or created further suspicion. Charges were drawn up against Washburn, and even Madame Lynch rushed to the Legation to urge him to "confess" (and to pick up the small fortune she had deposited there).

Had he not believed, in his twisted mind, that Washington was considering sending aid for his cause, López would undoubtedly have stormed the Legation. In the event, when he departed for his new capital, he left behind a force of troops who literally put the Legation under siege. (Manlove made the mistake of going out of the Legation for a bit of air one evening, against Washburn's advice, and "fell into the hands of the police, who passed him from prison to prison before a firing squad ended his suffering in August." The Cochelets were permitted to leave when their replacements finally arrived. Senhor Leite-Pereira and a number of the other foreigners, not knowing how long López would respect the Legation's diplomatic immunity, decided to surrender and throw themselves on Paraguayan justice, confident that their innocence would be upheld. It wasn't.)

The State Department was not unaware of Washburn's predicament, and had ordered its envoy at Rio de Janeiro to do everything possible to rescue him. A ship of the South Atlantic Squadron, the *Wasp*, was sent up the Río Paraguay but was refused permission to go through the Allied blockade—until the American Minister at Rio threatened to break off diplomatic relations. López did not want to let Washburn go, even when the commander of the *Wasp* announced that Washburn was a personal friend of the recently elected President Grant, and that, furthermore, six U.S. monitors were "standing by, ready to knock Asunción around the López ears." When Madame Lynch argued that Paraguay could ill afford to get involved militarily with the United States at *this point*, López agreed to give Washburn and his staff their passports—but refused them permission to take along Masterman and Bliss.

Though reluctant to leave them behind, Washburn decided it was "Our united opinion . . . that if I could get away and give the alarm to our squadron as to their situation, it would be the best thing for me to do. They thought that probably before they would be killed, something would come to their relief. . . . We had got to the front door of my house, and just as we stepped off the corridor into the street, there were about 50 soldiers . . . who rushed in and caught Bliss and Masterman . . . and took them right off to prison."

Loaded down with heavy irons riveted to their ankles, Masterman and Bliss were sent to López's new capital at San Fernando, where they were thrown into an open prison that contained upwards of seventy priests (including Father Palacios), native Paraguayans (including Berges, his successor Benítez, and what others remained of López's original Cabinet, save for Vice President Sánchez), and a number of foreigners (including fifteen Italians, nine Spaniards, six Frenchmen, three Portuguese [including Senhor Leite-Pereira], two Germans, thirty-three Brazilians and twenty-five Argentinians). Masterman has written that "many were in the last stage of misery, almost, some quite naked, covered with wounds." Bliss subsequently testified that they "received no food, except bits of entrails of animals thrown to them twice a day which they were obliged to cook for themselves."*

By now Padre Fidel Maiz had won his release from prison by writing a nauseating encomium on the "greatness of Mariscal López, the Savior of our Country," and was serving as the "Savior's" Chief Inquisitioner. His favorite instrument of torture was the *cepo uruguayo*. Alonzo Taylor, the English architect who had fallen into Lópezian disfavor (perhaps because he failed to complete the Palace), was one of the many subjected to this fiendish device. Taylor has written how he was forced to sit on the ground

> with my knees up; my legs were first tied tightly together, and then my hands behind me with the palms outward. A musket was then fastened under my knees; some more of them, tied together in a bundle, were then put on my shoulders, and they were looped together with hide ropes at one end; they then made a running loop on the other side from the lower musket to the others, and two soldiers hauling on the end of it forced my face down to my knees and secured it so. The effect was as follows: First the feet went to sleep, then a tingling commenced in the toes, gradually extending to the knees, and the same in the hands and arms, and increased until the agony was unbearable. My tongue swelled up, and I thought that my jaws would have been displaced; I lost all feeling in one side of my face for a fortnight afterwards. The suffering was dreadful; I should certainly have confessed if I had had anything *to* confess.

(Taylor goes on to describe how the prisoners "were of all nationalities and of all grades and positions, but with the heat,

---

* Dr. Cecilio Báez, the eminent Paraguayan statesman, who was also his country's outstanding scholar, claims that between June and December of 1868 "the number of executions of distinguished persons for imaginary crimes reached 1,000, without counting the seven or eight thousand soldiers shot for minor offenses, and the hundreds of families sacrificed by the lancers, for no purpose except to despoil them of their jewels and silver. Among the tyrant's victims, one counts hundreds of distinguished women and young ladies, whose only crime was in being mothers, wives, daughters or sisters of supposed conspirators."

wear and tear, the rain and wind, they were soon all alike, nearly naked . . . Amongst them were many women, some of them belonging to the best families in the country. . . . For my part, I do not believe that there was any conspiracy at all, unless on the part of the President himself and some of his tools to rob the foreigners of their money." Taylor was among the more fortunate ones who survived when "the Brazilians had got our range, and shells were flying over and close to us, and the Paraguayans [by then in flight] hoped to see us thus got rid of.")

6

On July 24, 1868, López received word that Humaitá had fallen to the Brazilians, who had finally gotten wise to the Paraguayan game of tactical deception. In the major assault on the fortress led by the Duke of Caxias, Colonel Alen and his pathetic band of defenders had acquitted themselves admirably, managing to hold off for more than three months until their supplies ran out. With his communications to López cut off, and seeing no hope of relief, Alen tried to commit suicide but, unfortunately, bungled the attempt. Realizing that Humaitá was being evacuated, Caxias, ever eager to cover himself with glory, threw 10,000 men into the final assault on the fortress; of this number, more than 2,000 Brazilians died in the carnage—which was probably more than twice the number of men Caxias actually needed to capture his objective. Guaraní troops too weak to escape surrendered to the Brazilians; about half of these subsequently managed to escape their captors and flee into the Chaco, where they were recaptured shortly thereafter when their ammunition —and their strength—ran out.

With the collapse of Humaitá, López thought it prudent to abandon his headquarters at San Fernando and withdraw farther upriver to Villeta. Before moving on to his new (rather, latest) capital, López paused long enough to torture and shoot Colonel Alen, and execute the wife and mother of Alen's second in command, who had surrendered the remnants at Humaitá to the Brazilians. Also eliminated by López were those pathetic few who had miraculously avoided capture by the enemy and had made their way back to San Fernando. As López moved on to Villeta, Colonel Thompson was left behind with a scanty battalion at Angostura, which commanded a strategic position along the river, and which was the last major fortress in Paraguayan hands. Angostura was vital to Francisco and Eliza, as it was through here that so much of the wealth they had accumulated was sent off to Europe on neutral vessels.

It was a curious caravan that set out for Villeta: López, Madame Lynch and their sons, and Von Wisner traveled in a convoy of landaus, sharing room with gaudy uniforms, magnificent ball gowns, Sèvres and Limoges china, the national records and treasury, the confiscated Church treasures, Madame's wine cellar, and, to be sure, Madame's piano. Surrounding the train was López's escort. Behind, on foot, came the principal prisoners: Berges; Benítez; the Baron R. von Fischer-Truenfeld who had built the telegraph line from Asunción to Humaitá; what remained of the López family, save for Doña Juana, who was by now under house arrest at her quinta at La Trinidad; Masterman; Bliss; et al. Bringing up the rear were slaves, camp followers, and, forming an outer perimeter, the young boys, old men, the crippled and walking wounded who made up the Paraguayan Army. Masterman recalled that "men, women, and children, in three divisions, were hemmed in by soldiers on foot and horseback, fully armed and with sticks in their hands, with which they thrashed those outside and those that fell from exhaustion; whilst the officers, with drawn swords, rode amongst them, dealing out blows right and left in wanton cruelty . . ."

On September 23, Villeta fell, and López and his caravan were on the move again, this time to the new provisional capital at Luque. Outside of Luque, the imported landau collapsed, and Madame Lynch & Friend (& Children) were forced to transfer to "an old Spanish carriage with high wheels and leather springs." They were also forced to jettison Madame's piano. (The spot where the piano was abandoned is today the Indian village of Piano, Paraguay.)

Also spared the travail of having to walk were the López sisters, Doña Inocencia de Barrios and Doña Rafaela de Bedoya, by now both widowed, who "were imprisoned, each in a covered bullock-cart, or *carreta*, about seven feet long, four wide, and five high. They remained, poor ladies, shut up in these moveable prisons for more than five months"—save on special occasions when they were permitted to crawl into their brother's Presence, make further "confessions," and submit to lashings. They, along with most of the important prisoners (brothers Benigno and Venancio had already been dispatched to their reward), were flogged periodically for having "in their grief and despair, expressed their detestation of the barbarous and unnatural cruelty of their ferocious brother."

It was now Mother López's turn. Under escort, she was summoned from her quinta at La Trinidad to Luque, where she was forced "before the altar of the church" to swear that she "recognized Francisco Solano alone as her child," and to curse her other children "as rebels and traitors." She was then sentenced to periodic floggings for *her* role in the "conspiracy," though she "piteously pleaded her advanced age [she was over seventy] and disease of the heart."

By early December, López was on the move again, this time to Lomas Valentinas, where yet another national capital was established. (Masterman relates how while on the march he and some of the other prisoners were overtaken by the carriage carrying López and Eliza. "She bowed with a gracious smile; we took off our caps to her, all well knowing that a word from her could send us to the scaffold, or worse, on the morrow . . . Madame Lynch was overheard to say to López, 'Oh, Your Excellency, how you have sacrificed yourself for the sake of your country, and these wicked men have conspired against you. Es muy triste, Señor. Oh very sad indeed!")

It was at Lomas Valentinas, on December 12, that López accepted the credentials of Washburn's successor, General Martin T. McMahon, another political appointee. McMahon had withheld his government's recognition of Paraguay until López agreed to surrender Bliss and Masterman, pursuant to a promise the new envoy had made to his predecessor.

Prior to leaving Asunción, Washburn had advised the two to say anything they liked against him if it would help them at all, and this they proceeded to do (thereby giving López further "proof" that Washburn had been, after all, his personal antichrist). Masterman bought time for himself by attending to the medical needs of his fellow prisoners—in itself a herculean task, since his instruments had been taken from him. Bliss bought time by agreeing to write a diatribe entitled *The Secret History of the Mission of the North-American Citizen Charles Amos* [*sic*] *Washburn* . . . , which López immediately had published. (As Warren notes, "No intelligent person could accept it as being anything but a complete fabrication; for those who might be somewhat obtuse, Bliss not only misspelled Washburn's middle name but also threw in many stories and charges that obviously were fantastic.")

Anxious to retain American recognition—and fearful that the American squadron which had brought McMahon upriver from Buenos Aires might take action—López agreed to surrender the two. (Immediately on reaching the United States, Bliss published a complete retraction of the book the writing of which had saved his life. Masterman returned home to write his own memoirs, *My Seven Eventful Years in Paraguay*, one of the few authentic primary sources for the history of the Lópezian era.)

For López, it proved to be a wise exchange. McMahon immediately fell under the spell of Madame Lynch and wound up becoming one of Francisco's major apologists. Indeed, so taken with the new American Minister was López, that eleven days after presenting his credentials McMahon was named executor of the Marshal-President's last will and testament:

> I, the undersigned, Marshal-President of the Republic of Paraguay, by this present document, declare formally and solemnly, that, thankful for the services of Madame Elisa A. Lynch, I make in her favor a pure and perfect gift of all my goods, rights and personal actions, and it is my will that this disposition be faithfully and legally complied with.

And when McMahon left Paraguay the following July, according to Báez, he carried in his baggage a small fortune in gold and silver dollars to be deposited in the Bank of England to the account of López's physician, Dr. William Stewart, who had (allegedly) given Madame Lynch a signed statement that the treasure was hers whenever she got around to claiming it.

Washburn claimed that McMahon carried in his baggage quite a personal hoard that one does not normally associate with a departing diplomat. The two were subsequently called before a Congressional committee investigating how the U.S. Navy almost got caught up in the Paraguayan debacle. In what amounted to a direct refutation of all Washburn's charges, McMahon offered, under sworn oath, such gems as "López treated his mother and sisters as the first ladies of the land . . . and on many occasions it occurred to me that his devotion to [Doña Juana] was exceedingly filial." After hundreds of hours and thousands of pages of sworn testimony, those who conducted the *Investigation into the conduct of the late American Minister to Paraguay and of the officers commanding the South Atlantic squadron since the breaking out of the Paraguayan War Commenced in Washington, D.C. on March 30, 1869* (Report No. 65, U.S. House of Representatives, 41st Congress, 2nd Session) were able to agree only on the fact that both Washburn and McMahon had acted in a manner unbecoming accredited representatives of the United States Government; thus two foreign service careers came to an inglorious conclusion.

There are those who, having sided with McMahon, claim that

Washburn's charges against López and Madame Lynch were no more than outrageous fabrications predicated on a not unnatural detestation of the two; those who take the opposite tack believe that McMahon came out of Paraguay a much wealthier man than when he went in. After having pored over the testimony, which drifts back and forth between the sophomoric and the soporific, the present writer, fully appreciative of the confusion that must have prompted the committee to hand down an inconclusive judgment, has come down on the side of Washburn. Perhaps some readers will decide to the contrary.

Four days after having made out his will, López was on the move again. After landing 35,000 men above Villeta—where they engaged in a few pitched battles which took a toll of 5,000 Paraguayan "troops": old men, young boys, cripples, and even women —the Duke of Caxias launched an all-out attack on Lomas Valentinas. At a loss of 10,000 of his own men, Caxias routed the pitiful remnants of the López Government—and, predictably for Caxias, allowed López to escape. The Brazilian commander was anxious to get to Asunción and declare the war at an end.

On January 21, 1869, Caxias made his declaration. For the Emperor, this was wonderful news indeed. Expenses for the war had been running at $60 million a year (Argentina and Uruguay had long since stopped sending even token contributions), a sum Dom Pedro could ill afford. Also, the Government at Rio, along with the general populace, had been demanding an end to it all.

Actually, the war was at an end only insofar as Caxias was concerned.

López felt differently. . . .

End of a Dream

Historians are fond of referring to the last phase of the War of the Triple Alliance as a Golgotha-like waging of guerrilla warfare on López's part. In the literal sense of the word, it was indeed a "little war." But guerrilla warfare as it has come into general usage connotes a variation on the martial arts whereby a small, highly maneuverable band harasses a numerically superior enemy by staging lightninglike raids on his sources of supply and communications. López's band was highly maneuverable; but instead of harassing the enemy, he irritated the enemy by leading the Brazilians on a miserable year-long chase through the jungles and bogs of Paraguay. The strategy of the Allies for the first four years of the war had been to move in fits and starts; now instead of giving pause every time they scored a victory, the Brazilians pursued their quarry relentlessly. Dom Pedro II vowed that he would not recall his forces as long as López remained alive on Paraguayan soil.

It is doubtful, as some chroniclers claim, that López was merely trying to escape; had that been the case, he could have fled immediately into Bolivia, instead of persisting in patching together a succession of piecemeal "armies," establishing, and being forced to abandon, a succession of "national capitals," and otherwise waging a war the outcome of which had long since been determined. Nor is it to be considered seriously that López had realized that the war was lost but would not admit defeat until the last Paraguayan (including himself) had fallen; had that been the case, he would have holed up in one position, like Hitler in his bunker, and fought it out to the bitter end.

López's hope in prolonging the carnage was to get so far into the jungle that the Brazilians would abandon their pursuit, whereupon he would establish himself as a cacique or Indian chieftain among the natives of the deep interior, and, in Washburn's words, "continue for years to play the part of a despot, and be such a pest on the borders of civilization as to figure in the newspapers of other countries." Evidence exists that López went so far as to "sign a treaty with some chiefs of the miserable tribes of the region" whereby they were to furnish him with provisions and manpower. Copies of these treaties he "contrived to get published by having them fall into the hands of the Brazilians"; they were then republished "by his faithful agents" in the United States and Europe, "to prove that he was still invincible, and that it was the duty of foreign powers to interfere and put an end to the war."

López's determination was, according to all laws of reason, inexplicable; Madame Lynch's decision to be part and parcel of her Friend's lunacy is incomprehensible. Why did she not surrender with her sons to the oncoming Brazilians, instead of fleeing with the remnants of López's government every time a capital was about to be overrun? Was it, as some of her defenders maintain, a sense of loyalty toward López that precluded her abandoning him? Was it López's refusal to let her go? Or was it, perhaps, the surrender of Angostura, the last point of egress from the country on a neutral ship? Is it even possible that her pride would not permit her to admit defeat? Can it be that she shared with the putative cacique the delusion that somehow the major powers could be brought into the war on Paraguay's side? It must have been any one or more of these factors that compelled Eliza to drag herself and her sons along on this mad hegira.

As has been indicated, that legend about Madame Lynch going into battle on horseback is dismissible; Madame Lynch went "into battle" in a fairly well equipped carriage. Washburn, relying on accounts of those foreign observers who were on the scene to the bitter end, and whom he interviewed prior to completing his two-volume history, has written that throughout the year-long farce-tragedy one of López's "constant cares had been to provide that in no contingency should the means be wanting for supplying his own table. . . . During the latter part of the retreat, nearly all the carts and oxen left to him were employed in transporting the elegant camp, equipage and provisions, wines, and liquors that were intended only for the use of himself and Madame Lynch, and their joint progeny." (Alfredo d'Escragnolle Taunay, later one of Brazil's outstanding authors, was a captain in the cavalry force that overran López's capital at Piribebuy in August 1869. According to his memoirs, it was Taunay who discovered the Lynch-López wine cellar: "Unfortunately, the quantity of champagne was quite small." He also discovered a magnificently bound second volume of an edition of *Don Quijote*, and "many silver coins in the house.")

When the Duke of Caxias allowed him to escape at Lomas Valentinas, López had made his way to Cerro León (ironically, his original encampment at the outbreak of the war), along with Madame Lynch and their sons; those prisoners who had been unable to surrender to the Brazilians; that rather extraordinary wagon train containing his mother, sisters, and a few cast-off concubines; the remnants of López's Cabinet (including the aged and infirm Vice President Sánchez, who was forced to travel on shank's mare); the camp followers and female laborers; and a meager military escort of barely a thousand half-starved and ill-clad Guaranís. Carried along in the Lynch-López carriages, in addition to their wine cellar and other household amenities, were, of course, the national treasury and archives and the Church treasures. As Eliza had remarked on an earlier and less exigent occasion, "The seat of government is wherever you are, dear Francisco." *In toto*, it all resembled not so much a government in retreat as a broken-down troupe of vaudevillians striving to keep one step ahead of the sheriff.

The Duke of Caxias, after accepting the surrender of Asunción from its willing inhabitants and establishing a provisional government the nuclei of which were the anti-López exiles who had rushed up from Buenos Aires, returned home to accept the glory he had sought. But when Dom Pedro learned that López was still alive and obdurate about accepting the war's end, the Emperor ordered his son-in-law, the Comte d'Eu, to hurry on to Paraguay and end this nonsense once and for all time. (There was an irony, perhaps intended, in this appointment: the Comte d'Eu was the husband of Princess Isabella, whom Francisco Solano would have made his empress.)

At the end of January, learning that the Comte d'Eu was coming after him, López left 300 men at Cerro León and retreated farther into the Chaco, where he established his new capital at Piribebuy—a collection of whitewashed brick or stone houses laid out around a large square whose central feature was a church that dated back to 1767. López immediately ordered the village semicircled with deep trenches facing east, south, and west; to the north was the escape route. (López always left himself an escape route.)

Between February and August, the Marshal-President managed, incredibly, to patch together a new "army" of 13,000—boys of nine and ten, men of seventy and eighty, the wounded and the crippled, and even women of all ages and degrees of infirmity— and twenty-one pieces of artillery.

On August 12, 1869, at six-thirty in the morning, the Comte d'Eu attacked in force. Leaving behind a rear-guard force of 1,500—who were reduced to having to "fight" with stones, bottles, broken glass, and even, *in extremis*, clods of dirt—López and his caravan fled to the north. In his precipitous escape, the Marshal-President either forgot to take—or had perhaps lost—the national archives and treasury as well as the Church treasures, which are believed to have fallen into Brazilian hands. (Like the fabled loot of the Spanish galleons believed to lie on the floor of the Caribbean, legend persists that these treasures were buried along the route López and Eliza followed in their last flight, and that those who buried them went down with the treasures. To this day Paraguayans speak of *espíritus* who guard *los tesoros escondidos del Mariscal López y su Concubina*.)

Between the fall of Piribebuy and the following February, López & Company led a fugitive existence through the swamps of the Alta Paraná and Amambay regions, establishing and losing temporary capitals almost monthly: Caraguatay, San Estanislao, Curuguati, and then eastward to the heights of Panadero, always barely one step ahead of the oncoming Brazilians. General Correa da Cámarra had replaced the Emperor's son-in-law as chief of the posse (it is said that the Comte d'Eu considered the waging of a war on such terms as quite beneath his royal dignity). Early in 1870, Cámarra drove the fugitives across the Maracaju range, and on February 6 the Marshal-President established his latest (and last) capital at Cerro Corá on the banks of the Río Aquidaban, approximately two hundred miles north of Asunción near the Bolivian frontier. His total resources: 1,200 "men" and six pieces of artillery, and a decimated battalion of female laborers.

On March 1, 1870, the Brazilians attacked. When López learned that their cavalry, personally led by General da Cámarra, had broken through the pass which guarded the entrance to his cave-headquarters, he ordered the remnants of his "army" to form a human wall to keep back the invaders, and then hauled himself onto his horse and tried to effect an escape into the jungles of the Matto Grosso.

It was now everyone for himself.

In the confusion that accompanied the overrunning of the camp by the Brazilians, López managed to flee into the woods behind Cerro Corá and start across the Aquidaban; unfortunately, the river at this season was little more than a broad marshy brook, and López's horse floundered and became stuck in the mire. López dismounted and straggled back to the river bank—and practically into the arms of Cámarra. The Brazilian commander called out to his soldiers to disarm López, not to kill him. As a cavalryman—one Chico Diablo—moved forward to obey his commander's orders, López drew his revolver and was about to shoot Cámarra; Chico Diablo, in the words of one observer, "thrust at the tyrant with a lance and he fell headforemost into the muddy stream. But he instantly scrambled up, and was upon his knees when he was hit by a shot from an unknown hand [some chroniclers believe it may have been a Paraguayan hand] and fell again in the mud, and there he expired. His last words were: 'I die with my country!' "

López's mother and sisters, whom he had condemned to death barely hours before the Brazilians penetrated his defenses, surrendered themselves to Cámarra. (Sánchez and the remnants of the "Government" were killed by enemy cavalry as they sought to flee across the Aquidaban on foot.) Cámarra brought the López Ladies over to view the remains of their son and brother upon which maggots and other swamp creatures were commencing to indulge themselves in an orgy of feasting. Mother López, her back and shoulders raw from the fresh scars caused by the blows of the double lasso inflicted at her first-born son's orders, stared down upon the carcass in an attitude of maternal affection and sorrow. Her daughters, however, were less forgiving. As the two "looked unmoved" upon their brother's corpse Doña Rafaela said to the sorrowing Doña Juana, "Mother, why do you weep? He was no son, no brother; he was a monster!"

When the Brazilians broke through, Madame Lynch had rushed to her carriage, "which was always kept ready for such an emergency," and attempted to flee with her younger sons, escorted by a few ragged boy soldiers under the command of the sixteen-year-old Pancho. They were overtaken by a Brazilian cavalry detachment, and Pancho was ordered to surrender; as the cavalry officer turned to give an order, Pancho lunged at him, whereupon one of the Brazilians ran him through with a lance.

General Cámarra personally led Madame to the spot where her Friend lay, at the same time posting a guard to protect her: had they been permitted to do so, the Paraguayan women would have fallen upon her and, in the words of one chronicler, "stripped her of the elegant furs and rich jewels she still wore, and thrust her mutilated body into the Aquidabán, to become food for the alligators." Cámarra generously acceded to Eliza's request that she be allowed to give Francisco and their eldest son the semblance of a decent burial.

Using only their hands and bits of stick, Eliza and her remaining sons scraped out a shallow grave into which the bodies were shoved, and then placed some heavy stones upon them—a futile attempt to ward off the wild beasts who circled the perimeter awaiting the departure of the humans so that they might be permitted to feast freely on the remains. As soon as the surviving Paraguayans in the encampment realized that the tyrant was truly dead, they broke out into an ear-shattering cacophony of joy. Observers to the scene claim that it was necessary for Cámarra to post sentinels around López's makeshift grave to prevent the women from further defiling the remains of the Marshal-President.

When word was received at Asunción that López was no more, a great ball was held to celebrate his demise. (The present writer was shown one of the original invitations by a Lynch-López grandson who remarked bitterly, "How could people who would celebrate so callously the glorious death of a great hero, the greatest hero of our nation, pretend to call themselves Christians!")

It was the only ball in eight years that had not been arranged by Madame Lynch.

2

Eliza and her sons, along with the López Ladies, were marched to Concepción, the nearest port, where they were put aboard a Brazilian gunboat and taken to Asunción. No record survives of that melancholy journey, but it can be presumed that the López

Ladies steered a wide berth of Madame Lynch, for whom they entertained a hatred that, while justified, was nonetheless beyond the scope of human comprehension.

At Asunción, López's mother and sisters, after a few days of surveillance, were permitted to return to their homes. Madame Lynch and her sons, however, were detained as prisoners aboard the Brazilian gunboat—for their own safety. The Ladies of Asunción who had survived the war were all but maniacal in their eagerness to wreak vengeance upon the woman who had spent the better part of a decade wreaking vengeance upon them. When the Brazilian authorities refused to surrender Eliza to the Provisional Government, which demanded that she be bound over for trial by tribunal—surely an act of mercy on the part of her captors, who realized Eliza would probably not have survived long enough to stand trial—the Ladies drew up a formal petition in which they claimed to have been forced to surrender their money and jewels "under the pretense that they were for the defense of their country"; charged Madame Lynch as an accessory before the fact in the wanton murder of their husbands, brothers, fathers, and sons; and begged "that she might not be permitted to leave the country and carry away the property of which they had been robbed to spend in other countries."

Indubitably out of some sense of chivalry—there is no evidence that they were bribed—the Brazilian authorities rejected the petition. The gunboat sailed for Buenos Aires, where Madame Lynch and her four surviving sons were put aboard a ship for Europe.

When Eliza Lynch first came from the Old World to the New, she had had six weeks on the Atlantic in which to contemplate a glorious future. Now as the ship bearing her began its slow trek from the New World back to the Old, Eliza Lynch would have six weeks in which to reflect on a disastrous past.

The forty-four-year-old "emperor" was dead, the thirty-five-year-old "empress" was headed into exile, and the stillborn "empire" now lay in total ruin, its economy devastated, its population decimated. The two races that made up the Paraguayan strain—the Spanish and the mestizo descendants of the early colonials, and the Guaraní Indians—had been all but obliterated. A nation that had boasted a prewar population of 525,000 had been reduced to a nation of 221,000 war-weary, emaciated, hate-filled, and miserable human beings—of whom a mere 28,700 were males, most of them under the age of eight or over the age of eighty.*

When the protesting survivors at Asunción saw the gunboat bearing Madame Lynch weigh anchor and move downriver toward Buenos Aires, they assumed they were through, once and for all time, with the Irish Concubine.

But the Irish Concubine was not through with them. . . .

---

* Some historians claim the prewar population at more than a million, and have revised upward the statistics on losses and survivors correspondingly. The figure of 525,000 has been corroborated by prewar census records which somehow managed to survive.

PART THREE

THE SURVIVOR

The Litigant

Of all the myths surrounding Madame Lynch to which her partisans cling most tenaciously, the one most easily exploded is that she left Paraguay as a pauper. The more reliable (and conservative) estimates place at approximately $500,000 the value in jewels and specie she had managed to ship out to her Paris banker, Antoine Gelot, prior to the Brazilian capture of the port of Angostura.

But the fall of that port had not stopped Eliza. Having cultivated the admiration of not only the American Minister (McMahon) but also the Italian Consul, she had had them carry out in their baggage, and deposit in the Bank of England for her reclamation, more than four thousand ounces of gold (value approximately sixteen dollars an ounce).* It is believed that the envoys delivered the monies as promised; at least, there is no evidence that Eliza had to take either of them into court—although there is a strong suspicion, admittedly unsupportable historically, that McMahon deducted a handsome "commission" for his efforts.

Also in the custody of Gelot was a tidy sum which López had

---

* Also taken out by McMahon, according to captured documents, were "500 ounces more to be delivered to Emiliano"—López's first-born son by the ill-fated Juana Pesoa, who was at the time serving abroad in Paris in his father's legation. He returned to Paraguay around 1876 in order to press his claim as a López heir, but died shortly thereafter from a pulmonary infection.

shipped out late in 1868, to be deposited to Eliza's account in case he could not appear on the scene to claim the money in person. And then there was that real estate which López had willed to her, plus the parcels which Eliza had forced the Paraguayans to sell to her at deflated prices (and in exchange for worthless scrip), not to mention a cache of jewels and specie which she had been obliged to leave behind in the rapid evacuation of Asunción (or so she would have us believe) and which she maintained was hers as López's testamentary heiress.

Mention should also be made of the booty Eliza carried with her. It is true that in their frenzy of relief at the death of López, the surviving women at Cerro Corá had fallen upon Madame Lynch's wagon and seized her gowns and silver plate. But in the confusion, Madame had managed to hold on to a large casket which she guarded as zealously as would a true believer guard a nail from the True Cross. On March 21, 1870, aboard the Brazilian gunboat *Princeza*, which had brought her from Concepción to Asunción, the contents of the casket—which she was permitted to keep—were inventoried by the Brazilian authorities.

The inventory is worth taking note of, if only to demonstrate Madame Lynch's eclecticism as a collector. In addition to "6 bars of gold," a variegated collection of specie ranging from 14,000 worthless dollars ("paper of the Republic of Paraguay") to 391 ounces of gold, and the two promissory notes signed by the American and Italian diplomats, the casket contained:

55 assorted pieces of valuable jewelry (including 40 gold rings)
23 valuable buttons (including "5 of gold for waistcoat and 6 of gold for cuffs")
16 bracelets ("including 2 of human hair")
10 pairs of earrings
 1 gold diadem
20 watch guards and chains
11 gold watches (including 9 men's)

6 *bombillas* "for the taking of *yerba maté*" trimmed in gold
5 *maté tubos* (spoon straws) made of silver
4 head combs (3 in gold, 1 in diamonds—presumably "sub-scribed" by a few of the more successful Asunción whores whose soubriquet, *peinetas de oro*, derived from the golden combs they wore as a badge of their profession)
1 crucifix and 2 rosaries "of gold and coral"
1 "commander of the order of Christ, and a pendant of the same order worked in gold and diamonds"

There was more. Thanks to the Brazilians who guarded her so chivalrously when it became apparent that the frenzied mob at Cerro Corá was set on stripping her to the bones, literally, Eliza had managed to salvage "19 sets of children's toys (including 12 of gold of different tastes)" and some remembrances of the dead Marshal: 1 gold cigar holder, 2 gold snuff boxes, 2 albums (1 of gold, raised by national subscription; the other of mother-of-pearl, awarded him by the people of Buenos Aires when he "settled the Argentine civil war" in the 1850s), 1 tube "containing rosaries of gold chains" (which may have been filched by López, or perhaps Eliza, from his devout mother), López's diamond-encrusted mar-shal's baton, and "1 whip with the initials F.S.L. in diamonds."

The inventory concluded with "1 box" belonging to Rosita Carreras (one of López's love children, whom Eliza had either taken under her protection or hired on as a servant, depending on which sources are to be believed) containing "51 pieces of jewelry and 7 pairs of toys of gold and topaz." (According to Eliza's daughter-in-law Maud Lloyd López Rancia in a letter to author William Barrett sometime prior to her death at the outbreak of World War II, when Eliza learned that the Carreras girl "born to one of her rivals, was being raised in poverty," she "brought the girl to Europe and raised her as her own daughter, providing an education equal to that which she gave to her own sons." Maud also wrote that she knew Eliza "intimately in London" at the time of her marriage to Enrique, whom she subsequently divorced. Since Maud married Enrique in London in 1885, more than a decade after Eliza had decamped that city never to return, and has followed through on the unfounded legend that Eliza was buried as a pauper, Maud's *Recuerdos de mi Suegra* [*Memories of my Mother-in-Law*], published posthumously, are not above suspicion. Incidentally, it is the contention of the Lynch-López descendants that Maud's granddaughter, Alicia, became the first United States Senator from Alaska. When advised by the present writer that records both in Washington and Juneau fail to support this extraordinary contention, Jorge Manuel Solano López, the family historian, replied most courteously, "Forgive me, Señor Brodsky, but the American authorities are in error.")

Madame Lynch arrived back in France with her booty and her party of ten (four sons, the Carreras girl, and a quintet of servants) sometime toward the end of May. It was only then that the thirty-five-year-old exile learned of the change that had come over the beloved city from which she had departed sixteen years before, presumably to live and die as an empress-consort. Baron Haussmann had miraculously transformed the once slumlike Paris into the city of *son et lumière;* but the miracles Haussmann had worked were as nothing when compared to the miracles that other master builder, Bismarck, was working. Having outrageously gulled France into a war she could not possibly win, through no less a device than a forged telegram, the Iron Duke was now in the midst of completing the unification of Germany and the destruction of the Second Empire—a destruction that would be finalized the following September at Sedan when López's "good friend" Emperor Louis Napoleon III would surrender his armies, and his consort would be forced to flee for her life. (Like Eliza, Eugénie appears to have provided well for her future; she lived on for fifty years in England, enjoying not only the luxuries but, as an adopted friend of Queen Victoria, the prerogatives of an empress.)

That other exiled "empress," Eliza Lynch, had looked forward to enrolling her sons in a proper French school. The boys were already familiar with the language (their parents are said to have conversed in French when *en famille*), although that seems to have been the extent of their education. (No records survive regarding the boys' schooling while in Paraguay; perhaps they were tutored at home by their mother.) But two factors militated against Eliza remaining on in France. First, the realization that, what with the war, it might be safer to place the boys in an English school. Second—and more urgent—the realization that, or so she claimed, Eliza had been bilked by a wily Scotsman in whom she had placed much of her trust and a healthy amount of her wartime gleanings.

While Eliza would have been dismayed at the turn in the Empire's political fortunes, she must have been outraged beyond measure at the turn in her personal fortunes. For on arriving in Paris she was advised by Monsieur Gelot that when he, in his capacity as her and López's European representative, had gone to claim some of the monies which Dr. William Stewart had allegedly agreed to send out of Paraguay for them, payment had been stopped.

Pausing barely long enough to provide herself and children, and, one would hope, her servants, with wardrobes, Eliza led her entourage across the Channel. After entering the three older boys at either the Saint Joseph College, a private academy in the London suburb of Croydon, or an unnamed school in Richmond (sources are unagreed on this point), Eliza engaged a solicitor. On July 30, William Mason "signeted" on his client's behalf two summonses against Stewart in the Edinburgh courts.

Thus began a period of more than a year during the course of which Madame Lynch would be bogged down in attempts to reclaim two fortunes, totaling (allegedly) close to $200,000, which may or may not have been rightfully hers, depending on whose testimony is to be believed. Known respectively as the Yerba Case and the Specie Case, the two actions would prove to be the most frustrating experiences in Eliza's event-filled life to date.

2

Neither the plaintiff (or, to use the court parlance, "pursuer"), Eliza, nor the "defender," Stewart, appeared in court; indeed, neither appeared in Edinburgh.

Stewart, who was being sued *in absentia*, is referred to in the summonses as "sometime residing in Paraguay, thereafter in Edinburgh, and now or lately residing furth [*sic*] of Scotland (but whose place of residence is unknown to the pursuer)." He had, or so he informed the court through his solicitor, been captured at the end of 1868, when one of López's many "national capitals" was overrun by the Brazilians, and subsequently released as a national of a neutral power. (Eliza informed the court through *her* solicitor that Stewart had "willfully surrendered to the Brazilians," a charge that is decidedly more credible than the fantastic charge made by one of her more ardent chroniclers to the effect that Stewart had "capped his desertion from the [Paraguayan] army by tricking Colonel Thompson into his surrender of Angostura.")

The doctor could well have been in London when the summonses were issued, for it is known that around this period he met there with Washburn. The former American Minister to Paraguay had made a quick trip to the British capital in order to take a sworn deposition from Stewart and enlist him as a witness (*in absentia*) on his behalf for the aforementioned "trial" Washburn was about to undergo in the House of Representatives. (It is only questionable as to whether Washburn had succeeded in bringing out of Paraguay a fortune belonging to Stewart and his wife which had been left for safekeeping in the American Legation. Against the claim made by Stewart that the fortune had been left behind, and had fallen into López's hands, is the contention made by some Washburn critics, ergo Lynch loyalists, that Washburn not only succeeded in getting the treasure out of Paraguay but had brought it to Paris—and used it to "purchase" Stewart's favorable testimony in his support at the upcoming Congressional hearings. To be sure, Washburn denied the charge. Perhaps it was an honest denial.)

Eliza had decided to remain in London throughout the litigation —to avoid the hazards of Edinburgh's unpredictable clime, to be near her children, and, presumably, to spare being publicly humiliated by the "vile words of mendacity" which she must have known Stewart would introduce into evidence in his defense. (Whether some of Stewart's charges were truly mendacious is only questionable, though they were certainly "vile.") Thus the charges, denials, and countercharges (and counterdenials) were carried on through sworn depositions; and if these depositions suggest nothing else, they suggest that neither Pursuer nor Defender felt particularly averse to lying under oath.

A native of Perthshire, Scotland, and qualifying as an M.D. in 1852, William Stewart practiced general medicine for two years in Argyllshire before volunteering to serve eighteen months in Her Majesty's Service during the Crimean War. At war's end he went out to the Argentine province of Corrientes in charge of a boatload of colonists sent by the British Government. When the colony failed, Stewart made a visit to Paraguay; his fiercest detractors (that is, Eliza's staunchest defenders) maintain that he arrived in Asunción as a penniless vagrant, which is rather difficult to accept on faith. Had that been the case, it is doubtful that he could have so ingratiated himself with the Anglophobic young Minister of War and Hero of the Corrientes, Francisco Solano López.

For ingratiate himself Stewart did. In March 1857, Francisco prevailed upon his father, the old President-Dictator Carlos Antonio, to appoint Stewart Surgeon to the Government of the Republic. Five years later, upon his friend's accession to the presidency, the doctor became Senior Medical Officer in the Paraguayan Army. He was also personal physician to López, Eliza, their sons, and the entire court. He organized a school of medicine at Asunción and was, at a salary of eight hundred pounds sterling per annum, the highest-paid foreigner in López's service.

From letters and other accounts of the period, we learn that Stewart was one of the Lynch-López favorites; he must have shared their sumptuous table as often as did that other Court Favorite, Baron von Wisner. If, as Stewart swore on oath, López, as a concomitant of his mounting xenophobia when the war began to go sour, fell into the habit of failing to pay his salary with any sense of regularity, this probably posed less a problem of finances than a matter of principle. Stewart had by then married one of the few legitimate Paraguayan heiresses (that is, one not a member of the López family), whose dowry included cattle ranches and other estates in the interior plus some select parcels of real estate in Asunción proper.

In September 1865, finding himself pressed for cash and unable to carry on any semblance of international trade, López requested Stewart to export on his behalf a large quantity of *yerba maté* for sale on the Buenos Aires market. Stewart's brother, George Drummond—a merchant residing in the Argentine capital, and not, as the pro-Lynch chroniclers maintain, a director of the Royal Bank of Scotland whose God-given role in this life was that of Eliza's nemesis—was assigned as broker on the deal.

Stewart claimed that the *yerba* was a personal gift; Eliza counterclaimed that the proceeds of the sale—it was estimated that the crop would fetch upwards of $112,000 on the open market—had been intended by López to be set aside for her and their children against any future exigency. As proof, she had her solicitor introduce into evidence a letter from Stewart to his brother, dated January 17, 1867—two years after the tea had been shipped out of Paraguay—assigning Eliza as recipient of the proceeds of the sale. Thus the Yerba Case.

Also introduced as evidence was a letter from Stewart to Eliza, dated October 17, 1868, acknowledging that $70,000 in gold coins which Stewart had sent out to Scotland on an Italian merchant ship was rightfully hers. ("The defender undertook to transmit the said specie to this country, to lodge the proceeds thereof in the Royal Bank of Scotland in his own name, and to hold the same for behoof, and on account of the pursuer, until the amount should be restored to her.") Thus the Specie Case.

Stewart did not deny writing the letters. Rather, he maintained that Eliza had coerced him into doing so "under force and fear . . . that if he had refused," Eliza "would have used her influence with López to have had him tortured or executed for some pretended offence." Perhaps. But militating against Stewart's probity are the various tactical maneuvers to which he resorted in order to uphold his defense. These ranged from the technical charge of *forum non competens* (that is, that the cases could be tried only in the Paraguayan courts), which was thrown out by the Scottish magistrate, to the charge that Eliza had no right to sue: she was a married woman, and the funds she was attempting to reclaim belonged by law to her husband, Xavier Quatrefages. (It was then that Eliza's solicitors introduced the aforementioned power of attorney granted her by Quatrefages, and a reiteration of that power of attorney, dated December 7, 1870, wherein Quatrefages, by now happily married and the father of a grown brood, eagerly asseverated that he wanted no part of the action.)

When these ploys, and a few others even more audacious, failed, Stewart had introduced into evidence a decree by the Paraguayan Provisional Government, dated May 4, 1870, embargoing all of Madame Lynch's assets in Paraguay, declaring that both she and her Friend had stolen any and all monies and property on which she might make any future claim, and setting aside López's will; and a decree assigning Stewart the proceeds of the *yerba* sale as compensation for back salary owed him by López and compensation for Mrs. Stewart's estates which López had allegedly "confiscated." Also introduced by Stewart's solicitors was a long statement by Manuel Antonio Maciel, López's private secretary throughout most of the war, in which Eliza and Francisco are portrayed in a less than desirable light (a portrayal which

Eliza subsequently tried to rebut through a series of hysterical letters in the Buenos Aires press).

In August 1871, after much deliberation, a special jury agreed that, as regarded the Specie Case, Stewart had indeed been coerced into signing the promissory note. However, the court—either out of compassion for the Pursuer or out of suspicion of the Defender—denied the jury's decision and suspended resolution of the matter until Eliza could produce fresh evidence to the contrary. Since this proved impossible, she was compelled to drop the case. As for the Yerba Case, the court concluded that Eliza, as López's rightful heir, that proclamation of the Paraguayan Provisional Government to the contrary, was entitled to what remained after, as Stewart swore, avaricious customs officials at Buenos Aires and transmitting agents in England had deducted what was probably more than their fair share of the proceeds.

But Eliza's victory was a pyrrhic one. After swearing in deposition that the net proceeds of the *yerba* sale amounted to considerably less than what was owed him by López in back pay, Stewart filed for bankruptcy. (Concurrent with her suits of reclamation against Stewart, Eliza had, as a British subject, initiated litigation aimed at having the Provisional Paraguayan Government's abrogation of López's will set aside; involved were considerable sums in British banks which López had shipped abroad years before in his own name. These sums, argued the Paraguayan Government's Scottish solicitor, were "by the now existing law of Paraguay" the property of that government. In a landmark decision, the Edinburgh Court of Probate and Divorce ruled, on June 20, 1871, that "the succession to property in England of a deceased foreigner is regulated by the law of his place of domicile as it existed at the time of his death . . . and, therefore, that the Government of Paraguay had no *locus standi* to contest the validity of the will." But for Eliza the decision was an academic one. Since no one could determine precisely *what* the law was during López's reign, and since she could not prove to the court's satisfaction that López's will had been validly executed, Eliza was compelled to settle for yet another pyrrhic victory.)

Madame Lynch's failure to gain acceptance by the Paraguayan ruling class had, as has been demonstrated, triggered in her a transmogrification from a *soi-disant* inordinately altruistic pseudo-missionary into an assumedly avaricious schemer bent on seeking what she considered to be only fair and just compensation for myriad wrongs unjustifiably inflicted upon her. Now, having met with material failure in the British courts, she underwent still another metamorphosis.

She became, in her eyes, a pitiable widow who must—if need be, to her dying moment—fight to regain not only her own good name (and those of her children and dead "husband") but the inheritance that she considered hers by both moral and juridical law but which was being denied her by "satanic forces." It was a role she played to the hilt; and if she failed to convince the world at large that she was the innocent victim of a gross miscarriage of justice, it was not for her want of trying. God knows she managed to convince herself—as well as so many of her partisan chroniclers down through the years, all of whom approach, and quote from as gospel, the *Exposición y Protesta* with a fervor equal to that with which Church hierarchs approach, and quote from, the Revelation of St. John the Divine.

Stewart eventually returned to Paraguay, where he went on to build up the great fortune which survives, in a somewhat vitiated state, to this day—a fortune which the Lynch-López descendants regard as rightfully theirs, through periodic claims which the Stewart heirs dismiss as, in the words of one of their number, "perpetual aberration." As for the wronged Pursuer, she remained on in London—preparing herself for the onslaught she was determined to launch against the Paraguayan Government on its own ground.

Cunninghame-Graham has written that as a young child he saw her "several times in London in 1873 or 1874, getting into her carriage at a house she had, I think, in Thurloe Square or Hyde Park Gate." (A fact that is unsupportable by census records, which has led some biographers to conclude that she was by then back in Paris. But since the evidence that Eliza was in London at the time is overwhelming, it is quite probable that she lived there under an alias. Also, there is no evidence that she made any attempts to contact survivors of her immediate family, providing there were any; nor is there any evidence that, as still others maintain, she made a sentimental pilgrimage to Ireland.)

"She was then," Cunninghame-Graham continues, "apparently about forty years of age, of middle height, well made, beginning to put on a little flesh, with her abundant hair just flecked with grey." Then revealing a staunch English prejudice, he goes on to report that "in her well-made Parisian clothes, she looked more French than English, and had no touch of that untidiness that so often marks the Irishwoman. She was still handsome and distinguished-looking [an evaluation substantiated by a surviving photograph of Eliza dating from this period]. Her face was oval, if I remember rightly, and her appearance certainly did not seem that of one who had looked death so often in the face, lived for so long in circumstances so strange and terrifying, buried her lover and her son [Pancho] with her own hands and lived to tell the tale." (She had also buried by then her youngest surviving son, Leopoldo Antonio, whose congenital malaria, according to the Lynch-López family history, "had debilitated him to the point where he was unable to tolerate the inclemencies of the London climate.")

It is probable that Cunninghame-Graham saw her in 1873 at the latest, for by 1874 Eliza was back in Paris; this time she was having her problems with the French Government.

Prior to leaving Asunción ahead of the invading Allies, Eliza had granted power of attorney to her French lawyer in Paraguay, one Edmon Berchon des Essart, in whose safe she had deposited the bulk of her "proof" that the property she had cadged from the Paraguayans in the period predating the fall of the capital city had come by her through honest negotiation. (Eliza claims in the *Exposición y Protesta* that the "only reason" she bought the property was because López's brother Benigno had put his own holdings on the market, thus stampeding the citizens into fearing that "the war was about to end in a manner fatal to Paraguay"; she then went on a property-buying binge in order "to avert a panic" by showing that if Madame Lynch was investing in real estate, then surely the war would be won by Mariscal López. Too, she insisted most urgently that "the only properties I bought are those situated near the Palace, because I wanted to build high buildings with shops." Suffice it to say, there is no evidence to support Eliza's further and even more absurd contention that "when I was a Brazilian prisoner in Asunción Harbor, I offered to return the titles of all properties, provided those who had sold me them would give me back my money, but this they refused, because they wanted to keep the property *and* the money.")

Though the Paraguayan Government had, in addition to embargoing all her assets in the country, nullified the deeds, Eliza was convinced that if she were to produce the "proof" which she had left with Des Essart, her claims would be upheld; that even in a Paraguayan court, her good name (not to mention that of her dead Friend) would be vindicated; the world would be brought to realize that she was in fact an innocent victim of "base calumnies" put abroad by "heartless men in power and authority" who were incapable of experiencing compassion for "a pathetic, wronged lady of virtue and probity."

To hear Eliza tell it, God Almighty knew that she was "a defenseless woman" totally at the mercy of "malicious multitudes" who had "repaid the countless kindnesses I have always shown toward these unfortunate people" by "castigating scurrilously my good name, and that of my innocent children, sons of the Hero of the Nation, and trying to deprive me of all that which is legally mine."

But Eliza was pragmatic enough to realize that God Almighty would not be able to take the witness stand in her defense. Nor, for that matter, would Monsieur des Essart. While involved in her litigation against Stewart, Eliza received the disturbing news that the French attorney had been assassinated—to her way of thinking, by a crazed Paraguayan mob intent on precluding her "vindication" by destroying the land deeds, the "proof." Luckily for Eliza, however, the French consul at Asunción had managed to prevent the looting of Des Essart's house; but since everything on the premises was technically the possession of a French subject, the papers in question were sent back to France. After communicating through the mails for a year or so with French authorities, and meeting with no success, Eliza crossed over to Paris early in 1874 to retrieve her papers in person.

Surely anyone who has ever become entangled in French bureaucracy can empathize with Madame Lynch in her frantic attempt to recover those papers. To compound matters, she was now a total stranger in this city where less than a generation before she had been hailed up and down the boulevards as the foremost "instructress in languages." Perhaps if some of Eliza's former "students" were still around, doors might have opened more quickly, bureaucratic heads would have risen from bureaucratic somnolence more readily. But, alas, she was, in her own words, "alone, without power, and with my bosom open to the poniard." That Eliza succeeded within the comparatively brief period of one year to recover what was legitimately hers is testimony both to the energy she expended and the money she expended. By the spring of 1875, having raised considerably the income of a brace of Parisian lawyers, Madame Lynch, her "bosom" still "open to the poniard," was ready to return to Paraguay in order to recover what she considered to be rightfully hers and her children's.

Spurring her on—not that Madame Lynch needed much spurring—was a letter she had received from the new (rather, the latest) President of the Republic, dated March 23, 1874, and urging that "it is convenient for you and your interests that you come as soon as possible." Or so Eliza would have us believe.

3

The six-year occupation of Paraguay saw that pathetic, prostrate nation caught up in a cat-and-mouse game between the two major powers, Brazil and Argentina. Each hated the other; both involved themselves in Paraguay's pitiful attempts at political and economic reconstruction to serve their own ends. Each feared the other was attempting to absorb Paraguay territorially; both probably were. Undoubtedly what saved Paraguay from total extinction as an independent nation was the animosity that prevailed between the two conquering powers. (The Brazilians, who were the major occupying force, are said to have fomented insurrections in Argentina and Uruguay in order to keep their quondam allies bogged down and out of Paraguayan affairs.)

Following the adoption of a revised constitution, Cirilo Rivarola had been named President on November 25, 1870. A fierce anti-Lópezian (it was Rivarola who signed the decree embargoing all of Madame Lynch's holdings in Paraguay and setting aside López's will), Rivarola was a pro-Argentinian and a political naïf. He was greatly influenced by his minister of finance, Juan Bautista Gill, a politically ambitious schemer and a Brazilian tool. After being formally charged by the Senate with misappropriating national funds (a charge that had merit), Gill proved his political acumen by forcing Rivarola to resign (1871) and to be succeeded, as the Constitution demanded, by his vice president, Salvador Jovellanos, who was totally subservient to Gill. Within three years Rivarola had been assassinated, Jovellanos had been deposed, treaties had been signed with all of the Allied powers (the called-for indemnities were never paid; Paraguay was in total bankruptcy), and Gill, who had been forced into political exile in Brazil, was now back at Asunción and in the presidency.*

Did Gill, in inviting Eliza back to press her claims as López's heiress, hope to "capture" her, as it were, and get his hands on those land deeds? Or were his letters of invitation simply forgeries on Eliza's part, to give some semblance of legitimacy to her return? We shall never know. Gill was himself assassinated a year after he took office; nowhere among his personal papers was there discovered any evidence as to why he might have urged Eliza to "come as soon as possible"—if indeed he had.

Accompanied by her eldest son, Enrique, Eliza arrived at Rio de Janeiro during the week of June 17, 1875, aboard the Royal Mail packet *City of Limerick*. (There appears to be no foundation for the claim advanced by many that Eliza's youngest surviving son, Carlos, also accompanied her; those who maintain that he did are, perhaps predictably, the same chroniclers who seem to have been unaware of the existence of that third surviving son, Federico Noel.) A month later she was in Buenos Aires—and either being received as befitted her position as the maligned widow of a great South American patriot, or tied up in still further litigation, depending on which sources are to be believed.

Henry Lyon Young, who can be said to reflect the non-litigious school, writes that "she found she was not forgotten and was taken to see a play based on the story of her life, entitled *Madame Lynch*." Barrett, on the other hand, who has established his credentials as the leader of the loyal opposition

---

* In terms of stability, the politically immature Paraguay would appear to have fared better as a dictatorship than as a democracy. In its first fifty-six years of independence, the nation was led by only three men (Francia and the two Lópezes). Between 1870 and 1954, when the incumbent dictator, Alfredo Stroessner, seized power, the country was subjected to forty-one chief executives, which means that on the average each served out little more than one half of his constitutionally authorized four-year term. In one year alone, 1949, no less than three men took the oath of office—a record which even postwar Italy has yet to beat.

to Madame Lynch's detractors, and who has drawn in equal doses
on historical evidence (liberally interpreted) and liberal imagination (historically unsupported), writes that Eliza

> found South America filled with the writings of pamphleteers
> who had drawn heavily upon Washburn and Masterman and
> Porter Bliss for their material. The old pre-war gossip of her
> early days in Asunción was revived in these books and pam-
> phlets as were the atrocity tales of the propagandists during the
> war. Her anger was stirred and she fought. She entered a dozen
> or more suits for slander and for defamation of character. The
> lawyers gathered around Ella Lynch and when she won her claim
> against the Argentinian government, attorney fees took all of
> the settlement except a few dollars which she spent on a trip to
> Asunción.

For the record, the only litigation of which evidence has survived was Eliza's suit against the Argentine Government, wherein
she charged that her furniture was "adorning the rooms of the
National Government building." Far from having "won her
claim," Eliza suffered the indignity of seeing it laughed out of
court (though this would not necessarily indicate that the Argentinians had *not* in fact looted her Asunción homes). "Unable
up to the present moment to obtain a resolution proving that the
furnishings were indeed my own," as she wrote in the *Exposición
y Protesta*, Eliza "decided not to stay any longer in Buenos Aires
and to go to Asunción." She was prepared—nay, eager—"to
answer the charges made against me, to confront all my enemies
at the very arena of their power, having no other support than
that of my conscience, and that of my acts."

When this intention became known—Eliza seems to have gone
out of her way to make sure that the readers of the Buenos
Aires press were dutifully apprised of all her comings and
goings—an anonymous letter appeared in the September 26 issue
of *La Tribuna* (the leading Buenos Aires newspaper) to the
effect that she dare not enter Paraguay lest she be "kidnapped

and tortured to tell where the wealth of Paraguay's treasure was buried." Or so she has written.

On October 11, Eliza and Enrique and her Guaraní servants boarded the *Cisne* for the upriver journey to Asunción, where they arrived a week later. Even Eliza must have been appalled by the transformation that had overtaken this once paradisiacal land whose leadership she had eagerly anticipated sharing with an uncouth lover who had transported her here twenty-one years before (though it is extremely doubtful that Eliza could have considered herself in any way responsible, however remote, for that transformation). Alberto Amerlan, a sort of Germanic Sir Richard Burton, who visited Paraguay during this period which Professor Warren has aptly described as "those days of despair," found that "poverty, want and corruption now reign. . . . Outcasts, tramps and adventurers corrupted with vices, the scum of humanity . . . removed here after the termination of the war, to appropriate to themselves the estates of the perished Guaranís and to console the hundreds of thousands of bereaved widows and maidens, over their losses."

Thanks to Eliza, those widows and maidens found amelioration, however transitory, in their bereavement; that is, according to Eliza's recounting of events. For when the word spread that "Madame Lynch has returned, Madame Lynch has returned!" she was, in her own words, "received at dockside by Paraguayan women who almost drowned me with affectionate embraces. The quay was literally infested with people, and all of them, without exception, saluted me kindly." As she walked along to the custom house, the Madame was "surrounded by people who embraced me, kissed and shook my hands; all of them wanted to touch me and talk to me, and everybody greeted me kindly. As we walked along the streets, people in their doorways recognized me and greeted me kindly. The merchants in the San Francisco Square surrounded me with expressions of happiness and affection and joined in my procession . . ."

And on and on it goes. In rhapsodic passages that summon to

mind some fictive recounting of the Resurrection by a pious purveyor of penny dreadfuls, Eliza recalls how the entire populace struggled cacophonously to touch her fingers, kiss her skirts, and otherwise accord her the sort of homage that might be paid a saint returned to earth.

After making her way to the home of one of her former courtiers, Eliza sorted out her *papeles de prueba* and awaited the anticipated invitation from President Gill to drop by at the Palace with those "papers of proof" and, over a cup of tea, to chat about Madame's suit to regain her status as her Friend's heir. Instead, what came from President Gill was an invitation to pack up her papers and leave Asunción on the next tide. And lest his invitation be in any way misinterpreted, the President sent a detachment of troops to escort Madame to the vessel which the Government had thoughtfully placed at her disposal.

It seems that on learning "Madame Lynch has returned, Madame Lynch has returned!" a group of the Ladies had hastily convened at the home of one of their number and drafted a petition to Gill. "In the name of the victims that the woman Eliza A. Lynch had sacrificed, we, their daughters, wives, mothers or sisters, using the rights that the Constitution gives us" demanded that Madame Lynch either be expelled from the country immediately or brought to trial on criminal charges. Possibly fearing that Eliza's deeds might hold up in court, but more probably wishing to be rid of what he quite properly considered to be *una irritación vengativa*, Gill opted for expulsion. Eliza remained convinced, to her dying day, that Gill had incited the Ladies into filing that petition—a conviction that is doubtful in the extreme.

A week later, Eliza and Enrique were back in Buenos Aires, where she divided her time between bombarding the newspapers with hysterical letters of justification and writing and having published her *Exposición y Protesta*. (Some sources claim that she failed to pay the printing costs for which she had contracted and was threatened with still another lawsuit.) She then signed over to Enrique all rights to her investments in Paraguay, urging him to press the fight for what was legally his as "the son of a great hero" and the "bearer of a great heritage," and sailed off to France—and yet another round of litigation.*

In 1876, the Paraguayan Government brought a suit of reclamation in the London court at Westminster against one James Currie of Leith for the sum of approximately $33,000 plus interest and court costs. Apparently Currie had acted as López's broker in some prewar business deal, quite possibly a sale of *yerba* or tobacco to offset some of his outstanding debts in London; the details were never established. The Paraguayan Government maintained that since anything belonging to López had been stolen from the people, the money was rightfully theirs.

Quite probably from Enrique, Eliza learned of the action against Currie, for in the following year she sent word to her London solicitor to enter her into the lists in her capacity as "administrator of the estate of the deceased Francisco Solano López, former President of Paraguay and also as an individual." Casting a plague on both their houses, Currie posted a small bond with the court, suggested that both "pursuers" fight it out among themselves, and disappeared. The Westminster magistrate adjudicated in Eliza's favor, and she was awarded the bond. Since Currie was a Scot, and, of more consequence, because the Scottish courts had already determined that Eliza was López's heiress, Eliza next sent her solicitor up to Edinburgh to reclaim the bulk of the money. Currie had disappeared, the Paraguayan Government refused to be bound by the decision of a foreign court, and as a consequence the case died.

---

* Enrique was subsequently joined by his brother Carlos, who came out to Buenos Aires upon completion of his schooling to assist in the chase of the Paraguayan Government through the Argentinian courts (where the López boys felt they stood a better chance). It was a futile chase.

The inflation that had wreaked havoc on the French economy in wake of the disastrous war with Prussia had cut into the fortune Eliza had laid aside in her Paris bank. There was still enough for her to get by on, on a regal scale. But instituting lawsuits costs money, and after all these pyrrhic victories, Eliza must surely have realized that if she kept up all this litigation much longer, she might well sue herself into poverty. Be that as it may, Eliza's days as a "Pursuer" were at an end.

According to the papers filed in the action against Currie, Eliza was living at Number 1 Avenue Ulrich, in the fashionable Seventeenth Arrondissement. Nine years later, according to her death certificate, she was living at Number 54 Boulevard Pereire, in the same fashionable part of town. Since 1 Avenue Ulrich was a private mansion, and 54 Boulevard Pereire a rather glorified rooming house for elderly ladies of limited means, the removal from the one to the other was less a change of address than a change of station in life. It is easier to suggest *why* Madame Lynch made the move (her funds had undoubtedly run low) than *when*. According to the Lynch-López family historian, Eliza refused to seek financial assistance from her children, especially Federico Noel, who was "a successful executive with the Paris telephone company," and "a typical Parisian boulevardier." When asked by the present writer if it was a matter of pride, he was told "*Quién sabe?*"

To be sure, many theories abound regarding how Madame Lynch spent the remaining years of her life—indeed, as many theories as there have been chroniclers of her life and style. And since, with the exception of the Paraguayan period, so little documentation has survived, no problems obtruded to preclude Madame Lynch's biographers from treating with her later years as they have treated with the earlier ones: passing off as "fact" whatever seemed to have struck their fancy. Did she truly spend her last years lapsing into terminal melancholia? (God knows she had enough to be melancholy about.) Did she really make that pilgrimage to the Holy Land as, in Cecilio Báez's words, *"una penitente"?* (She certainly had enough to feel penitent about.)

A careful perusal of newspapers dating from this period has failed to turn up Eliza's name, which would indicate strongly that she led a subdued life.

Nor is she mentioned in any of the countless books which chronicled the Paris of the late 1870s and early 1880s—which would indicate that a skeptical approach is warranted in light of the claims made by a number of biographers to the effect that she had resumed her pre-López activities as one of the shining luminaries in the worlds of art, music, and literature—the world of the salon. If, for instance, as has been contended, Franz Liszt, on again encountering Eliza a few years before their respective deaths, expressed his disappoinment that she had not followed his earlier advice and made a career on the concert stage, the encounter would have been conducted under the most guarded of circumstances. How else to explain that nowhere in the vast literature on Liszt is Eliza's name ever mentioned. It is possible that his biographers were as determined as the many biographers of that other titan of the age, Victor Hugo, not to sully the reputation of their subject by having it recorded for posterity that his life had been touched by the notorious Madame Lynch. It is more logical to assume that the two had never, in fact, enjoyed the opportunity of making the lady's acquaintance.

Obviously, the money Madame Lynch had set aside for her "exile" could not last indefinitely—especially in the hands of one such as she, who enjoyed much more than the basic amenities of living, not to mention a few of the headier luxuries. (She had been practically addicted to champagne, an addiction not easily shrugged off.) But while it lasted, Madame Lynch made the most of it. The house on Avenue Ulrich, which still stands, suggests strongly that its mistress could well have been a retiring lady who spent her mornings discussing the evening's menu with her housekeeper; her afternoons riding quietly in the Bois de Boulogne, weather permitting; her evenings entertaining a few select acquaintances at a quiet dinner, to be followed by a round or two of another of Eliza's addictions, whist.

At least it is safe to assume that Madame Lynch did not go out of her way to draw any attention to herself. Had she become so consumed with bitterness that she felt she could find some measure of surcease only in solitude—well-upholstered solitude? *Quién sabe?* Her descendants claim that she spent much of her time carrying on a one-way correspondence with the Paraguayan Government, attempting to set aside the embargo on her assets, and, more, attempting to "redeem her good name" and that of her dead lover. A careful check of Paraguayan archives has failed to bring to light any of these communications (though not to be dismissed is the possibility that any mail which came from either 1 Avenue Ulrich or 54 Boulevard Pereire was destroyed unanswered).

And then there is the theory, put forth by many historians but for which no evidence has come down, that after Eliza's funds ran out she went to work in a brothel: that toward the end of her life, Madame Lynch became Madam Lynch.

Admittedly, the charge cannot be proved; conversely, it cannot be *dis*proved.

A surviving formal portrait of Madame Lynch, purportedly taken in the closing years of her life, reveals that she had put on a considerable amount of weight and suggests that she had abandoned the habit of bedecking herself modishly in favor of austere gowns of subdued color. As in the few other photographs of her which survived, this presumably ultimate one shows its subject's eyes staring penetratingly, focusing not so much on the camera as on eternity. The mouth is slitted in a cryptic smile (perhaps smirk would be more apt). The hands, which seem to be embracing the tail end of a necklace, are cupped piously.

Who, in truth, is this bloated lady with the Gioconda smile

who stares out from this photograph? Is she a lady of gentility who has made her peace with the world? A lady prepared to die in the conviction that she was grossly maltreated and maligned by those seemingly omnipresent "satanic forces"? A lady who has plummeted from imperial heights to the indignity of having to work for a living within the milieu from which she had been rescued by a lunatic who would have made her an empress—a lady who, broadly speaking, has come full circle and is accepting her fate with equanimity?

Her defenders see Eliza Lynch as an embodiment of Christian virtue whose entire life was a sacrifice to a legion of enemies; her detractors see nothing more (and nothing less) than a nineteenth-century Agrippina. She was neither the one nor the other. But she did fall somewhere in the middle ground between the two extremes. As to where exactly—well, *Quién sabe?*

The Death of Madame Lynch

To quote from the Official History of the Lynch-López family (which as of this writing exists only in manuscript form):

Our sanctified grandmother, Madame Eliza Alicia Lynch-López, after being unwarrantedly asked to leave Paraguay by the treacherous Provisional Government in 1875, retired to Paris. There she lived on in genteel obscurity, struggling heroically to prove to the world that she and our sainted grandfather, Mariscal Francisco Solano López, the greatest Hero our country has ever known, had been calumniated beyond all comprehension and human decency by enemies both within and without the Republic. Her efforts were, alas, in vain. And only in the long sleep of Death was Madame Lynch to find a measure of surcease from her worldly woes, an easing of the sorrow she had carried with her as tenaciously as she had carried on the valiant struggle against the barbarian foe, a welcome escape from the litany of vilification that had been imposed upon her by satanic forces against which she, a God-fearing Christian but nevertheless a mortal soul, was powerless. She died in the knowledge that she had been wronged by her enemies as Joan of Arc had been wronged by her enemies. And like Joan of Arc, she died the death of a Martyr, content in the belief that History would vindicate her noble name, would restore her stolen reputation, and would enshrine her in the uppermost reaches of that region of Heaven reserved for the spiritual remains of the greatest women South America has ever known.

She may have died a martyr like Joan of Arc, but unlike the Maid of Orléans Eliza Lynch underwent her apotheosis without an audience. On July 27, 1886, at nine o'clock in the morning, police broke down the door of Madame's rooms at 54 Boulevard Pereire. Perhaps they had been summoned by her physician, or even Federico Noel, who had not seen her for a few days and was concerned; perhaps it was a kindly neighbor who had not seen Eliza about the premises of late; or perhaps, as some have claimed, the summoning agent was the noxious miasma that lingers on when the Angel of Death has come and gone unnoticed. In the event, the "sanctified grandmother's" remains were discovered, according to the *Minutes des actes de décès* now on file in the Mairie of the Seventeenth Arrondissement; also discovered was the fact that Madame Lynch had died two days previously—ironically, on what may well have been her Friend's sixtieth birthday. (Historians are unagreed as to whether López was born on the twenty-fourth or twenty-fifth of the month.)

If, as one might expect, there was a coroner's inquest, the records have not survived. According to the family historian, Jorge Manuel Solano López, the cause of death was "either malnutrition or stomach cancer, I am not sure which."

Interestingly enough—quite probably at the insistence of Federico Noel—Eliza was given in death the respectability she had never enjoyed in life: the death certificate refers to her as "the Widow of Francisco Solano López." Also of interest is the listing of the deceased's occupation—a necessary inclusion on all French death certificates. Whether out of some sense of delicacy on the part of the French authorities, or, again, at the insistence of son Federico—or even perhaps because it was the abject truth, those claims that Eliza died in dire poverty to the contrary—the Widow Lynch's occupation was listed as *rentière*. The word translates as "one who lives off investments."

Also militating against the widespread belief that Madame

Lynch died completely estranged from her children, that they did not learn of her passing until a few years after the event, and that she was buried as a ward of the municipality of Paris, is the following documentation, which has never been published in any of Eliza Lynch's biographies. On the day that his mother's body was discovered, Federico Noel, who was living at Number 4 Rue Chateaubriand, appeared at the Préfecture du Département de la Seine to make financial arrangements for the funeral, and to purchase, for four hundred francs, a Perpetual Concession for his mother in the Père Lachaise Cemetery. (He also paid the obligatory hundred francs *"en faveur des pauvres ou des hôpitaux"* of Paris.) A week later, after the appropriate number of Masses (paid for by Federico) had been celebrated to her memory, Madame Lynch was interred.

In this busy cemetery, as in many others, bodies are often buried in layers. Over the succeeding fourteen years the remains of six other individuals were interred atop those of Madame Lynch. The last to enjoy this honor was one Estelle Martín, who died on February 18, 1900, and whose family capped the seemingly crowded plot with a gigantic rectangular tombstone. Although the officials at Père Lachaise will not commit themselves on the matter, one is tempted to suspect that Eliza's sons decided to cut costs in memorializing their mother. Instead of erecting a monument to mark what they only assumed was to be her final resting place, they waited until the Martín family put up the four-foot-high marble slab, and then had inscribed along its northern side the legend *"Paz y Justicia."* Concurrently, they had affixed to the Martín tombstone a small marble plaque which bears the inscription (in Spanish):

Monument Erected
by
Enrique, Federico
and Carlos Solano López
To the Illustrious Memory
of their Always Beloved and Unforgettable Mother

Señor Doña Elisa Alicia
Lynch-López
Died 25 July 1886

In the early 1930's, when the "reconstruction" of Francisco Solano López was begun by the Paraguayan Government, replicas of the seal of Paraguay and the nation's flag were placed over the grave of the Widow Lynch-López.

The plaque erected by Eliza's sons, as well as the stone seal and flag of the nation over which she had set out to reign as empress-consort, remain to this day at Père Lachaise. Not remaining there, however, are the remains of Eliza. Seventy-five years after her interment, Madame Lynch—or what remained of her, presumably*—was shipped back to Paraguay, where her valiant struggle to "escape from the litany of vilification that had been imposed upon her by satanic forces" was finally realized.

But in death as in life, it was a monumental struggle—one that pitted the state against the Church.

---

* One functionary in the Père Lachaise administrative office told the present writer, in response to a rather pointed question, "We are not perfectly sure that the correct remains were disinterred and shipped to Paraguay—but if you quote me by name I'll deny I said it!"

PART FOUR

MADAME LYNCH

& FRIEND

REDIVIVUS

The Making of a Hero

The carefully orchestrated transformation of Francisco Solano López from a national embarrassment into a national hero can be said to have been precipitated by a war that equaled in insanity the war that had precipitated his immolation. The Chaco War was hardly justified, yet it was decidedly inevitable. Having been profoundly humiliated by its losses as a result of the War of the Triple Alliance, Paraguay sought vindication of its national honor by extending its borders at the expense of the militarily and politically vulnerable Bolivia.

The two nations professed strong claims, dating back to the colonial period, on the largely uninhabited void of dense forests, scrub lands, and swamps that separated them: the Chaco Boreal. Against the Paraguayan argument that settlers and missionaries from Asunción had long since established and maintained outposts in the disputed, and worthless, region was the landlocked Bolivia's argument that it was in desperate need of ports on the Paraguay River which would give her access, through the Río de la Plata, to the Atlantic. A war against Chile (1879–1884) had cost Bolivia her access to the Pacific.

Both arguments were valid, and could have been compromised through negotiation. But by the opening of the twentieth century, the contestants—as if by tacit agreement—would seem to have concluded that the issue could only be resolved militarily.

Exacerbating the situation were the rumors—unproved to date
—of huge oil deposits in the Chaco. In 1907, both countries began to enlarge their frontier garrisons, and despite outside efforts
to defuse the rivalry, the slow but irrevocable march toward open
warfare was under way. The Paraguayan press broadcast the
charge that Standard Oil of New Jersey, which held a concession
in Bolivia (which proved to be worthless), was openly financing
that nation's army; the Bolivian press countercharged that Argentina, in concert with Great Britain, was inciting Paraguay to
attack. The Bolivian charge held slightly more validity, at least
so far as regarded Argentina.

Though Argentina was indeed "encouraging" Paraguay, it
must be admitted in all fairness that Bolivia was being egged on
by, and offered the support of, Chile, which felt, quite logically,
that a Bolivian attempt to break through Paraguay to the Atlantic
would obviate any attempt to again contest Chile for access to the
Pacific. For two decades the hawks of Paraguay and Bolivia,
backed up by their respective neighbors, indulged in a propaganda war. As Hubert Herring has noted, "The polemicists of
both nations used barrels of printer's ink to prove the validity of
their claims. Cynics in Asunción and La Paz spoke derisively of
the learned disputants as *doctores en Chaco*."

In December 1928, Paraguayan patrols stormed a Bolivian
fort at Vanguardia; it was the first of a series of "border incidents" which, four years later, marked the transition from a war
of words to a war of bullets. Militating in Bolivia's favor was
the fact that its population was three times greater than that of
Paraguay, and that it enjoyed the material support not only of
Chile but of Germany (the Spanish Civil War was not the only
"training ground" on which Germany rehearsed for World War
II).

However, the Bolivian government was weak and vacillating.
Too, the Boliviano Indians—most of whom were conscripted by
force and, more often than not, transferred to the battlefront in

chains—were congenitally acclimated to the two-mile-high Bolivian Altiplano and were thus physically unable to adapt to the Chaco lowlands. Conversely, Paraguay enjoyed the total support of its people, who had been brought by their government to see in the struggle a defense of their homeland.

Though outmanned and outweaponed, the Paraguayans not only managed to overrun most of the Chaco but to invade eastern Bolivia as well. Were it not for the sophisticated German weaponry on the Bolivian side, and total exhaustion on both sides, Paraguay's army quite probably would have taken La Paz and ended the war on its terms.

By June 1935, six Western Hemisphere governments including that of the United States prevailed upon the physically (and financially) spent combatants to submit to arbitration. Paraguay was adjudged the victor; it was a victory that, in Professor Warren's words, "won them 20,000 square miles" of uncultivable jungle "at a cost of about three Bolivians and two Paraguayans per square mile." Thus ended what has gone down in the books as one of South America's—and history's—most senseless wars.

In February 1936, the government of Eusebio Ayala was overthrown by a military revolt; the Army felt that Ayala—Paraguay's last respectable President to date—had been too "weak" in the peace negotiations. Riding into power as a result of the coup, Colonel Rafael Franco became the nation's thirty-fifth President in sixty-six years. After proclaiming himself military dictator, Franco proclaimed Paraguay a totalitarian state. Then, in order to rally patriotic dissidents and thus further entrench his regime, Franco resorted to a standard ploy among military dictators since time immemorial: glorifying (and sanctifying) the nation's greatest militaristic figure of the past. Casting about for someone to fit the bill, he came up with Francisco Solano López. Militating in Franco's favor: The Paraguayan people, demoralized at the loss of 40,000 of their finest young men, not only *needed* a hero figure but *wanted* one. Their latest dictator accommodated them.

On March 1, the sixty-sixth anniversary of López's death, President Franco decreed a nationwide celebration to honor his memory. Both Argentina and Brazil professed to see in Franco's nauseatingly laudatory references to López a deliberate attempt to antagonize them; the Paraguayans, whether out of choice or ignorance, might see López in a new light, but the Brazilians and Argentinians felt no pressing urge to rewrite history.

Predictably, Franco turned their protestations to his own advantage. After decreeing that "all laws derogatory to the memory of López are hereby annulled," Franco went on to "remind" his people that Argentina and Brazil—those "barbarian foes" of yore—had "unjustifiably invaded the Fatherland," and that the invasion had been "gloriously repulsed" by "the great Hero of the Nation, Mariscal Francisco Solano López," who "surrendered his precious life on the battlefield of glory" so that Paraguay might remain "as it remains today a bastion of democracy and freedom."

The resurrection of López was on.

Statues of the Martyred Marshal astride his horse sprang up throughout the country.

Streets were renamed in his memory.

The government-controlled Paraguayan press all but stripped its gears in grinding out effusive encomiums to the memory of "this Noble Son of Paraguay."

And before Franco himself fell from power a year later, idealized portraits of the Hero were staring down from the walls of all government buildings (as they continue to stare down to this day).*

To climax the entire farce, what are purported to be the

---

* The reconstruction of López's historical image was extended to a reconstruction of his physical image as well. One of the most frequently reproduced photographs, purporting to show López in the last months of his life, reveals a tall, trim, exceedingly handsome man on the brink of middle age. The photo may be that of one of López's aides; to the present writer the man in the picture bears a remarkable resemblance to the ill-fated Emperor Maximilian of Mexico. At any rate, it is most definitely not López.

Hero's remains were brought from Cerro Corá and, amidst much panoply, enshrined in the Panteón de los Héroes. López's wish to be buried in a setting exactly like that where his hero Napoleon Bonaparte allegedly lies was finally realized. (In a conversation with one of the pro-Stroessner Church hierarchs, the present writer—admittedly tactlessly—questioned how the bones borne from Cerro Corá could possibly be those of López; his "grave" had been little more than a shallow pit covered over with rocks, and eight decades at the mercy of the elements, not to mention vultures and marauding animals, must surely have militated against its contents remaining intact. Replied the good padre, "Ah, Señor, a mortal man's remains would have disappeared over the years, as you argue. But Mariscal López was no mortal man.")

And then came the books. History must be rewritten; historians must be found to fulfill the task.

Of all those who came forward to write "the truth," the most revisionist—and least likely—was Juan Emiliano O'Leary. O'Leary's mother and many relatives had been tortured by López. How, then, to explain his transformation from a bitter anti-Lopista into a craven worshiper? The Argentinian scholar Arturo Rebaudi attributed it to a gift of fifty leagues of land by Enrique Solano López. It's as good a reason as any.

By the turn of the century, perhaps adopting the time-honored thesis that when you can't fight 'em, join 'em, Enrique had abandoned his fight against the Paraguayan Government in the Argentinian courts, and with brother Carlos had moved on to Asunción, where he involved himself in the politics of the politically distressed nation. He became one of the kingpins of the Colorados, the nation's ruling political party, as well as its only legally tolerated one; and he distinguished himself as a brigade commander in the civil war of 1901 that resulted in a Colorado victory. Or so his heirs claim. At any rate, when he died in 1917, Enrique was mourned as a "hero of the nation." Brother Carlos lived in obscurity until his death in 1929; brother Federico Noel had died in Buenos Aires, where he had gone in order to help the Argentinians construct their first telephone system. Of the three surviving sons of Francisco by Eliza, it appears that Enrique was the most determined to "clear" his parents' names. At the time of his death he was fairly well off financially; perhaps, as some wags claimed, the Paraguayan Government had settled a sum on him, with the stipulation that he stop dragging them through the courts.

If O'Leary was indeed "bought off" by Enrique, it must be admitted that he kept to his end of the bargain, as this panegyrical introduction to his biography of López would suggest:

> Ridiculed by the diatribe of his enemies, exalted by the praises of his admirers, he has known in life and afterward in death the most resplendent heights of glory and the deepest shadows of condemnation. Meanwhile his cyclopean figure [surely a curious choice of words here] has remained alone but firmly set on its high pedestal, defying the hurricane of passion and the destructive action of time, without anything being able to cast it down, nor anyone being able to detract from his tragic grandeur. . . . Over his gigantic tomb, over his mountain mausoleum, there has always burned a funeral lamp that no wind will ever extinguish. And through its tremulous and uncertain splendors posterity has seen him as in a dim twilight, limned magnificently on the far horizon, treading the earth with his feet, touching the sky with his great brow thoughtful in Promethean sorrow.

As the "cyclopean figure" continued "defying the hurricane of passion," his chief apologist went on to become the house historian in the various Colorado *gobiernos* that rose and fell rhythmically about that "mountain mausoleum." When O'Leary died in the late 1950s, he was mourned as the nation's greatest belletrist and historian. Though denied the Nobel Prize (it is doubtful he was ever nominated)—a denial which the more reactionary Paraguayans consider a gross oversight on the part of the Swedish Academy—O'Leary must have mounted his own "high pedestal" secure in the knowledge that he had given his *amigo y patrón,* Enrique Solano López, a damned good return on his land. (O'Leary's grasp of history would seem to leave something to be desired—provided, of course, that he actually *believed* that the flattering portrait of López which complemented his rhapsodic verbal elegies to the Hero had been, as he claimed, executed in 1853 by Jacques Louis David. The French artist died in the year preceding López's birth.)

No sooner had the presumed remains of López been enshrined in the Panteón and a sorry episode in Paraguay's history undergone a verbal transmutation into a glorious epoch, when it all had to be temporarily forgotten. Political upheaval broke out anew.

Eighteen years (and six presidents) later, yet another Army coup brought to power Colonel Alfredo Stroessner (he grandly promoted himself to General)—a tippling, Teutonic-looking, mild-mannered, and quite humorless son of a German immigrant and a Paraguayan mother, who takes umbrage at being described as a "dictator." (It was on the occasion of one of Stroessner's periodic "constitutional elections" that a foreign correspondent was moved to observe, "Were it not for an occasional headless body floating down the Paraná River, it might be possible to consider the gaudily uniformed and bemedaled dictator of Paraguay—the last of the breed in South America—a character out of Gilbert and Sullivan.")

In 1959, after laboring four years to secure the grip on the nation which he retains to this day,* Stroessner, following through on Franco's thesis that the best way to finesse dissidence is to give the masses a god figure, completed the rehabilitation of López. On March 1 of that year, the eighty-ninth anniversary

---

* The present writer, who was living in Paraguay at the time of the Stroessner seizure of the government, recalls how the local bookmakers, not to mention the politically astute among the foreign Diplomatic Corps, were giving odds that he would not last out the year. Thanks in no small measure to the United States Government (and the American taxpayers), Stroessner overcame the odds.

of the "glorious death of our glorious Hero," an idealized statue of López was unveiled in the Panteón over a plaque bearing the legend "Venció Penurias y Fatigas con la Espada en la Mano y la Patria en los Labios al Frente de sus Ultimos Soldados y sobre su Ultima Campa Batalla. . . ." ("He overcame Indigence and Exhaustion with Sword in Hand and the Country on his Lips, at the head of his Last Troops and on his Last Battlefield. . . .")

The resurrection of her Friend was complete.

It was now Madame Lynch's turn.

The Making of a Heroine

As was the case with the Roman Catholic Church, which did not get around to proclaiming the Dogma of the Assumption until as recently as 1950—two millennia after the presumed event, and many centuries after the cult of Maryology had taken root —the Paraguayan Government did not get around to what amounted to proclaiming the secular adoration of Eliza Lynch until years after the cult of "Lynchology" had taken root. The Church was compelled to come to terms with Mary worship by fixing as immutable "that the immaculate mother of God, the ever Virgin Mary, when the course of her earthly life was run, was assumed in body and in soul to heavenly glory." True, the Lynch worship was nowhere nearly as widespread—nor as justified—as that of Mary. Nevertheless, the Paraguayan Government was compelled to come to terms with "Lynchology" by proclaiming that she was "our national heroine and our national martyr."

When a high official in the Stroessner Government who was a close friend of the present writer when he lived in Paraguay twenty years ago was asked to explain—strictly off the record— this extraordinary phenomenon, he replied, "In truth, the question has never been raised seriously. In truth, it is probably a question that does not merit an answer. In truth, there may well be no answer. The Government has never been compelled to rationalize its attitude toward Madame Lynch. Or to explain that attitude in any way. Perhaps there is no explanation, no 'rationale,' if you will, that would satisfy your curiosity. Then again, perhaps that is the answer you seek: that there is no answer."

But there is indeed an "answer." For it is probable that the elevation of Eliza Lynch to exalted status was the inevitable culmination of a determination on the part of a minuscule band of propagandists *that got completely out of hand*. And here the subjunctive "probable" is used advisedly. How else to explain the quasi deification of a woman who helped to destroy the very country which now, by government fiat, looks on her as the greatest woman in its history.

At this point, a fine line must be drawn between the Lynch loyalists and the Lynch propagandists.

The loyalists are, of course, the descendants in the third and fourth generations who, like their progenitor Enrique Solano López, lived on in Paraguay and, also like Enrique, chose to throw in their lot with the ruling Colorado Party. Jorge Manuel, the family historian, is a minor functionary in the Government; his less self-effacing brother, Miguel Cirilo, is his nation's ambassador to Washington (he had also been its ambassador to the United Nations); and their niece, Gladys Margarita, the most outspoken of the lot, is La Decana (Dean) of the one-professor Facultad de Filosofía at the government-controlled University of Asunción.

These three had *hoped* that the powers that be would bring together in death their two most adored ancestors. They may even have made murmurings toward that end; but there is no evidence that they brought any pressure on the Government to reconstruct the Madame's historical image (or that they were even in a position to do so).

And then came the propagandists—the novelists. Their original intent was not to deify their heroine. But where they are to be faulted is in their failure (perhaps unwillingness is more appropriate) to concede that what they were passing off as "biographies" were no more than works of fiction.

When the dictator Franco began the rehabilitation of López's historical image, all of Madame Lynch's contemporaries were long since dead; the Madame herself was, by and large, a forgotten woman.

Books averse to López dealt perforce with Eliza; but these were—with one exception—either not available in translation or long out of print (e.g., the Washburn and Masterman memoirs), or banned from the country (e.g., Cunninghame-Graham's *Portrait of a Dictator*, published in London in 1933). The one exception was Cecilio Báez's *El Mariscal Francisco Solano López* (Asunción, 1926). Báez, who was Paraguay's outstanding historian-statesman and scholar, as well as its greatest Liberalista had served briefly (1906) as President when the Colorados suffered one of their periodic, temporary falls from power. Succeeding Colorado governments permitted publication of Báez's corrosive indictment of Francisco and Eliza (Professor Warren notes that the author "used his blackest ink effectively") mainly because Báez—and the Liberal Party—were still powers to be reckoned with. A decade later, having secured their iron grip on the nation, the Colorado Party made sure that Báez's biography of López was no more than a memory among the enlightened few.

Then, in 1938, came William Barrett's *Woman on Horseback: The Biography of Francisco López and Eliza Lynch*, a rather curious hybrid: a romantic novel passed off as nonfiction history, which when translated into Spanish won its author wide praise in Paraguay—actually, wider praise than it won the author in his native United States. This was followed, four years later, by *La Dama del Paraguay*, another sympathetic treatise (though not in fiction form) whose author, Héctor Pedro Blomberg, was a grandson-in-law of the book's heroine. (An appendage of this tome was the aforementioned *Recuerdos de mi Suegra* by Blomberg's own *suegra*, Maud Lloyd López Rancia.)

What was amounting to an unintended rehabilitation of Madame Lynch through the medium of the printed word gained momentum after World War II. Flattering romances were published in Mexico, Argentina, and Spain. Apparently operating on the theory that the more sympathetic your heroine, the greater your audience, these authors all but allowed their imaginations to run amok. (For some reason—perhaps because their literary content is, by and large, rather dreadful—none of these romances has gone into English translation. A few are, however, available for scrutiny in the New York Public Library's American history reference section and in the Library of Congress, for those who read Spanish and who may wish to satisfy their curiosity.)

The rehabilitation peaked in the mid-1950s with the publication of two curious apologias: *Madama Lynch* by Henri Pitaud, and *Madame Lynch: Evocación* by Paraguay's "Grand Old Lady of Letters," the aged (and now infirm) Doña María Concepción L. de Chaves. Both became instant best sellers in Paraguay.

Doña María Chaves recorded for posterity a number of "unequivocal facts" including "definitive proof" that: Eliza matriculated at Dublin's Trinity College at the age of nine; that she was the daughter of "a great British Naval hero"; and that she was "sold" to López by her husband Quatrefages "for a not inconsiderable sum of money, ostensibly to take her off his hands." Among Pitaud's many, and equally absurd, contentions are that Eliza was a virgin when she met López, that this *"última de las enamoradas románticas"* followed López to Paraguay "out of pure love" (Pitaud also "proves" that López was an intellectual giant who was "pursued and courted assiduously by the great titans" of Paris's literary and social worlds), and that while Madame was, admittedly, at first disliked intensely by the Ladies of Asunción, she "quickly won them over with her many kindnesses and great intellect."

Even the Lynch-López descendants tend to dismiss these and similar hagiographies as "amusing romances"—although this has never stopped them from quoting as gospel the more flattering snippets when it serves their purpose. As one Paraguayan scholar commented to the present writer, "In all probability, if the Pitaud and Chaves books, not to mention that Barrett nonsense, had included the descendants' ridiculous claim that López and Madame Lynch were legally married in Paris, they would by now have petitioned the Vatican for the canonization of all that literary trash."

By the late 1950s, the Pitaud and Chaves "authentic biographies" were becoming authentic embarrassments to the Stroessner Government. More so in the case of the Pitaud work, which is cast in the form of a nonfiction memoir dictated by the Madame in the last year of her life, replete with bogus "letters" and complimentary items from unidentified French newspapers. Pitaud, a transplanted Frenchman, had cleverly assured himself a wide reader audience by having his good friend Juan O'Leary— the Colorado Party's favorite *"historiador de la Guerra del Paraguay, glorificador del Mariscal López, y bardo de los héroes de la epopeya"*—write an effusive *prólogo* wherein the book's heroine is portrayed in terms usually reserved for inhabitants of the Calendar of Saints.

The book quickly received wide circulation, less because of its sympathetic treatment of Madame Lynch than because of its extraordinary treatment of her Friend. It became "suggested reading" for all Paraguayan schoolchildren. And—a sure-fire guarantee that it would be a perpetual bestseller—Pitaud shrewdly dedicated the third edition of the book, with proper groveling obsequiousness, to "Excelentísimo Señor Presidente de la República del Paraguay, General de Ejército don Alfredo Stroessner." The "Excelentísimo" expressed his gratitude by issuing an *"orden general"* wherein the book was *"declarada útil para las Fuerzas Armadas del Paraguay."* (In Paraguay, where dictators rather shamelessly glory in the title "General of the

Army," what is good for the armed forces is considered good for the country as a whole.)

Pitaud became a rich man. (Sales on the Chaves book, which the Government also makes sure is always in print, are nothing to sneer at.) And thanks to his book, the vast majority of Paraguay's unenlightened became acquainted with a Madame Lynch who bore little resemblance to historical reality. Inevitably, people began to wonder why, if she had been so vital to, and inextricably a part of, the Hero's life, Madame Lynch was not lying at the Hero's side.

In 1961, this demand was satisfied. More or less. Eliza's remains (or at least what are assumed to be her remains) were exhumed from that crowded plot at Père Lachaise and brought to Asunción.

There are two widely disparate versions of how the exhumation and transportation were effected: the official government version, as transmitted to the present writer by Dr. Hipólito Sánchez Quell, and "the other version," as propounded by Señor Teófilo Chammas, an abject worshiper of the memory of Madame Lynch, and one of the most picaresque characters the present writer has yet to encounter.

Sánchez Quell is a handsome, courtly man in his late sixties —naturally, a Coloradisto—who after a career in his nation's foreign service is now Director of the National Archives. According to Dr. Quell, who was Paraguay's ambassador to France at the time of Madame's return, when the Stroessner Government decided to bring her remains back to Asunción Teófilo Chammas—in Quell's words "an immodest entrepreneur" and "the head *contrabandista*"—decided to get into the act.

Quell had made official representation to the French authorities for the exhumation, and had assumed everything was proceeding properly—when he was notified that the remains had been "hurriedly packed and shipped under mysterious circumstances." If what Quell claims is true, Chammas—obviously a man with connections—managed to spread a few francs around Père Lachaise, had stolen the remains, and had shipped them off in a sealed coffin containing four kilos of pure Lebanese hashish. The casket was allegedly opened by the Buenos Aires customs authorities (were they tipped off by the Paraguayan Government or the French?), at which point the Stroessner Government petitioned the Argentinian authorities for Madame's remains, which were then brought up to Asunción by gunboat. (As to why Chammas never got into any trouble anent the hashish, provided one accepts the validity of Quell's charges: smuggling is the leading "industry" in Paraguay; the contraband comes in across the Argentinian border and is winked at by the authorities on both sides.)

Teófilo Chammas is a Lebanese Paraguayan over six feet tall, weighing more than 250 pounds, who walks with a pronounced limp and has about him a "Sidney Greenstreetish" aura. He flits back and forth from continent to continent; while in Asunción, he "holds court" in the cantina of the Hotel Guaraní. (It was the present writer's great fortune that one of Chammas's periodic trips to Asunción coincided with his own visit there to complete research on this book. During our conversations, spread over four days in June 1974, strange characters would rush up to our table periodically, delivering to Chammas telexes: e.g., "Ship 20,000 kilos coffee on the seventeenth from São Paulo," "30,000 kilos of sugar enroute for off-loading New Orleans," and the like.) A close friend of Jorge López and of Juan O'Leary's son, Chammas is so ardent a devotee of Madame Lynch that one gets the impression that he periodically lights votive candles to her memory. (He says that his house in Beirut contains a shrine to Madame Lynch, with authentic relics including a swatch of her hair.)

Chammas claims that it was he who arranged the entire deal regarding Madame's exhumation: "I went through a personal fortune doing it. It was my way of expressing my gratitude to Paraguay, in bringing her home. Her one desire was to return to

Paraguay, you know. She literally starved herself to death in frustration over not being allowed back. Of course she died in poverty. She was a pauper when she left here after the war. All I want from the Stroessner Government is a simple 'thank you for bringing her back.' That's all; just a simple, 'thank you.' I ask them for a 'thank you,' they give me shit. Sánchez Quell is a dirty liar, and I'll tell him that to his face."

The "real story" regarding Madame's return, according to Teófilo Chammas:

The Père Lachaise had been petitioned by the Paraguayan Government for the body, but had refused, as "it is against their laws to exhume bodies, you know." (Not true. A.B.) Admittedly under cover of darkness ("I certainly couldn't do it in broad daylight, you know!"), Chammas had the remains dug up. "When I opened the coffin, Madame Lynch's long, jet-black hair [!] turned instantaneously to a luminescent golden yellow, like a sunburst; it was a miracle! I cut off a swatch and gave it to Jorge Solano López; it's hanging on his dining-room wall." (*Something* is hanging on Jorge's dining-room wall, and even though he told the present writer it is his grandmother's hair, it looks more like the sort of stuff used for making dolls' wigs.)

After the exhumation, or so Chammas claims, he had the remains brought over on a French ship, but while awaiting transshipment at Buenos Aires the coffin was embargoed by customs officials "because the Argentina Government didn't want Madame Lynch back in South America." ("I know Sánchez Quell and the rest of them are saying I set up the whole thing to smuggle in some hashish. Bullshit!") For three months—to continue the Chammas account—he prevailed upon the Buenos Aires customs officers to let the remains through. Then, one dark night in May, he "managed to have the remains transferred to a suitcase, which I personally flew up to Asunción on a chartered seaplane; but the Paraguayan officials had heard I was coming, and as soon as I stepped off the seaplane they grabbed the suitcase and hid it on the docks till July, when they pretended they had brought

Madame Lynch from France on a Paraguayan warship. *What*
warship? This country didn't even *have* a warship in sixty-one!"
(They still don't. A.B.)

Chammas also allowed that "I have seen absolute proof—letters,
documents, so on—that there was a secret marriage between
Madame Lynch and López in Paris—but all this material was
sealed for eternity at the orders of Charles de Gaulle." Apparently, or so Chammas would have it believed, López had
prevailed upon Napoleon III to grant Madame Lynch a divorce
from Quatrefages—"the first ever granted in France"—so that
he could marry her, but the marriage "had to be kept a secret
because as a practicing Catholic, López could never marry a
divorced woman. López took his religion very seriously." When
asked why Charles de Gaulle, of all people, "sealed the documents for all eternity," Chammas confided that "Madame Lynch
had a lot of 'dirt' on some very high officials in the French Government, which De Gaulle never wanted publicized; all very
embarrassing."* When asked how, if the documents were sealed,
he managed to see them, Chammas replied, "I have connections."

In one final conversation with this charming rogue and excellent host, the present writer was told, "I am leaving for
Paris in a few days to arrange an important deal with President
Giscard d'Estaing; millions of dollars involved. Maybe twenty
million. Because I like you, and because I want to prove that
Madame Lynch was married to López, I'm going to tell Giscard
that the whole deal is off unless he agrees to open those archives.
Give me your address in the States. As soon as I force Giscard to
open the archives, I'll send you a cable: 'Come quickly. Chammas.' You'll fly over to Paris on the next plane, and see for yourself."

---

* In her *Exposición y Protesta*, Madame Lynch makes a fleeting allusion
to "the book on my life which I will publish later." The Lynch-López
descendants believe the book was written but was lost before publication
whereas Chammas claims it is the repository for all that "dirt" and is thus
one of the documents "sealed for all eternity."

The address was duly given; as of the publication of this book, the cable has yet to arrive.

2

The Government had planned to place Eliza's remains in the Panteón, but the Church had other ideas. She was not, in their eyes, a married woman; and the Panteón is sanctified ground.

When the Stroessner Government pressed ahead with its plans, the Church authorities issued not an interdict but an *advertencia:* under no circumstances could Madame Lynch lie alongside her Friend, unless the Government was willing to exhume her Friend and bury him elsewhere.

There still remained fresh in the Government's collective memory the knowledge that it was the Church which had brought down Stroessner's good friend Perón six years before. (The Argentinian Caesar had not only rendered to himself what he should have rendered to God, but had gone so far as to petition the Vatican for canonization of his late wife, the charismatic Evita, widely believed to have been an ex-whore. The Church likes their saints to be pure in body as well as pure in heart.) The Stroessner Government was fairly secure: its most vocal dissidents were by then either in jail or in exile. But there was a rather powerful underground Liberalista movement which, though lacking much cohesion, and thus posing a minimal threat, could create problems for the Colorados if given enough encouragement by the powerful Church hierarchy.

After months of wrangling—while Madame Lynch was, in a manner of speaking, dividing her time between the docks of Buenos Aires and the docks of Asunción—a compromise was worked out that satisfied ecclesiastical sensitivities and saved the Stroessner Government face.

July 25, 1961—the seventy-fifth anniversary of Eliza's death, and the one hundred and thirty-fifth anniversary of Francisco's birth—was declared by Government edict *Un Día de Homenaje*

Nacional. At ten o'clock in the morning of this Day of National Homage, the people of Asunción and the surrounding hamlets —ever ready to enjoy a fiesta—trooped down to the quay below the Plaza de los Héroes. There they were joined by all the government officials, from Stroessner on down. Stroessner, as is his wont, was decked out in one of his many uniforms which equal in meretriciousness those favored by the lover of the woman who was being honored. As the Paraguayan Army Band played the national anthem (a delightfully tuneful piece which sounds not unlike the overture to some yet to be discovered Rossini opera), the urn bearing the collected remains of Madame Lynch—an exact replica of the urn bearing the purported remains of her Friend—was brought off the Paraguayan gunboat in which it had reposed for either weeks or months, depending on whose version of events is to be believed.

After proclaiming her to have been "our national heroine, our national martyr," Stroessner, in his capacity as Chief Pallbearer, led the procession that wended its way up from the docks, along the Plaza de Palma, and into the Panteón de los Héroes—at which point the urn was whisked out the back door and rushed over to the Ministerio de Defensa Nacional (ironically, in Avenida Mariscal Francisco Solano López).

There it remained for nine years in a large area of the second floor which had been set aside as the "Lynch Museo"—a rather shabby *museo* composed of an idealized (and terribly garish) portrait of Madame Lynch, a large volume allegedly containing 87,000 names "A Homenaje a Madame Elisa Alicia Lynch," a rusty sword said to have belonged to López—and a hand-painted sign containing an arrow and the word "*Caballeros.*"

Somewhere between Père Lachaise and the Asunción docks— perhaps in Señor Chammas's suitcase—Madame Lynch had lost her status as "the Widow López."

By 1970—a century after the event—the history of the War of the Triple Alliance had been satisfactorily rewritten; instead of celebrating the centennial of the conclusion of a national tragedy, the Paraguayans were celebrating the centennial of "a heroic epoch in our glorious history."

As part of the celebration, it was decided that "the national heroine, the national martyr" was more deserving of a final resting place than that musty *museo* on the second floor of the National Defense Ministry, equidistant between the outer corridor and the men's toilet.

At considerable expense, a large, meretricious marble mausoleum was erected at the national cemetery at La Recoleta, a few kilometers from where Eliza's quinta "Patiño" is believed to have stood, and a few meters from the tomb that adorns the grave of her only daughter. Atop the mausoleum—the tallest in all of Paraguay (and, in the words of one of that nation's leading architects, the ugliest)—was placed a life-size statue of the Madame holding two crosses aloft: one symbolizing her own martyrdom, the other symbolizing the martyrdom of the Paraguayans over whom she had hoped to reign (and whom she had helped to martyr).

On the one hundred and forty-fourth anniversary of López's birth, and a few months past the hundredth anniversary of his death on the banks of the Río Aquidaban, the urn bearing Madame Lynch's remains was carried in procession down the boulevard that bears her Friend's name, to its final resting place.

Again decked out in one of his more ostentatious bemedaled costumes, General Stroessner read aloud before the assembled multitude the legend on a bronze plaque which had been affixed to the north wall of the mausoleum:

Homenaje Del Pueblo, Gobierno y F.F. A.A. de la Nación a Elisa Alicia Lynch, Que Con Abnegación Accompañó Al Héroe Máximo de la Patria Mariscal Francisco Solano López Hasta Su Immolación En Cerro Corá.*

---

* "Homage of the People, Government and Armed Forces of the Nation to Elisa Alicia Lynch, who with Abnegation Accompanied the Greatest Hero of the Nation, Marshal Francisco Solano López, until his Immolation at Cerro Corá."

Madame Lynch had failed in her ambition to go down in history as the Empress of Paraguay; but considering the *homenaje* she received from the heirs of her putative subjects, one is compelled to admit that she came damn close. . . .

Epilogue

Every Saturday afternoon following the siesta, weather permitting, it is the custom among the people of Asunción to visit La Recoleta—which is, in addition to being the *national* cemetery, the *only* cemetery—there to put flowers on the graves of their dear departed ones and those of their favorite figures from the past. But only civilian figures. All military heroes are in the Panteón with López. Indeed, as one Paraguayan remarked cynically to the present writer, "If this country comes up with many more 'heroes,' the walls of the Panteón are going to burst at the seams."

On a balmy Saturday afternoon in June, La Decana Gladys Margarita Solano López, who in addition to being Madame Lynch's great-granddaughter is her greatest devotée, drove me out to visit the mausoleum. The Dean is a rather humorless woman in her middle fifties who, with her bobbed hair and rather chunky physique, bears an uncanny resemblance to her great-grandfather.

En route to the cemetery, La Decana informed me, with quiet pride, that the mausoleum is not only considered a national monument by the government, but is regarded as such by the people at large: "Masses stream out here constantly to place flowers at the tomb, to remind themselves of the greatness of that woman."

Upon our arrival at the cemetery, La Decana purchased a bouquet from one of the many *floristas* who do a thriving business at the front gate. We then advanced to the mausoleum, a short walk up a knoll. With reverence, La Decana unlocked the doors of the mausoleum and bade me follow her in. Two feet from the doors—stone executions of the delicate *ñandutí* lace for which Paraguay is famous—is a low shelf on which rests the urn.

After murmuring a silent prayer, La Decana opened the urn, and gently rearranged the folds in the soiled scarlet bag that contains (presumably) her revered ancestress's mortal remains. She solicitously inquired if I would care to "caress the *restos* of Madame Lynch"—an invitation which I murmuringly declined with equal solicitude.

Five minutes later, outside the tomb, as La Decana prepared to offer another silent prayer, I excused myself on the grounds that I would like to purchase a bouquet of flowers as my own "homenaje" to Madame Lynch. La Decana nodded appreciatively, and then assumed an attitude of meditation, staring through those beautiful stone doors at that ghastly bronze urn.

As I made my purchase at the front gate of the cemetery, I asked the *florista* if there was any reason why the "masses" had picked this particular day not to "stream out." Replied the flower lady, "The only one who ever comes out here to Madame Lynch's tomb is that crazy lady there. She comes practically every Saturday and plays with the bones."

At that moment, as if by some tacitly prearranged signal, we both turned in the direction of the mausoleum—and watched a long moment as La Decana stood before the shrine in an attitude of total transfixion.

When the *florista* wondered if I were by chance a tourist—a rarity among rarities in Asunción—I told her that I was writing a book on Madame Lynch and López, and hoped to get at the truth.

To this she responded, with a vehemence rarely encountered among the truly gentle Paraguayan people, "The truth? I'll give you the truth! Mariscal López was a tyrant, a madman. Madame Lynch was his whore. The Government tries to tell us different. Well, let the Government say that Mariscal López was our greatest hero, that Madame Lynch was a martyr for our people. The Government can say what they want to say. But among the Paraguayans, memories run deep." . . .

ALYN BRODSKY

Harbor Island, Florida

Bibliography

Alberdi, Juan Bautista. *Historia de la Guerra del Paraguay*. Buenos Aires, 1962.

Amerlan, Alberto. *Bosquejos de la Guerra del Paraguay*. Buenos Aires, 1904.

Ayala, Victor Queirolo. *Historia de la Cultura en Paraguay*. Asunción, 1966.

Báez, Cecilio. *Resumen de la Historia del Paraguay*. Asunción, 1910.

———. *Política Americana*. Asunción, 1925.

———. *El Mariscal Francisco Solano López*. Asunción, 1926.

———. *Historia Colonial del Paraguay y Río de la Plata*. Asunción, 1926.

———. *Historia Diplomática del Paraguay*. Asunción, 1932.

Barrett, William E. *Woman on Horseback*. New York, 1938.

Belgrano, Manuel. *Memoria Sobre la Expedición al Paraguay 1810–1811*. Buenos Aires, 1910.

Benítes, Gregorio. *La Triple Alianza de 1865: Escapada de un Desastre en la Guerra de Invasión al Paraguay*. Asunción, 1904.

Benítez, Justo Pastor. *Los Comuneros del Paraguay, 1649–1735*. Asunción, 1938.

———. *El Solar Guaraní*. Buenos Aires, 1947.

Benítez, Luis A. *Historia Cultural: Reseña de su Evolución en Paraguay*. Asunción, 1966.

Beverina, Juan. *La Guerra del Paraguay*. Buenos Aires, 1921.

Bliss, Porter Cornelius. *The Secret History of the Mission of the North-American Citizen Charles Amos Washburn against the Government of the Republic of Paraguay*. (Translated from the original Spanish text believed to have been published in Luque in 1868.)

Blomberg, Héctor Pedro. *La Dama del Paraguay* (appended with Maud Lloyd López Rancia's *Recuerdos de mi Suegra*). Buenos Aires, 1942.

Box, Pelham Horton. *The Origins of the Paraguayan War.* Champlain, Ill., 1930; reissued by Russell & Russell, New York, 1967.

Bray, Arturo. *Solano López, Soldado de la Gloria y del Infortunio.* Buenos Aires, 1945.

———. *Hombres y Épocas del Paraguay.* Buenos Aires, 1957.

Burchell, S. C. *Imperial Masquerade: The Paris of Napoleon Third.* New York, 1971.

Burton, Sir Richard Francis. *Letters from the Battle-fields of Paraguay.* London, 1870.

Cancogni, Manlio, and Boris, Ivan. *El Napoleón del Plata—Historia de una Heroica Guerra Sudamericana.* Barcelona, 1972.

Cardozo, Efraim. *Hace Cien Años: Crónicas de la Guerra de 1864–1870.* Asunción, 1967.

———. *Paraguay Independiente.* Barcelona, 1949.

———. *Vísperas de la Guerra del Paraguay.* Buenos Aires, 1954.

Charlevoix, Pierre François Xavier de. *The History of Paraguay (An Account of the Jesuits).* Dublin, 1769.

Chaves, Julio César. *Compendio de Historia Paraguaya.* Buenos Aires, 1958.

———. *Historia General del Paraguay.* Asunción, 1968.

Chaves, Maria Concepción L. de. *Madame Lynch: Evocación.* Buenos Aires, 1957.

Cova, Jesús Antonio. *Solano López y la Epopeya del Paraguay.* Buenos Aires, 1948.

Cunninghame-Graham, Robert Bontine. *Portrait of a Dictator, Francisco Solano López.* London, 1933.

Dalegri, Santiago. *El Paraguay y la Guerra de la Triple Alianza.* Buenos Aires, 1964.

Deberle, Alfred Joseph. *The History of Nations,* Vol. XXI. Translated by Philip Patterson Wells. New York, 1907.

Decoud, Héctor Francisco. *Sobre los Escombros de la Guerra: Una Decada de Vida Nacional, 1869–1880.* Asunción, 1925.

De Lasserre, Mme. Duprat. *Sufferings of a French Lady in Paraguay.* Buenos Aires, 1870.

Garay, Blas. *Compendio Elemental de Historia del Paraguay.* Madrid, 1896.

Garcia, Manuel. *Paraguay and the Alliance Against the Tyrant Francisco Solano López.* New York, 1869.

Gonzalez, Juan Natalicio. *Solano López, Diplomatico.* Asunción, 1948.

———. *Solano López y Otros Ensayos.* Paris, 1925.

———, and Ynsfran, Pablo M. *El Paraguay Contemporaneo.* Asunción, 1929.

Great Britain. Foreign Office documents dealing with the entire River Plate area, most notably "1867–1868. Nos. 1 & 2. Correspondence Respecting Hostilities in the River Plate."

Herring, Hubert. *A History of Latin America* (third edition). New York, 1968.

Hutchinson, Thomas Joseph. *The Paraná: With Incidents of the Paraguayan War and South American Recollections, from 1861–1868.* London, 1868.

Koebel, W. H. *Paraguay.* London, 1916.

Kolinski, Charles J. *Independence or Death? The Story of the Paraguayan War.* Gainesville, Fla., 1965.

Krüger, Hilde. *Elisa Lynch, o la Tragedia Como Destino.* Mexico City, 1946.

Laconich, Marco Antonio. *El Paraguay Mutilado.* Montevideo, 1939.

League of Nations. "Dispute Between Bolivia and Paraguay (Report of the Chaco Commission)." Geneva, 1934.

Levey, George Collins. *A Handy Guide to the River Plate.* London, 1890.

Lynch, Eliza Alicia. *Exposición y Protesta.* Buenos Aires, 1875.

McMahon, Martin T. "The War in Paraguay," in *Harper's New Monthly Magazine,* XL, pp. 633–647. "Paraguay and Her Enemies," in *Harper's New Monthly Magazine,* XL, pp. 421–429. New York, 1870.

Maiz, Fidel. *Etapas de Mi Vida.* Asunción, 1919.

Martin, Michael Rheta and Lovett, Gabriel H., *Encyclopedia of Latin-American History.* Indianapolis, 1968.

Masterman, George Frederick. *Seven Eventful Years in Paraguay: A Narrative of Personal Experience Amongst the Paraguayans.* London, 1869.

Meyer, Gordon. *The River and the People.* London, 1965.

Mitre, Bartolomé. *Cartas Polémicas Sobre la Guerra al Paraguay.* Buenos Aires, 1940.

———. *Páginas Historicas: Polémica de la Triple Alianza . . .* Buenos Aires, 1897.

Molas, Mariano Antonio. *Descripción Histórica de la Provincia del Paraguay.* Asunción, 1880.

Moreno, Fulgencio R. *La Ciudad de la Asunción.* Buenos Aires, 1926.

Munro, Dana Gardner. *The Latin American Republics: A History.* (New York City, 1950).

O'Leary, Juan Emiliano. *El Libro de los Héroes: Páginas Historicas de la Guerra del Paraguay.* Asunción, 1922.

———. *El Mariscal Solano López, El Héroe del Paraguay, en el LX Aniversario de su Gloriosa Muerte.* Montevideo, 1930.

———. *Nuestra Epopeya (Guerra del Paraguay).* Asunción, 1919.

———. *Páginas de Historia.* Asunción, 1916.

Page, Thomas Jefferson. *La Plata, the Argentina Confederation, and Paraguay.* New York, 1859.

Pendle, George. *The Lands and Peoples of Paraguay and Uruguay.* New York, 1959.

Pereyra, Carlos. *Francisco Solano López y la Guerra del Paraguay.* Madrid, 1919.

———. *Solano López y su Drama.* Buenos Aires, 1962.

Peterson, Harold F. *Efforts of the United States to Mediate in the Paraguayan War.* Durham, N.C., 1932.

Pitaud, Henri. *Paraguay, Terre Vierge.* Paris, 1950.

———. *Madama Lynch.* Asunción, 1956.

Quell, Hipolito Sánchez. *Política Internacional del Paraguay.* Asunción, 1935.

———. *Estructura y Función del Paraguay Colonial.* Buenos Aires, 1955.

Raine, Philip. *Paraguay.* New Brunswick, N.J., 1956.

Rebaudi, Arturo. *Guerra del Paraguay: La Conspiración Contra Su Excelentísimo el Presidente de la República, Mariscal Don Francisco Solano López.* Buenos Aires, 1917.

———. *La Declaración de Guerra de la República del Paraguay a la República Argentina.* Buenos Aires, 1924.

Robertson, John Paris and W. P. *Letters on Paraguay: Comprising an Account of Four Years' Residence in that Republic under the Government of the Dictator Francia.* London, 1838.

Seeber, Francisco. *Cartas Sobre la Guerra del Paraguay 1865–66.* Buenos Aires, 1907.

Thompson, George. *The War in Paraguay, with Historical Sketch of the Country and Its People and Notes upon the Military Engineering of the War.* London, 1869.

Toro, David. *Mi Actuación en la Campaña de Chaco.* La Paz, 1941.

United States. Documents dealing with the entire River Plate area during the period under discussion, and most notably "Correspondence and other Documents Concerning the Relations of the United States with Paraguay, the Argentina Republic, Uruguay, and Brazil during the Paraguay War: Papers submitted by the State and Navy Depts."; "Report No. 65, U.S. House of Representatives, 41st Congress, 2nd Session."

Varela, Héctor Florencio. *Elisa Lynch, por Orion* [pseud.]. Buenos Aires, 1870.

Versen, Max von. *Historia de Guerra do Paraguai: Episodios Viagem na America do Sul.* Rio de Janeiro, 1914.

———. *El Lopezmo: Trozos Selectos de la Obra "Viages en America y la Guerra sud Americano."* Buenos Aires, 1923.

Vittone, Luis. *Tres Guerras, Dos Mariscales, Doce Batallas.* Asunción, 1967.

Warren, Harris Gaylord. *Paraguay, an Informal History.* Norman, Okla., 1949.

Washburn, Charles A. *The History of Paraguay, with Notes of Personal Observations and Reminiscences of Diplomacy Under Difficulties.* Boston, 1871.

Wilgus, A. Curtis, ed. *South American Dictators during the First Century of Independence.* Washington, D.C., 1937.

Wilson, E. *Paraguay, a Concise History of Its Rise and Progress; and the Causes of the Present War with Brazil . . .* London, 1867.

Young, Henry Lyon. *Eliza Lynch, Regent of Paraguay.* London, 1966.

Zinny, Antonio. *Historia de los Gobernantes del Paraguay 1535–1887.* Buenos Aires, 1887.

Also: Scottish Record Office (Edinburgh): unpublished records dealing with Madame Lynch's various lawsuits in the Edinburgh courts. The Archivos Nacional and Bibliotéca Nacional in Asunción, Paraguay. The following newspapers, issues of which deal with the period covered in the text: *Edinburgh Times, London Times, New York Times, Patria* (Asunción), *Semanario* (Asunción), *Tribuna* (Buenos Aires). Note: A check of French newspapers extant covering the period 1849–1886 has failed to record any mention of Madame Lynch.

Index